NEW MEDIA AND EDUCATIONAL PLANNING

NEW MEDIA
AND
EDUCATIONAL PLANNING

M.U. Qureshi

ANMOL PUBLICATIONS PVT. LTD.
NEW DELHI - 110 002 (INDIA)

ANMOL PUBLICATIONS PVT. LTD.
4374/4B, Ansari Road, Daryaganj
New Delhi - 110 002
Ph.: 23261597, 23278000
Visit us at: www.anmolpublications.com

New Media and Educational Planning

First Published, 2006

ISBN 81-261-2565-9

PRINTED IN INDIA

Published by J.L. Kumar for Anmol Publications Pvt. Ltd., New Delhi - 110 002 and Printed at ARORA Offset Press, Delhi.

Contents

Preface

The media in its new 'Avtar', plays a major role in informative and reformative spheres. Sweeping changes in the Information Technology have made this world a global village. The students are benefited from information through T.V., Radio, Newspapers, Periodicals and Internet, etc.

The new media has an unprecedented impact on education. The information in a remote corner of the world can be gathered at the click of a mouse.

Now, Media has been grown into a big industry which can employ a large number of educated, skilled and semi-skilled people. As the educational planning takes new dimensions, the significance of media also keeps growing. In this modern age, educational planning without media's participation would prove to be an imposing task.

This book is a meticulously tailored work on media in its present form and educational planning. It consists chapters such as; educational planning, media's impact, the evolution, rapid growth, planned development, systematic scheming, the organisation and structural set-up etc.

It is beyond doubt that this study would make an interesting reading and would prove to be useful for students and as well as general readers.

—Editor

Preface

[illegible]

1

Educational Planning

The Central language institutions relating to Hindi, Indian Languages, English, Urdu, Sanskrit and Foreign Languages implemented a variety of schemes relating to training of language teachers, publication of language teaching materials, assistance to voluntary organisations, support for Urdu Calligraphy Centres etc. The National Book Trust (NBT) was involved in the work relating to preparation of literature for neo-literates under the NLM and preparation of a Central list of books for the libraries of 5.5 lakhs primary schools under the OB Scheme.

The NBT's Nehru Bal Pustakalya and Adan-Pradan Schemes have also made a mark. Besides continuing the schemes relating to national scholarships and scholarships for the talented children from the rural areas, in 1988-89 a new scheme for upgradation of merit of SC/ST students through remedial and special coaching was started as part of NPE.

Universalisation of elementary education, eradication of illiteracy in the age group of 15 to 35 and strengthening of vocational education (VE) so as to relate it to the emerging needs in the urban and rural settings are the major thrust areas of the Eighth Plan in the Education Sector. Utilisation of formal, non-formal and open channels of learning would be the strategy for this purpose.

The changed approach, improved methodology of teaching, increased participation of NGOs and student volunteers have infused a new vitality into the literacy programme and have given it a fresh momentum. The aim would be to impart a similar vitality and momentum to the universal primary education programme with a definite edge in its favour. The programmes of AE and UEE are complementary and there are situations where the Elementary Education (EE) programmes may benefit from the spin-off effect of the AE programmes. The improvement in the literacy percentage in the decade 1981-91, after allowing for statistical adjustment due to the exclusion of age group 0 to 6 is as much due to the higher literacy rate of school age cohorts and attrition of old-age cohorts with low level of literacy as to the special efforts on the AE front.

The need for according the highest priority to UEE is, therefore, well-established. Within the overall school-age population, the focus would be on girls, who account for two-thirds of target, and among adults the focus would be on women's literacy which has a beneficial impact on children's literacy as well as other national objectives like population control and family welfare.

So far as UEE is concerned, the NPE stress on retention, participation and achievement, rather than mere enrolment, would be reinforced. Enrolment data are easily available and enrolment is a pre-condition for any further action. However, special attention would be paid to increase retention, improvement of quality, specification of minimum levels of learning (MLL) and their attainment by the learners.

Elementary Education: Projected Enrolment for Eighth Plan (1992-97)

(Figures in Crores)

Sl. No.	*State*	*Population by 1997*		*Population with overage/ underage children*		*Enrolment achieved upto 1991-92*		*Addnl. Population to be enrolled by 1997*	
		Total	*Female*	*Total*	*Female*	*Total*	*Female*	*Total*	*Female*
1	*2*	*3*	*4*	*5*	*6*	*7*	*8*	*9*	*10*
1.	Elem. Edn	16.64	8.09	19.14	9.30	13.53	5.54	5.61 (67%)	3.76
	(a) Primary (I-V)	10.53	5.12	12.11	5.89	10.09	4.24	2.02 (82%)	1.65
	(b) Upper Primary (VI-VIII)	6.11	2.97	7.03	3.41	3.44	1.30	3.59 (59%)	2.11

In regard to literacy, the emphasis would be on sustainability of literacy skills gained and on the achievement of goals of remediation, continuation and application of skills to actual living and working conditions.

In view of the employment orientation of the Plan and the need to establish meaningful linkages between the world of work and the world of learning, VE would be another priority area. This would not be confined to higher secondary stage but permeate the whole arena of secondary education and non-formal education/training. A combination of vocational and academic courses would be offered at secondary stage with open education (OE) as an important channel, preparing the students for wage employment and self-employment. In the service sector, expansion of health-related courses having a rural orientation would be emphasised. In the rural areas, agro-based and technology-based vocational courses would be developed by combining the strengths of existing institutional structures with OE institutions.

Stimulative and Purposeful

It is estimated that additional enrolment to be achieved during the Eighth Plan to reach universalisation is approximately 5.61 crores children. These data are based on the assumption of 15 per cent incidence of overage/underage phenomenon both at the primary and the upper primary stages. Enrolment of about 4.38 crores would be achieved through formal schools, about 1 crore through non-formal centres and the rest through the open learning channel of upper-primary stage. These targets are much higher than the Seventh Plan achievement. They are, however, within the realm of possibility, if the requisite will and mobilisation of organisational and financial resources are brought to bear on the task and innovative schemes like voluntary primary schools and OE at the upper primary stage are introduced. The NDC Committee on Literacy recently appointed is expected to give a lead in this regard. Working targets in relation to retention and achievement based on institutional capabilities and consultations with State Governments need to be laid down. The details of enrolment targets are given in Table.

According to the 1991 Census, the number of illiterates in all age-groups is 33.6 crores. It is estimated that there will be 11.2 crore illiterates in the 15-35 age group of whom 70 lakhs would have become literate by the end of March 1992. Thus, the target to be covered during the Eighth Plan will be about 10.5 crores, compared to the achievement of 2.65 crores during the Seventh Plan. In the context of the emphasis on sustainability of literacy and on continuing education, suitable targets in this regard need to be laid down after consulting State Governments.

In the VE, the target is to cover 15-20 per cent of students of higher secondary stage by the end of Eighth Plan.

The main strategy for achieving the targets would be : (a) adoption of the decentralised approach to educational planning and management at all levels through Panchayat Raj

(PR) institutions; (b) combining this approach with a convergence model of rural development involving integrated utilisation of all possible resources available at Panchayat, Block and District level for activities relating to elementary education/literacy, child care/development, women's socio-economic empowerment and rural health programmes; (c) large scale participation of voluntary agencies and (d) development of innovative and cost-effective complementary programmes including open learning system (OLS) supported by distance education techniques.

In specific terms, the following measures will be adopted :

1. The formal school system will be expanded and improved.
2. The non-formal system mainly catering to the needs of children working for wages, children working whole-time in domestic or household duties and children in schoolless habitations will be expanded, improved and strengthened in the matter of supply of teaching-learning materials, instructional delivery and achievements.
3. A voluntary school scheme will be introduced. At present, elementary education is considered a responsibility of State and local bodies. However, there is scope for providing part-time non-formalised education to a large number of learners who are not able to avail of the facility of formal full-time school or non-formal education centres. Voluntary agencies would be encouraged in a big way to start non-formal part-time schools, thus catering to the learning needs of urban working children and children in the tribal, hilly and inaccessible areas.
4. A well-defined open learning system will be developed with a network of educational opportunities relevant to the needs and circumstances of learners, especially

girls, women, SCs/STs, and the poor, the unemployed and the untrained. The major thrust of OLS would be on the acquisition of life-skills, vocational skills, directly contributing to productivity and inculcation of habits of self-learning.

5. The MLL with reference to class III, V and VIII will be laid down for improving learning achievement. The educational system will be required to ensure that every child who completes any of these stages of learning reaches the minimum level of achievement. Measures for improving classroom teaching like introduction of a comprehensive evaluation system and a continuous in-service training of teachers will be taken up simultaneously. The MLL approach will be decentralised, each planning unit being able to determine its present levels of achievement, adopt appropriate MLLs and define a realistic timeframe within which to achieve the mastery level, through additional efforts and inputs where necessary.
6. District Boards of Education (DBEs) would be set up. They are conceived as the nodal agency for planning and management of education at the district level comprising formal education, AE, NFE and teacher training, vertically linked to Block/or Mandal Education communities and Village Education Committees (VECs) in a decentralised framework.
7. The school complexes would be developed as the basic unit for educational planning, mobilisation and supervision, building organic linkages between educational institutions, DBEs and the Panchayati Raj Institutions.
8. The involvement of the people in school management would be operationalised by giving VECs a more prominent role in planning and management of

educational programmes at local level so that VECs, which know the micro-level problems, needs and expectations of the local community, will be accountable for the enrolment, retention and achievement of children and teachers.

9. The methodology of Mahila Samakhya (MS) project of mobilising women's groups to voice their needs would be extended in conjunction with the involvement of local community to create a favourable environment to serve as a monitoring mechanism for promoting UEE and adult literacy.

10. The district will be treated as a unit of educational planning in the Eighth Plan. For grant of central assistance under CSSs during Sixth and Seventh Plans, a number of States were characterised as educationally backward. The Gross Enrolment Ratio was considered as a benchmark for the identification of backwardness. It was considered that there is a need for special assistance to the educationally backward States to overcome the historically obtaining disadvantages and also for reduction of regional disparities in educational development. The district-wise data of various indicators of educational development, however, show that the inter-District variations are more significant then the inter-State variations. Moreover, the State is too large and variegated an area to serve as a homogeneous unit for educational planning. Therefore, educationally backward districts would be identified and special inputs would be provided in proportion to the degree of backwardness. The Working Group on early childhood and elementary education had ranked the districts in terms of a composite indicator giving equal weight to four parameters of general/female literacy and general/female GER - primary. Although, almost all districts in the top 200 backward districts

were from backward States, there is no guarantee that assistance to backward States will necessarily flow to backward districts within them. During the Eighth Plan; accordingly, the backward districts irrespective of the State where they are located, will be targeted. A more systematic study to identify the criteria for educational backwardness of districts and the ranking of the districts in terms of the selected indices on the basis of latest Census data, as a basic tool for investment decision would also be initiated.

11. Special efforts will be made to bring down construction cost of school buildings and other educational structures using available materials and adopting locally relevant architectural styles. Attention will be given as much to full utilisation of resources as to larger allocation, e.g., more intensive use of buildings by operation of double shifts in schools and of equipment by inter-institutional sharing.

12. In the case of teacher education, the stress will be on improving the standard of pre-service teacher education institutions and the quality of its programmes, providing continuing education of a suitable kind to every teacher educator and to a substantial number of teachers and on creation of a system to discourage setting up of substandard institutions and phasing out of existing sub-standard ones.

13. Time-bound, area-specific and cost-effective TL campaigns by involving all sections of society, specially students and non-governmental organisations would be expanded. While the whole adult education programme will be debureaucratised, the strategies of ensuring continued political commitment, strong administrative support, use of traditional and non-traditional media and cultural and art forms will be adopted. Students and teachers of universities, colleges

and schools would be involved in a big way not only by awarding marks to students for their literacy work but also by making literacy work as a part of curriculum.

14. Apart from consolidation, and expansion of secondary education increasingly through the open channel, the stress during the Eighth Plan will be on qualitative upgradation of secondary education through reorientation of its content and process, examination reform, diversification by way of vocationalisation and modernisation by way of technological inputs.

N.B: The revised policy formulation relating to the NPE, 1986 which was placed before parliament on 7th May., 1992 should be kept in view while working out details of programmes under General Education, University and Higher Education and Technical Education.

Fresh Plan

The Eighth Plan is being launched in the backdrop of acceptance by the NDC of the recommendations of the Report of the Narasimha Rao Committee which has removed the uncertainties regarding the continuance of CSSs in Education Sector. All the existing CSSs will be continued. Introduction of new CSSs would require approval of full Planning Commission but they may be taken up in the priority areas when justified.

Basic Level

(1) *Early Childhood Education (ECE):* would be expanded by attaching pre-primary classes to selected primary schools. Voluntary agencies and other NGOs would be encouraged and provided financial assistance by reorganising the scheme of ECE. Integrated Child Development Scheme (ICDS) model would be supplemented by Balwadis, Creches and Vikas Wadis.

(2) *Non Formal Centres :* Primary schools or alternatives to primary schools like non-formal centres etc. would be provided to every child within a walking distance of one kilometer, with suitable adjustment for special cases. Voluntary agencies, factories, cooperatives etc. would be encouraged to set up part-time primary schools to serve several groups of children belonging to hilly, desert, marshy, forest areas and nomadic tribes, seasonal migrants, urban poor etc. with freedom -to adjust the number of school days, instructional hours and appoint teachers on contract basis.

(3) *Shikshakarmi :* Innovative programmes like Shikshakarmi which have given good results in an experimental project in Rajasthan would be expanded. Besides, a range of activities that suit the requirements of specific groups of learners, who are usually left out of the ambit of large scale projects, would be taken up. Opening of night schools in urban areas, pre-primary and lower primary centres for children of 3-9 years of age, 'half-time' instructors and special projects to tackle educational problems of areas with concentration of child labour would be tried out.

(4) *Open Schools :* Open schools would involve themselves in the post-primary stage education on an experimental basis to provide wider access to children who are working or not in a position to attend regular schools due to socio-economic or any other reasons.

(5) *Increase Enrolment :* Special efforts will be made to increase enrolment rates and improve participation rates at the upper-primary stage especially in respect of girls. Hence, while ensuring effective universal access to all children at the primary stage, the infrastructure at the upper-primary stage will have to be considerably expanded.

(6) *Quality of Education* : Besides expansion of school facilities, there will be need to improve the quality of education by providing existing schools with sufficient facilities. Therefore, the "Operation Blackboard" scheme will not only be continued and completed during the Eighth Plan in relation to primary schools but also extended to upper primary schools. The eventual aim would be to move towards a situation where every class has a classroom and a teacher.

(7) *Universalisation of Education* : In order to expedite universalisation of middle stage education and increase the enrolment of girls, the ratio between primary and upper primary schools would be brought down from the existing 1: 4 to at least 1: 3 with the ultimate aim of 1: 2.

(8) *Tribal Sub-Plan* : Apart from expanding Tribal Sub-Plan (TSP) and Special Component Plan (SCP), special measure are required for promotion of education of SCs/STs. Certain sub-castes, tribes and communities need particular attention because literacy rates among them are extremely low. The existing scheme of residential ashram schools will be expanded to cover classes from I to X and scholarship schemes for talented children at the secondary level would be expanded. This will be supplemented by the scheme of voluntary schools wherever possible. Suitable incentives will be provided to all educationally backward sections of society, particularly in rural areas. Hill and desert districts, remote and inaccessible areas and islands will be provided adequate institutional infrastructure. Greater attention will be paid to the educationally backward minorities keeping in view the recommendations of the Empowered Committee on Minority Education (1991).

Fundamental Structural Foundations

A system of incentives to overcome social, economic and educational handicaps, which lead to high incidence of dropout has been an integral part of educational planning for universalisation since long. A recent evaluation of these schemes has made a positive assessment but has also emphasised the need for paying adequate attention to management aspects of the system so that they yield the desired results. A comprehensive package of incentives and support services for girls, SCs, STs and children of the economically weaker sections of society will be provided. The emphasis will be on provision of facilities that have special relevance for retention of girls, such as establishment of Day Care Centres for pre-school children and infants, provision of free uniforms, textbooks and stationery, attendance allowance and coordination of support services such as drinking water, fodder and fuel to release children, especially girls as well as women from related domestic chores.

A National Evaluation Organisation (NEO) will be set up to undertake assessment of student learning on national scale on a sample basis to implement the strategy of MLL.

Expansion and Development : Annual sample studies to estimate the completion rates as envisaged in NPE, vis., "number of children of about 11 years of age completing five years of schooling or its equivalent through the formal/non-formal stream" will be undertaken. The data of completion rates and MLL will be used to set targets for the States under the 20-Point Programme also:

> A comprehensive computerised institutional and related data base at the district level will be developed so that information, relevant not only to monitor the internal efficiency of the educational system, both formal and non-formal, but also to improve the planning and management at the

district level, is available in time. Computerisation would be extended to all districts of the country in phases.

Teacher Education

Statutory status will be accorded to the National Council for Teacher Education (NCTE) to lay down and maintain standards in institutions and courses. The schemes of DIETS, STEIs and IASEs would be continued and their coverage expanded with a view to strengthening the institutional infrastructure and programmes of teacher education. The scheme of strengthening of SCERTs would be sanctioned and implemented and suitable measures for selection and professional development of staff in SCERTs, DIETs and IASEs will be undertaken. A large number of teachers will be covered through in-service programmes, both institutional and distance education, and reputed professional organisations will be encouraged to conduct inservice and refresher courses for teachers.' Open universities at the national and State level will be encouraged to introduce induction teacher training courses to supplement the efforts of the existing training institutions. The bulk of seats in teachers' training colleges would be reserved for rural women.

Literacy programmes will be launched in districts/regions which are educationally backward or have high concentration of SC/ST population or have low female literacy. By the close of the Eighth Plan, 345 districts including about two-thirds of all districts in the educationally backward States would be covered by the TL campaigns, while the centre-based approach would be gradually phased out and confined to hilly, tribal and sparsely populated regions. The strategy for backward districts would be two-fold. First, a few blocks would be selected where the literacy campaign can achieve success within a reasonable period. The demonstration effect of the blocks would influence the backward blocks which, in course of time, could develop appropriate literacy programmes. Secondly, the voluntary base in educationally backward districts being somewhat weak, ways and means of identification, strengthening and expansion of the same would be evolved in consultation with the respective State Governments. It is also necessary to develop technical competence among voluntary agencies so that the partnership between the Government and the operating agencies becomes meaningful.

The possibility of further enhancing contributions from the community especially in urban areas and industrial towns would be explored so that apart from voluntary service, at least 20 per cent of the total expenditure on the campaign may be met.

In States, where library movement is strong, rural libraries should be integrated with the JSNs which are envisaged as innovative post-literacy and continuing education centres. Reputed NGOs, educational institutions, distinguished individuals, ex-servicemen, war widows, award winning teachers, etc., will be encouraged to set up and run JSNs. Particular attention would be paid to the availability of a variety of quality materials in adequate quantity to the neo-literates. Reputed printing presses and publishers would be motivated to print gratis literacy materials, posters and charts.

The academic and technical support to Adult Education programmes would be provided by the newly set up NIAE, which would be involved to a greater extent in various aspects of training, action research and monitoring, so that the Directorate of Adult Education can be phased out by the end of the Eighth Plan. At the State level, the State Resource Centres will be strengthened.

The scheme of SVs, which provide a variety of training programme to the industrial workers and their families would be extended to cover workers in unorganised sector and would also experiment with a variety of training models including distance education.

The contents of adult education would also include inculcation of values like secularism, national integration, scientific temperament, small family norm, concern for environmental conservation, cultural appreciation, and so on.

The expansion of secondary schools would be regulated and new schools opened on selective many avenues for continuing education in the context of the march towards a learning society, in which open schools and open universities would play an important role.

Basis, particularly to cater to the needs of deprived sections like girls and SCs/STs and in rural areas generally. Quality improvement and the raising of the internal efficiency of the existing (10 + 2) system would be emphasised. While an increasing number of students may like to discontinue their formal studies either temporarily or permanently after 10 + 2, there would be provision for there re-entry into the education system at a later stage. For this purpose, education would be linked to the world of work by expanding the facilities and improving the quality of vocational education as also provision of subjectwise examination credits.

For widening the reach, an open channel of education would be provided to those who do not have access to regular institutions because of socio-economic and locational constraints and those who have already entered the world of work but are keen to improve their skills and income generating capacity. Open education programmes will be imparted with the help of multi-media packages and contact centres.

Door-to-Door Education

The NOS will continue its existing programmes and revise the syllabi and textbooks for the secondary/senior secondary courses and bring out a fresh set of instructional materials for the bridge course. It will develop and introduce vocational courses, especially in the areas of health, agriculture and rural development in collaboration with the concerned departments. The coverage is expected to increase progressively with registration of more and more accredited institutions, which now number 191. It should also coordinate and standardise the work of similar State-level mechanisms. The idea of starting state level open schools in all the States as recommended by the Conference of Boards of Secondary Education should be pursued. The NOS is expected to provide programme and resource support to State-level Open Schools. The setting up of a national Consortium on Open Education to facilitate accreditation of courses and of maintenance of quality through a process of networking and evaluation should be pursued by NOS in cooperation with the Indira Gandhi National Open University (IGNOU).

Professional Streams

The courses which have already been started would be consolidated. Special attention will be given to paramedical vocational courses to meet the needs of health manpower in the Eighth Plan. In addition to vocational courses. In addition to vocational courses forming part of the higher secondary courses, efforts would be made to offer varied courses of suitable duration to women, rural and tribal students and deprived sections of society. These courses may be coordinated with the working of Krishi Vigyan Kendras/organisations which offer training for self-employment. Non-formal, flexible and need-based vocational programmes would be made available to neo-literate youth who have completed primary education, to the school dropouts, to persons engaged in work and to the unemployed or partially employed persons. Institutions of Open Education will be actively involved in this area. Suitable programmes would also be started for the handicapped.

Candidates who have completed vocational courses should have ample opportunities for career improvement and professional growth. For this purpose, bridge courses which would give them an opportunity to take up higher technical and professional courses should be a necessary component.

It is essential that experimental projects with other vocational education models are also tried out, e.g., pre-vocational education at the lower secondary level, exposure to various occupations right from the primary level for attitudinal change, etc. It is also proposed to involve major industrial houses and all large projects and to prevail on them to include human resource development as part of project cost. The services of commercial agencies and NGOs will also be utilised.

The target for the Eighth Plan would be to cover about 200 blocks by following the composite area approach to the planning and implementation of the integrated education for the disabled. Crucial areas like health, physical and art education should be made an integral part of school curriculum and accorded parity with other subjects. It is necessary that the work of NCERT in the area of Value Education is supplemented by work at the State level by SCERTs and measures to enrich teacher education. The CSS for introduction of Yoga in schools should be implemented more effectively and comprehensively. The activities of the national Population Education Project would be directed, in addition to the formal schools, towards the non-formal sector for which the curriculum, material development and facilitator orientation would have to be specially developed.

It is proposed to continue assistance to State Institutes of Educational Technology (SIET) and to extend in a phased manner facilities for Educational TV programme production. The government is committed to the establishment of Navodaya Vidyalayas in each of the districts of the country. The construction work for the existing 275 Vidyalayas would be completed. The possibilities of reducing the cost of construction and expenditure towards infrastructure will be explored. The setting up of new NVs in all the remaining districts will be appropriately programmed keeping in view the stipulated target date. In view of the key role of computers in modernisation of Secondary Education, the CLASS Project will be continued in a modified form and would cover 15,000 higher secondary schools by 1997.

The project will be implemented with the collaboration of private agencies, with the elements of accountability and monitoring built in. The physical facilities and characteristics of the selected schools will be ascertained prior to the launching of the project. Full-time teachers will be provided for computer literacy by the private organisation and this subject will be taught during the normal school hours unlike the earlier practice of teaching it beyond school hours. The existing schemes of improvement of science education and environmental orientation to school education would be strengthened by improving teacher training inputs. A new scheme for improvement ox teaching of Mathematics at school level is being started. The NCERT would undertake Sixth Education Survey and a scheme for examination reforms apart from watching implementation of National Curricular Framework and MLL.

Language Development

For the implementation of the Three Language Formula in a uniform manner, 100 per cent financial assistance for appointment and training of modern Indian language teachers in Hindi-speaking States is envisaged. The Bureau for Promotion of Urdu would be accorded an autonomous status as per the recommendations of Jafri Committee. The long pending Sindhi Vikas Board would be established. The Education Department would collaborate with the Department of Electronics (DE) in the project 'Technological Development in Indian Languages'.

For promotion of classical languages, a national level body is proposed to be set up for maintaining, coordinating and improving teaching of Sanskrit and classical languages as also Arabic and Persian.

Sanskrit organisations for promoting Sanskrit learning would be fully utilised by reorganising and developing the existing ones. Vedic learning and its linkage with modern scientific development under the Rashtriya Veda Vidya Prathisthan (Vedic Endowment) will be strengthened. The scheme of scholarships to upgrade the merit of SC/ST students would be revised with respect to number of awards and amount in consultation with State Governments.

The number of awards under other schemes would be suitably enhanced so as to increase coverage and make them attractive. To foster book mindedness in the country, a Readers' Club Movement would be introduced. The National Book Trust intends to set up a National Centre for Children's Literature with the aim of producing 3000 titles every year. Under its Adan Pradan Scheme, translations of a large number of significant books from various Indian languages would be brought out. Besides developing manuscripts for neoliterates and school dropouts by organising workshops in various States, the NBT would provide assistance to publishers and voluntary agencies for production of books The school Library Programme under OB would continue. A National Society of Authors is envisaged to oversee the interests and needs of authors.

Supervision and Regulation

The Eighth Plan would focus on decentralisation of planning and management activities; providing autonomy to educational institutions; building capabilities for the involvement and participation of the stake-holders in the educational process and building up of capabilities and professional competence among the administrators and voluntary associations and

NGOs. The State Advisory Board of Education (SABE) would provide strong advisory support for training, research and dissemination of information on methodologies of planning and management strategies appropriate to the State level and to the district-level bodies, namely the. DBEs referred to earlier. The existing bodies like Central Advisory Board of Education (CABE), UGC, NCERT and NIEPA would be strengthened.

The CABE needs to be reorganised and should have a number of sub-committees to continuously review and monitor the progress in specific areas of education. A standing committee of CABE on Open Education is proposed to be set up. For streamlining the flow of information and developing the planning capacity at the district level, an Educational Management Information System (EMIS) covering all the districts in the country needs to be operationalised by the end of the Eighth Plan. The National Informatic Centre (NIC) has already developed a comprehensive computer network linking all the districts with computers. There is need to coordinate the working of educational management information system with NIC network. Following steps are also necessary to improve the system of educational statistics:

(1) Compulsory registration of non-recognised educational institutions; (2) More extensive use of sample surveys to monitor the progress in respect of some critical indicators of educational development; (3) Continuation of educational surveys conducted by NCERT by clearly defining their frequency and objectives vis-a-vis other sources of data; (4) Construction of composite indicators of educational development of various States/districts and periodical monitoring of their behaviour; (5) Coordination between various sub-sectoral agencies for sharing of information; (6) Development of a comprehensive methodology and a sound data base on private costs of education to rationalise and to improve the efficiency in the use of financial resources.

The NPE statement that from the Eighth Plan onwards, the outlay on Education would uniformly exceed 6 per cent of the national income would be treated as a guideline for allocation of resources during the Eighth Plan. The present public sector allocation is much lower and requires to be appropriately stepped up a conscious effort to tap various avenues for raising resources for education needs to be made.

In view of the paucity of domestic resources, vigorous efforts to attract external assistance for financing educational programmes, especially priority programmes without compromising country's basic educational policies is necessary. While the external funding would be an additionality to the resources for education, the externally-aided projects would be in total conformity with the national policies, strategies and programmes and drawn up on innovative lines emphasising people's participation, improvement of quality, equality of education and substantial upgradation of facilities.

The project formulation would be the responsibility of implementation agencies. At present, India is availing of bilateral assistance for Shiksha Karmi Project in Rajasthan and Mahila Samakhya Project in Uttar Pradesh, Gujarat and Karnataka.

Within the broad objectives of the Eighth Plan, it is proposed to take up externally-aided projects, both bilateral and multilateral in various educationally backward States for promotion of basic education which includes : primary schooling, non-formal education, adult literacy, women's education and development and post-literacy and continuing education. Such projects are at various stages of development in respect of Bihar, Rajasthan, U.E and South Orissa.

The actual expenditure on general education sector in the Seventh Plan was Rs. 6549.57 crores, of which Rs. 2294.57 crores were in the Central Plan and Rs. 4255.00 crores in the State Plan.

Higher Level : Improvement of quality and consolidation continued to be the main concerns in the field of higher education during the Seventh Plan. The enrolment of students in 1991-92 was 44.25 lakhs — 36.93 lakhs in affiliated colleges and 7.32 lakhs in university departments. Women students totaled 14.37 lakh (34.2 per cent) and the enrolment, of SCs/STs was about 10 per cent. The growth of student enrolment which was 5 per cent per annum upto 1985-86, declined from 1986-87 onwards to around 4.1 per cent. The enrolment in the Correspondence Courses and Open Universities at the end of the Seventh Plan was approximately 5 lakh students, out of which the Indira Gandhi National Open University (IGNOU) alone accounted for more than one lakh students. The number of universities rose to 177, including 29 "deemed" universities.

The NPE had suggested: (1) creation of autonomous university departments and colleges; (2) State Councils of Higher Education (SCHE); (3) enhanced support to research; (4) strengthening of Open Universities (OUs) and Distance Education (DE); (5) consolidation of existing institutions and improvement of quality of teachers and teaching; (6) mechanism for delinking degrees from jobs; (7) establishment of a new pattern of Rural Universities; and (8) establishment of an apex body covering higher education in all areas.

Eleven more colleges were granted autonomous status, thus bringing the total number of such colleges to 106 till December 1991. Under the Academic Staff College Scheme for orientation of newly recruited and in-service college/university teachers, 48 academic staff colleges have been established, which organised 464 Orientation and Refresher Courses covering 12,970 teachers upto December 1991. An SCHE, may be elaborated, was established in Andhra Pradesh. The University Grants Commission (UGC) provided developmental grants to Central universities and 95 State universities, besides assisting more than 3000 colleges for general development programmes and for implementation of special programmes. About 295 departments received special assistance under different programmes such as Centres of Advanced Study (CAS), Departments of Special Assistance (DSAs) and Departmental Research Support. Under the Programme of Coordinated Strengthening of Infrastructure in Science & Technology (COSIST), 112 departments were assisted. To support educational broadcasts, the UGC has set up 7 audio-visual research centres and 7 education media research centres for production of softwares. As many as 2332 programmes, popularly known as Country-wide Classroom Programmes, have already been produced. A new organisation called Inter-University Consortium of Educational Communication (IUCEC) is being set up. Programmes like Teacher Fellowships and Research Fellowships for SC/ST candidates and remedial teaching for weaker sections including minorities were continued.

The UGC provided assistance for installation of mini/ macro-Computer Systems to 110 universities and 1216 colleges. In collaboration with the Department of Electronics (DE), several courses in Computer Science were run. An information and library network called "INFLIBNET" has also been proposed. With a view to providing common research facilities and services of the highest quality, inter-university centres in Nuclear Science, Astronomy & Astrophysics and Atomic Energy were established. The IGNOU widened the access to higher education by providing opportunities to learners from disadvantaged groups like women, people living in backward regions and hilly areas with an enrolment of 1.64 lakhs by March, 1992. The Research Councils — Indian Council of Social Science Research (ICSSR), Indian Council of Historical Research (ICHR) and Indian Council of Philosophical Research (ICPR) continued their activities relating to support of research in respective areas.

The higher education system at present suffers from several weaknesses, such as proliferation of substandard institutions, failure to maintain academic calendar, outdated curriculum, disparities in the quality of education and lack of adequate support for research. Recent consultations including the "Brain-Storming" session organised by the Planning Commission to consider future directions have underlined the following thrust areas :

(1) Integrated approach to higher education; (2) Excellence in higher education; (3) Expansion of education in an equitable and cost-effective manner, in the process making the higher education system financially self-supporting; (4) Making higher education relevant in the context of changing socio-economic scenario; (5) Promotion of value education; and (6) Strengthening of management system in the universities.

The strategy for achieving the goals in these thrust areas would be as follows :

1. At present, the higher education, system comprising of general, technical, medical and agricultural streams, is fragmented in terms of structures and policies. Greater cooperation among the streams should be encouraged by promoting networking, sharing of facilities and development of manpower including teachers' training/orientation facilities. There should be greater coherence in policy and planning. To adequately meet these requirements, the NPE had envisaged the establishment of a National Council of Higher Education (NCHE). This has, however, not made progress so far and a coordination mechanism should be constituted during the Plan period.
2. Several measures will be taken to promote excellence. The, NPE\POA proposal for establishment of a National Accreditation Council (NAC) would be followed up. Apart from continuing the existing programmes of

CAS/DAS, COSIST and the inter-university centres, IUCEC and the proposed INFLIBNET, new inter-university centres would be established to provide facilities in the emerging areas like Biotechnology, Atmospheric Science, Oceanography, Electronics and Computer Sciences. Facilities for computer education would be further strengthened in collaboration with the Department of Electronics. Model curricula for all disciplines have already been prepared but their implementation needs to be monitored. The suggestions of the working Group constituted by the Planning Commission to improve undergraduate courses in science and the teaching of mathematics at Indian universities/colleges would be implemented in a phased manner.

3. The additional enrolment in higher education during the Eighth Plan is estimated to be around 10 lakhs of which 9 lakhs will be at the undergraduate level. This expansion in higher education, keeping in view the present resource crunch has to be accommodated in an equitable and cost-effective manner mainly by large-scale expansion of Distance Education system and providing opportunities to larger segments of population, particularly the disadvantaged groups like women and people living in backward and hilly areas and by measures for resource generation. The programmes of Distance Education should absorb at least 50 per cent of the additional enrolment during the Eighth Plan and their cumulative enrolment should reach 15 lakhs, including 5 lakhs adult learners beyond the normal age-group 17-23 who have left school long back. Open universities should also start innovative programmes of a vocational nature for meeting the learning needs of rural areas. Opening of new conventional universities and colleges should not be

encouraged. Simultaneously, involvement of voluntary agencies and private sector participation in the opening and conduct of higher education institutions would be encouraged with proper checks to ensure maintenance of standards and facilities to make higher education as far as possible self-financing. However, the quality of education is not to be compromised at any cost. Upward revision of fee structure has to be considered but at the same time, the fees charged should not be exorbitant and should be supplemented by the provision of scholarships and other financial assistance to SCs\STs and students below the poverty line and loans to other students.

4. The tremendous potential of 44.25 lakhs students enrolled in higher education has to be utilised by actively involving them in the programmes of adult literacy, continuing education, population education and other constructive activities. Such extension activities of the universities and colleges would be expanded to cover 95 universities and 2,500 colleges during the Eighth Plan.
5. The significance of Value Education has been highlighted by several committees and commissions on education. The Planning Commission has recently constituted a Core Group on value orientation in education. The recommendations of the Group will be considered for implementation in consultation with the Ministry of Human Resource Development, UGC, Association of Indian Universities (AIU) and NCERT
6. Stress would also be laid on modernisation and restructuring of the management of university system which entails vigorous pursuit of the programmes of autonomous colleges and autonomous university departments. Facilities in universities and colleges,

including research facilities, would be consolidated and strengthened. The schemes of redesigning and restructuring of courses to meet the developmental needs of the country, examination reforms and teachers' training would be expanded.

The research activities of ICSSR, ICHR, ICPR and Indian Institute of Advanced Study (IIAS), Simla will receive specific attention for promotion of inter-disciplinary research. Action to support research in humanities which at present is neglected, would be taken up.

With a view to delinking degrees as a requirement for recruitment to services, the NPE visualised establishing a National Testing Service (NTS) to conduct tests on a voluntary basis and evolving norms of comparable competence across the nation to determine the suitability of candidates for specified jobs. Towards this end, the idea of setting up of an appropriate national organisation will be pursued.

A strong need has also been felt for providing training to personnel dealing with university administration, for which the existing infrastructure will be further strengthened rather than creating a separate organisation.

The Seventh Plan's actual expenditure on higher education was Rs.1201.13 crores, of which Rs. 659.96 crores was in Central Sector and Rs. 541.17 crores in State Sector.

Strategies, thrust areas and programmes as highlighted above, represent the priorities for implementation during the Eighth Plan. They are by no means exhaustive. Higher education is a vast sector and its significance as a source of new knowledge, research and manpower for preceding stages of education namely, elementary and secondary, should not be minimised. Adequate resources should be mobilised and provided to support the higher education sector so that the nation is fully equipped to face the challenges of the future, which is increasingly becoming information and knowledge-intensive.

Technical education including Management education is one of the most potent means for creating skilled manpower required for developmental tasks of various sectors of the economy. Technical education incorporates the technological dimension which is a vehicle for development. While this implies high costs of construction, laboratory equipment, library books and journals and high rate of obsolescence, such high cost, being directly related to development, should be viewed as an essential productive investment, yielding valuable returns to the society and contributing to socio-economic development.

The Seventh Plan emphasised consolidation and optimum utilisation of existing infrastructural facilities, their upgradation and modernisation, identification of critical areas and creation of infrastructure in new areas of emerging technology, effective management of the overall system and institutional linkages between technical education and other development sectors.

Under the thrust areas programme of technical education 510 projects with a grant of Rs. 53.43 crore were supported for strengthening of facilities in the crucial areas of technology where weaknesses exist, 685 projects involving a grant of Rs. 76.84 crore were supported for creation of infrastructure in areas of emerging technologies and 202 projects involving of Rs. 27.1 crores were supported for programme of new technologies. A comprehensive report of requirement of instrumentation engineers at national level for the period 1990-2000 has been prepared by the National Technical Manpower Information System (NTMIS). The number of Community Polytechnics (CPs) increased to 159 with an annual training coverage of 20,000 rural youth and women.

The following new schemes were started as part of the implementation of NPE

(i) *Continuing Education* : The scheme envisaged preparation and dissemination of course material packages suited to the needs of industry. Under the scheme implemented by 5 Indian Institutes of Technology (IITs) 4 Technical Training Teachers' Institutes (TTTIs), 1 Indian Society of Technical Education (ISTE), 4 engineering colleges/university departments and 4 polytechnics, more than 30,000 working professionals have undergone training.

(ii) *Institution-Industry Interaction* : Under the scheme, Proposals of 21 engineering colleges and 11 polytechnics have been approved for interaction with the industry.

(iii) *Research & Development in Technical Education* : 126 R & D Projects were supported.

Concept of Schemes

The perspective of development of technical education for the Eighth Plan would have to take into account the following imbalances and distortions :

(i) During the past four decades, there has been a phenomenal expansion of technical education in the country. Today, we have over 200 recognised technical education institutions (TEIs) at the first degree level and more than 560 polytechnics at the diploma level with annual admission capacities of 40,000 and 80,000 students, respectively. About 140 institutions offer facilities for postgraduate studies and research in several specialised areas with an annual capacity of 9400 students. (ii) The quantitative expansion has resulted in the lowering of the standards and there exists a structural imbalance of skill requirement of the business sector and the traditional curriculum followed by the educational institutes.

These factors give rise to problems of unemployment and under-employment. The wastage in the system is enormous, being 30 per cent at degree level, 35 per cent at diploma level and 45 per cent at post-graduate level. The situation in unrecognised institutions is still worse. A related phenomenon is that of brain-drain involving migration abroad of those trained in emerging areas in excellent institutes. (iii) The infrastructural facilities available in the vast majority of TEIs are extremely inadequate. There is an acute shortage of faculty with about 25 to 40 per cent of faculty positions remaining unfilled. In most of the institutions, there is hardly any R & D activity. (iv) The TEIs are functioning in isolation. Linkage and interaction between TEIs and user-agencies, such as industries, R & D and design organisations and development sectors are not sufficiently strong. Neither is there a strong interaction among institutions by way of sharing of facilities like equipments, libraries, teaching faculty and other resources. (v) There has been an enormous increase in public expenditure on education but little attention has been paid to the strategies for raising non-budgetary resources and maximising people's participation.

The Aims : The thrust areas for the Eighth Plan have, therefore, been identified as follows :

(1) Modernisation and upgradation of infrastructural facilities. (2) Quality improvement in technical and management education. (3) Responding to new industrial policy and industry-institution R & D labs interaction, (4) Resource mobilisation (5) Institutional thrusts.

The strategy to be adopted to achieve these objectives would be on the following lines:

Further Growth

Modernisation relates both to technical equipments and teaching methods. Technology development is a capital-intensive process. The country cannot afford to go on changing the technology every year. It is, therefore, imperative to adopt futuristic approaches for achieving modernisation and self-reliance in a sustained manner coordinated and concerted efforts would have to be made to upgrade and consolidate the infrastructural facilities in the existing institutions. The process of removal of obsolescence would include enhancement of computer facilities and establishment and interlinking of large computer systems with educational and research institutions through appropriate telecommunication facilities. Steps would be taken to strengthen and create the facilities in crucial areas of technology where weaknesses exist, in areas of emerging technologies and in new specialised fields. Upgradation of infrastructure would also include a crash programme for recruitment of about 10,000 teachers in polytechnics and colleges and strengthening of arrangements for teacher training.

Central Government has launched a massive project with the assistance of the World Bank to enable the State Governments upgrade their polytechnics in capacity, quality and efficiency for the period 1990 to 1999. The project is being taken up in two phases with a total outlay of Rs. 1,892 crores. The first phase would cover 296 polytechnics recognised by the AICTE in eight States- Bihar, Gujarat, Karnataka, Kerala, M.P, Orissa, Rajasthan and Uttar Pradesh. The second phase would cover 262 polytechnics in Andhra Pradesh, Assam, Haryana, Himachal Pradesh, Maharashtra, Punjab, Tamil Nadu, West Bengal and Delhi. The project has also a Central Sector Component for establishment of a national project implementation unit.

A holistic and need-based approach would be adopted to reorient the technical and management education (TME). A more, broad-based flexible system with provision for multi-point entry is required to enable a better response to the unspecified demands of the future. At the micro-level, the curriculum would be developed to encourage creativity and innovation in experimental work by introducing problem/ process oriented laboratory exercises. New technology-oriented entrepreneurship and management courses would be introduced in selected institutions having adequate infrastructural facilities. There would be greater emphasis on production engineering towards design and product development.

The Government has recently established a Technology Information Forecasting and Assessment Council (TIFAC). Its objectives include : evaluation of existing technologies, preparation of technology forecast reports and estimation of the nature and quantum of likely demands for goods and services in future. It would be desirable to couple the technology forecasting system with the system of manpower forecasting and planning. Universities and IITs are familiar with the frontiers of knowledge and hence should play an important role in technical forecast and technological assessment with the fruitful involvement of TIFAC, Institute of Applied Manpower Research (IAMR) and the Indian trade and industries associations. It should be possible to develop the right type of indigenous technologies to assess the related manpower requirements and to produce such trained manpower.

The existing facilities for continuing education and retraining are inadequate. There is a need to formalise the retraining programme for engineering and technology personnel engaged in all sectors and to make them mandatory. Increasing use of modern communication devices should be made. Programme-learning packages need to be created and distance learning methodologies employed to enable self-development and training of all scientific and technical personnel.

There is a need to establish linkage between industry, national laboratories, developmental sectors, professional bodies, technical education, vocational education and craftsmen training and to bring about networking among institutions. In the context of the new industrial policy, the priority may be assigned to interaction with industry as it holds the key to industrial competitiveness in a global market. A strategy may be evolved for effective interaction between industry and institutions and for promotion of interaction through apprenticeship opportunities, consultancy and sponsored research, continuing education programmes for industry personnel, adjunct professorships in institutions for willing and capable personnel from industry, seconding of institutional faculty to industry, involvement of industry in the development of curricula and courses etc. for this purpose, organisational mechanisms such as Industrial Liaison Board, Industry-Institution Cells, Industrial Foundation etc., will have to be set up. The R & D activities may be taken up through the support of industry.

In this context, a reference may be made to a model for university-industry symbiosis conceived and implemented at Jawaharlal Nehru Technological University, Hyderabad for bringing about a greater and more effective interaction between technological university and industry. The model envisaged the setting up of a Bureau for Industrial Consultancy and Research and Development (BICARD) in universities/technical institutes of higher education, preparation of a comprehensive directory of technology experts to operationalise various aspects of interaction like orientation of university curriculum, exchange of experts between teaching institutions and industries, involvement of teaching staff in industry, technological database and self-reliance of institutions, etc. A national cell to promote and coordinate the linkages between the promotional agencies university, industry and R & D organisations has also been suggested. The revised model could be adopted/adapted with benefit by other TEIs.

Since technical education is inherently expensive, concrete steps to ensure cost-effectiveness as an aspect of resource mobilisation are of vital importance. These include :

1. Avoidance of duplication of investment in TEIs located close to each other and proper maintenance of available facilities and instruments;

2. Developing institution-wise specialisation in respect of courses and technical manpower so that the institutions can have the most sophisticated and modern library and laboratory facilities in their chosen fields;
3. Weeding out of outdated and stereotyped courses and introduction of relevant courses in emerging areas;
4. Multiple use of infrastructural facilities through part-time courses, continuing education programmes and consultancy and testing services;
5. Marginal increase in intake capacities in areas of scarce manpower and decrease in intake of low demand areas. In this connection, an increase in the intake in better institutions by 10 per cent should receive urgent attention;
6. Introduction of multiple or at least double shifts in TEIs;
7. Maximum use of non-monetary inputs, like better planning, advanced technologies and practices, better system of supervision and administration, monitoring and review etc.; and
8. Commercialisation of research work of the institutions.

Reformative Measures

The Task Force appointed by AICTE to go into the question of laying down tuition and other fees and to suggest other sources of mobilisation of resources for technical education has suggested raising of fees in relation to Government, Government-aided and unaided institutions on a graduated scale. A beginning has been made by raising fees in the IIMs. The IITs and other TEIs are also required to raise the fees. The measure of raising fees, however, should be coupled with scholarships for SCs/STs and for students below poverty line and a loan scheme for other students.

Creation of a corpus fund can be another way of mobilising resources for an institution, especially in the case of IITs. Contributions to the corpus fund will have to come from various sources viz. industry, alumni, charitable trusts, etc., as well as Government. Another way of enhancing investment is to implement NPE/POA idea of requiring development departments to allocate a fixed percent of their annual budgets for development of TEIs. The question of collection of education cess from industry, which can thus share the cost of educating technical manpower and of giving tax exemption to industry for contributions made by it to development of technical education should also receive serious consideration.

The AICTE was given statutory status in 1988 in view of the need for maintaining and developing standards. It would be further strengthened to ensure coordinated development with its four regional committees located at Kanpur, Madras, Bombay and Calcutta. A Board of Accreditation is expected to be set up shortly and most of the schemes implemented by the Technical Education Bureau of the Department of Education are expected to be taken over by AICTE.

Elements of Technical Side

The UGC provides financial assistance to 32 institutions in engineering and technology for their overall development. Although some of the institutions in this sector like Indian Institute of Science, Bangalore, are centres of excellence and this sector as a whole accounts for 1,600 M.E/M. Tech students, the financial allocations tend to be limited, as they are part of the overall UGC allocations. A separate mechanism may be set up which would advise UGC regarding the financial needs and priorities of these institutions and the Planning Commission should allocate appropriate earmarked outlays for this sector covering not only post-graduate education as in the past but also undergraduate education on a selective basis.

Sixteen State Governments and 24 non-Government post-graduate institutions are being assisted by the Central Government with a view to developing specialised fields of engineering/technology having national relevance. The intake for post-graduate courses per year in engineering and technology is proposed to be increased from 10,000 to 11,000 by the end of Eighth Plan. The new Industrial Policy has created an environment which requires IITs to adopt a new role as leaders in current and futuristic technology development. The following four areas for further action have been identified in the light of consultations held by Planning Commission :

(1) Thrust areas of technology development, (2) International consultancy, (3) Resource mobilisation and setting up of Corpus Fund and (4) Industrial Foundation.

Renowned Institutions

The technology development through innovation and its subsequent transfer to industry by five IITs would be the first step towards the identification of project mission and creation of appropriate environment. These project missions are conceived in three groups :

1. Areas where gains are likely to be visible in the long-term such as biotechnology, fuel-efficient engines, micro-electronics, photonics.
2. Areas where short-term gains can be planned, such as communication and software technology, food processing, instrumentation and central integrated production engineering and design, non-conventional energy, remote sensing and transportation.
3. Areas where results in the intermediate term are possible like coal, computer, integrated manufacturing, natural hazard mitigation and new materials technology. It is expected that each of the IITs would select a few areas from among those to work on during the Eighth Plan.

The IITs have a potential to offer educational and industrial consultancy services at international level. The consultancy would cover: institution building, establishment of specialised laboratory facilities, development of curricula, organising continuing education/joint research projects and faculty development etc. There is good scope for international consultancy assignments for IITs in South-East Asian and other countries. This can be a source of additional resource mobilisation. Resource mobilisation measures would be taken up on the lines mentioned earlier, including corpus fund to which Government could contribute a block grant annually over a period of years subject to contributions from other sources. Ideas specific to IITs are: permitting them to charge from foreign students a full cost tuition fee in foreign exchange and obtaining an endowment grant from countries with an explicit commitment to training specified manpower for that country.

In order to facilitate interaction and collaboration with industry and other user-organisations in programmes of mutual interest, an industrial foundation needs to be set up in each IIT. The foundation would function as a registered society/ corporate body linked to the parent-IIT, with financial and administrative autonomy and adopt industrial culture and methods. Resource generation of these foundations would be through Government grant/corporate membership fees/ overheads on projects and service/donation and gifts etc. These foundations would render technical support to small scale industry and engineering entrepreneurs and develop products and processes at the request of industry. There would also be manpower exchange between IITs and industry.

There are 17 Regional Engineering Colleges in the country which are joint ventures between Government of India and State Governments. They are expected to be pace-setting institutions in their regions. They need academic autonomy and their funding should be from one source, preferably Central

Government. The ultimate aim should be to make them deemed universities. A proposal involving assistance of 6 million pound sterling to develop collaboration between RECs and some British Universities in the emerging areas such as design, materials, energy, informatics etc. is being worked out.

The four Indian institutes of Management set up as pace-setting and premier centres of excellence in management education and research have been instrumental in producing highly qualified managerial manpower. Their activities need to be revamped, particularly keeping in view the changing scenario both at the national and international level. A consultation held by Planning Commission led to the suggestion that there should be links between management institutes and training institutes in specific sectors like health, rural development, agricultural extension etc. It was also suggested that there should be an integrated view of management education and there should be resource mobilisation, corpus fund, mutual sharing of facilities and division of labour in the matter of thrust areas etc. A plan of action is being prepared in this regard.

Fiscal Elements

It is proposed to cover all the remaining polytechnics under the scheme of CPs by suitably reorganising and strengthening them in the light of the recommendations of the National Expert Committee set up to appraise them. The Community Polytechnics are expected to play a major role in rural manpower development and their outreach should be expanded by resorting to distance education methods.

The actual expenditure on technical education in the Seventh Plan was Rs. 1083.34 crores of which Rs. 610.96 crores was in the Central Sector and Rs. 472.38 crores in the State Sector. The Eighth Plan outlays in the State Sector are required to be higher to reflect the implementation of the World Bank-assisted Technician Education Project.

2

Media's Impact

CMS organised during 1994-95 a series of round-table discussions on the plus and minus points of the performance of the mass media in India and on steps necessary to enhance their contribution to nation building in the context of globe-encircling satellite TV.

Four of these colloquia were held in Delhi, and six in regional centres across the country: Lucknow, Bhubaneshwar, Vijayawada, Ahmedabad, Pune and Bangalore.

The first symposium in Delhi, on 18th February 1954, was on the emerging scene of satellite TV and India's response to the challenge.

Different Challenge of Transnational Television : Presented here are the salient points made by various participants, grouped under thematic heads.

Vasant Sathe, Former Minister of I & B : India does run a serious risk of cultural invasion, information imperialism and economic colonialism. We need not cave in. We have resources enough to stand on our own legs. It is our market of 250 million well-to-do consumers whom the foreign media and investors are after. We cannot ban cable TV. Rather, we should be competitive. Let us show better programmes on Doordarshan, of local interest, so that we retain the viewership. The low power transmitters should be enabled to transmit locally made video films.

P. Upendra, Former Minister of I & B : neither a ban on dish antennae, nor aping, will help. MTV will always be slicker in its presentation of mindless entertainment. We should offer programmes that are at once entertaining, socially relevant and useful. The appeal of foreign TV is to the urban viewers. There is no immediate threat in rural India. If we provide programmes of interest, in the regional languages, they will hold the attention and interest of the audience.

M.V. Desai, Veteran Journalist : The electronic media suffer from excessive centralisation. They use English and Hindi almost exclusively, whereas the majority of our people have mother tongues other than these. Doordarshan should offer locally relevant and useful programmes in local speech. Decentralisation is the best defence against destabilisation of the Indian ethos.

P.C Chatterji, Former Director General of All India Radio: Doordarshan and AIR should acquire credibility. Both blacked out the views on the Kashmir question expressed recently by Dr. Karan Singh, though he is an important political actor and observer vis a vis Kashmir. We should not drive viewers to alternative sources of news.

N. Bhaskara Rao : There is a class division in the world of information, as of economic life. There should be citizen involvement in the media. There are now no local advisory committees for the stations of All India Radio or Doordarshan. We have to promote responsiveness of media towards the public, and create awareness of issues. I have mooted the idea of 'social audit of the media' on a continuing basis, with involvement of independent professionals.

S.S. Gill, Former Secretary of I & B Ministry : If indigenous programmes are excellent and useful, no one will want to watch foreign programmes. It is' not as if we lack talented programme makers. Only, we must allow them to work under conditions that will permit credibility such as the BBC has.

Brahma Kumari Asha, Social Worker : The mass media should help to build national character. The need to preserve family values is being realised now in the West, and 1994 has been designated as the U.N. Year of the Family..

Hanumantha Rao : Dish Antennae for direct reception of foreign programmes via satellite are not allowed in China. This is the reason why Rupert Murdoch is turning to India, the next biggest market. Countries like Malaysia and Singapore are market-oriented in their economy but are zealous to preserve their cultural identity. Only India seems to be unconcerned. Do we want to pride ourselves that we are a media democracy, whatever be its consequences to our people ?

R. Vijay, Documentary Producer : Though TV is primarily a visual medium, there is far too much talking on Doordarshan, specially by political VIPs.

Nori Venkateswarlu, Broadcasting Engineer : Many excellent films are being made in the regional languages. These can be telecast with dubbing in the local language. Each low power transmitter can be utilised for telecasting locally made video programmes of relevance and interest.

S.B. Lal, Former Secretary of I & B Ministry : Our country boasts of the biggest cinema industry, and a widely appreciated Press. Why can't we have world class television too?

Ownership, Autonomy, Accountability of Media : P. Upendra : No government will be willing to give up its control over the national electronic media. While the government can retain the main TV channel for its purposes, ranging from information and education to propaganda, it should hand over other channels to private, competitive initiative.

Vasant Sathe : The government should retain one channel of Doordarshan and convert the others into independent commercial channels.

Kuldip Nayyar : Veteran Journalist: There is an increasing tendency, for persons who have made money in other industries to come into newspaper publishing. This is not a healthy trend.

N. Bhaskara Rao : There is an increasing trend towards cross-media ownership. This is ominous. We should beware of its implications.

Coarseness, Criminal and Consumer Nature : Kami Chhabra, The women's and family welfare movements, said that the low standard of Doordarshan's Chitrahaar and other filmy fare, specially on the Metro Channel, was debasing public taste. Instead of promoting gender equality and other dimensions of desirable social change, the advertisements and many of the entertainment programmes of Doordarshan present women as sex objects. This is contributing to increasing incidents of molestation of and crimes against women. The Indian mass media are shaking the foundations of Indian culture.

G.N.S. Raghavan : There have been many reports of the murder of employers by domestic servants in Delhi over the last year. This is not to be wondered at. Domestic employees watch along with members of the employing family Doordarshan's programmes, the most popular of which are punctuated by commercial advertisement of goods and services meant for the well-to-do. Why should they not aspire to the same luxuries ? The culture of consumerism spread by Doordarshan incites them to theft and murder.

H.B. Mathur, media critic, said that the visual medium is expensive and has an inherent tendency to become centralised and market-oriented. It treats the viewers as consumers rather than people to be served. The size and purchasing power of the audience determines profit. Zee TV and DD Metro tend to be oriented to the Gulf, which is now a zone of prosperity. Hindi cinema as a whole has become increasingly Gulf-oriented.

Mira Aghi, media specialist, said that the quality of Metro channel programmes was appealling and no better than the satellite entertainment channels. It is as if India's TV system is no different in its priorities and concerns.

Radio—the Cinderella : F.C. Chatterji said that All India Radio broadcasts excellent music programmes but there is no promotion of listening through advance announcement of the day's programmes. The use of FM in Delhi for broadcasting rap music is deplorable. As for news, why should the same bulletins be broadcast on different channels of AIR ?

P. Upendra : It is a pity that we are ignoring radio which is the common man's medium.

H.B. Mathur : In contrast to TV which is expensive and centralised, radio is closer to the people in a poor nation. It speaks to them in their own languages.

Maya Daruwalas of the Ford Foundation : Listenership of radio is double the viewership of TV. The use of FM for local-interest broadcasting, over a 50-km radius, can help to democratise the medium.

Hanumantha Rao : There has been a rejuvenation of radio programmes in several countries of South East Asia, with the novelty of TV wearing off.

Profit-driven Press

Some participants referred to certain statements by Justice Sarkaria (Retd.), Chairman of the Press Council of India, in which he had opposed the entry of foreign newspaper publishers into, the country. One discussant said that he had spoken as if he were the circulation manager of the Indian Press, while another described the uproar over the entry of foreign print media as a case of 'our profit versus their profit'.

Kuldip Nayar : A line should be drawn, in the process of globalisation and the encouragement of foreign investment, at the entry of external capital into the print media. Can foreigners start political parties ?

I. Rammohan Rao, Former Principal Information Officer: We should guard against the manipulation of our society by foreign media.

B.B. Nagpal of UNI : Foreigners may buy out our newspaper chains.

Brij Mohan : There can be a brain drain within the country, with foreigners hiring the services of talented Indian journalists.

S. Venkat Narayan : Opposition to the entry of foreign publishers into India is illogical, considering that there is extensive and increasing movement of people and of ideas between India and the rest of the world.

Inder Malhotra,. Journalist and Author : Why all this worry about foreign newspapers when our mainline dailies are devoting considerable space for reprinting material from those publications ?

Kuldip Nayar referred to a paper circulated in connection with the symposium, in which secularism had been cited as one of the subjects on which the Press had failed to educate the public. He strongly disagreed with the suggestion in the paper that secularism had become a 'nonsense word', thanks to its indiscriminate use by political parties.

S.B. Lal : There should be more space for local voices in our Press.

M.V. Desai referred to Article 19 of the Constitution which guarantees freedom of expression, and wondered whether this would apply to newspaper companies that might be established by foreigners, or with foreign capital participation. What did the Second Press Commission say on the subject ?

G.N.S. Raghavan, who had served as secretary of the Commission, said that in Chapter IV, on 'Constitution and Laws', the report notes that the Fundamental Right of freedom of expression (interpreted by the Supreme Court to include freedom of the Press) is available only to citizens, and not to companies. The Second Press Commission recommended that companies engaged in the business of communication, provided their shareholders are Indian citizens, should be deemed to be 'citizens' for the purpose of Article 19. However, the Government had not accepted this recommendation, taking the view that it would be discriminatory to give the status of citizen only to those companies that are engaged in the business of communication.

What's Media Teaching Today? : G. Ram Reddy, Chairman, University Grants Commission: There has been no convergence yet between the media and formal education. The media can play a big part in remedying a situation in which, out of 7600 colleges in the country, 3000 colleges are non-viable due to inadequacy of teachers, equipment and libraries. Even after the formation of the Indira Gandhi National Open University, Doordarshan gives only two hours to the programmes of the University Grants Commission in English and Hindi.

There are hardly any college-level educational programmes in the regional languages. In contrast, in Japan the NHK devotes 16 hours of a dedicated channel every day to education. Only six per cent of persons in the age group 17-23 go to college in India : in no civilised country is the percentage so low. Prof. Ram Reddy expressed regret that, having started with the objectives of education and national integration, the media have lost sight of priorities. He called for a dedicated TV channel for education.

S.B. Lal : Education and rural channels were to have been funded with money earned by the entertainment channel. This has not happened.

Gangwani: Television with its fleeting visuals does not render the teacher redundant. Students will continue to need the teacher for rechecking.

Technology Plays a Significant Role

R. Vijay : It is not modem technology in itself that makes for centralisation but advertising and financial considerations. Video technology now enables low-cost production of local-interest programmes.

S.B. Lal : The live telecast via satellite of the Republic Day parade in Delhi in January 1994 by Star TV has revolutionised the image of India abroad by making widely known the armed strength and confidence of the country.

Kamtekar, referred to a 'dynamic lock' that can be built into TV reception to keep out what is not desired.

A.K. Lal : Intellectuals tend to be distrustful of technology. They need to get over this attitude. India, too, can 'invade' other countries with its programmes—and at low cost.

3

Significant Issues

Mass Media in modern age has affected our society in many ways. 'Media effects' mean different things to different people. A psychologist, for example, has 'psychological' effects in mind when talking about media effects; the sociologist, the 'social' effects, the anthropologist, the 'cultural' effects, the political scientist the 'political' effects, the economist the 'economic' effects, the preacher, the 'moral' effects, the advertiser, the 'market' effects... and so on. Parents too are concerned about the amount of time their children spend with television, music, comics, and films, and the effects this might have on their children's behaviour and attitudes.

Then there are school teachers who worry about their students' exposure to adult material, and the police who scapegoat the media for social violence and delinquency. So, any attempt to understand 'effects' must necessarily take into account from whose perspective the 'effects' are being investigated.

'Effects' are of various types and various gradations too. They may be short-term, medium-term or long-term; they may be deep or profound, or transient or superficial as in the case of fashions, mannerisms, and life-styles. Then there are influences of a passing nature or a more permanent nature.

Can influences be termed as 'effects?' How are 'influences', 'effects' distinct from 'impacts', or are they mere synonyms for the same social phenomena? Few media sociologists have subjected the inadequacy of everyday language to fathom the complexity of media effects to any kind of critical scrutiny.

But what precisely are 'the media?' Are they the technologies (printing presses, the telegraph, telephones, radio and TV sets, audio and video recorders, video and movie cameras, satellites, computers, etc.) or the 'genres', the 'programmes' (the software) or the contents of individual media? Or, are they the cultural and entertainment industries which are today one of the fastest growing businesses owned by large media conglomerates? Or, are they the many media organisations involved in the production, distribution and exhibition of media materials? The sheer imprecision in all talk about 'the media' and 'effects' seems to be characteristic of the social sciences. But then, it must be conceded, the social sciences are not 'exact' sciences like the physical and natural sciences. For, while the social sciences study human beings and their behaviour in different situations, the natural sciences study minerals, plants, and animals.

Moreover, social scientists and media professionals rarely consider the infinite variety of 'uses' the different media and the different programmes are put to, in different contexts. In most cases, the use of the term 'effects' is misleading because it suggests that the media "do something" to people, as though people are inorganic creatures, who do not bring their own personalities to play in the communication process. It also implies that the media are actors, and that the people are acted upon. So while the media are active, audiences are unresponsive if not passive. These assumptions about media and audiences have their origin in Aristotelian linear models of communication where persuasion is seen as the primary goal of all communication.

The truth is that we have little precise knowledge or proven data about media effects since they invariably take place in combination with a whole lot of social, economic and cultural variables. Do effects relate to change, however slight, in attitude and behaviour (both elusive terms and comprehensive in meaning)? Perhaps. The extent of change (if any) depends on the variations in the desires and inclinations of individual members of an audience, and in the way they as individuals and as members of different social and cultural groups respond to various types of stimuli from the mass media.

It has to be noted, moreover, that people can be influenced without paying attention and without changing at all, that there is often no relationship between what a person learned, knew or recalled on the one hand and what he did or how he felt on the other. It follows therefore that one can learn things without believing them, believe things without doing them, and do things without learning or believing them.

How to Correlate? **:** The 'interaction' (a much more accurate term than 'effects') between media and human beings is an extremely complex phenomenon. It becomes even more complex when we realize that there are a great variety of media offering numerous programme genres, and also the fact that there are a whole variety of people and groups listening, viewing, reading in a countless number of socio-cultural environments.

Perhaps, the only safe conclusion on 'effects' (or 'interactions') of the media is that arrived at by Bernard Berelson several years ago: 'Some kinds of communication on some kinds of issues, brought to the attention of some kinds of people under some kinds of conditions have some kinds of effects."

Varied Principles

Several theories related to the effects or changes brought about by the media (largely television) on individuals and society have been propounded by both 'functionalist' and 'critical' schools of communication. The 'functionalist' theorists begin with the assumption that the media have a role and a function in society: to stabilise, reinforce and maintain the consensus in society. They do not see the question of power and conflict as a major driving force in society; they assume that the competition among the various groups in society allows for free and fair play, and all groups have an equal chance to dominate and to control. The 'critical' theorists, on the other hand, place the struggle for power among social classes/groups at the centre of society; the mass media are invariably employed by the dominant class to propagate its ideology. Further, while the 'functionalists' research media effects using empirical quantitative methods, the 'critical' theorists are so not much concerned with effects as the cultural and political context in which media experiences take place, the ownership and economics of the media, and the various ways in which audiences 'read' the media.

These theories range from one extreme position of all-powerful wide-ranging effects of the media, to the opposing extreme position where the media have no effects at all. At the one extreme are writers and researchers like Marie Winn who take the media, especially television, to be a 'plug-in drug'; at the other extreme is Joseph Klapper who concluded from his longitudinal research that media succeed only in 'reinforcing' old attitudes, habits, and beliefs. In between, are the 'negotiation' or interaction theorists who suggest that effects, like meanings of media texts, are ultimately 'negotiated' by audiences. This is sometimes termed the 'mediation perspective'. Most media theories deal directly with the 'effects' of the contents of programmes on opinions, attitudes, perceptions, beliefs and social behaviour. The theories have their basis largely in research on television and film, though some in speculation or personal experience. The largest number of studies have been on the effects of violence in television programmes on the behaviour of children and adolescents; others on the effects of propaganda on personal opinion and on voting behaviour. Since early effects research was based on the 'persuasion' model of communication (the Lasswell model and the Shanon-Weaver model, for instance) and carried out by social psychologists, the results often pointed to strong effects, for that is what they were looking for in the first place. The social contexts in which the media were experienced (say the family, the home, the theatre, the school or the peer group) were rarely taken into account. The stimulus-response experiments to measure effects were frequently carried out in laboratories using mechanical pre-test and post-test methods of research. Thus the results they obtained turned out to be along expected lines.

Reinforcement : Limited Effects Theory : Joseph Klapper and others, for example, believed that media reinforce existing values and attitudes. Only then, after all, can programmes of the media be popular with a majority of social groups which have an interest in the perpetuation of their own traditions and statuses. Lazarsfeld and Merton held that the mass media 'cannot be relied upon to work for changes, even minor changes, in the social structure.'

Some mass communication theorists (Lazarsfeld, Merton, and Winn for instance) argue that media have a 'narcotizing dysfunction' that distracts audiences from real problems and in fact prevents their doing anything about them. In other words, the mass media, have a drug-like addictive effect, lulling audiences into passivity and a sense of elation. Exposure to a flood of information, say Lazarsfeld and Merton, may serve to narcotize rather than energize the average reader or listener. As an increasing amount of time is devoted to reading and listening, a decreasing share is available for organized action. The interested and informed citizen can congratulate himself on his lofty state of interest and information and fail to see that he has abstained from decision and action. He comes to mistake knowing about problems of the day for doing something about them.

First proposed in 1948, the theory appears dated particularly after the galvanizing impact together with a combination of many other factors the mass media had in bringing the Vietnam war to an end, and in throwing Nixon out as a result of Watergate. In India, the press publicity given to excesses of the emergency, particularly through underground literature, did contribute to bringing about an end to the emergency.

Closely related to the 'narcosis' theory, is the 'cartharsis' theory of media effects. Seymour Feshbach, the main exponent of the theory, argued that the media may have a 'cathartic' effect on people that somehow purges them of many anti-social and unfulfilled desires, frustrations and feelings of hostility. In one of his laboratory studies, Feshbach subjected college students to savage insults and criticism at the hands of experimenters; the experimental group was then shown an aggressive film of a brutal boxing-match, while the 'control group' was shown a dull film. When they were later questioned about their opinions of the experimenters, those students who had seen the film on boxing felt less hostile to their experimenters than those students who were shown the 'control' film.

However, in an almost identical laboratory experiment by Leonard Berkowitz, the experimenters were introduced to the students as either a boxer or a rhetoric student. The students were then exposed to either a violent boxing film or a neutral non-violent film. Later, they had the chance to give electrical shocks (under the pretext of a separate experiment) to the 'boxer' or the rhetoric student. It was found that those students who had seen the boxing film gave the largest number of shocks to the 'boxer.' Berkowitz concluded that the boxing film was responsible for the aggressive response of the students. Other experiments have revealed that children in particular are likely to imitate violence in films if the violent actions in the film are rewarded.

Laboratory experiments are by their nature artificial for they cannot re-create the different conditions, environments, and states of mind in which violent films are seen. The reactions to violence in films can be very varied as is well demonstrated in Philip Schlesinger's work on 'Women viewing Violence.'

The 'narcosis' and 'catharsis' theories represent extreme views. So does Ernest Van den Hag's view that 'mass communications, taken together are demeaning, debasing and de-personalizing instruments of manipulation at worst; middle-class hedonism at best.' Yet another extreme theory is that of Frederic Wertham which says that the content of the media is 'corruptive in general and specifically teaches materialism, brutality, antisocial behaviour and callousness towards other humans.'

It is a Matter of Chance : In contrast, Aldous Huxley took the stand that media indeed do teach people things, but most of them are of no consequence; they also have effects, but mostly in unimportant and trivial facets of our lives although we may think that they are important. These trivial facets are fashions, mannerisms, mating habits, and food habits. As Schramm, Lyle and Parker found in their study of children and television, 'television could be an especially effective agent of incidental learning while the child is still young. This is because at that time it seems so real.'

By the 1950s and sixties, communication researchers began to fine tune their methods and their theories. Elihu Katz, Denis McQuail and Michael Gurevitch introduced what they termed the 'uses and gratifications' theory of media effects. They turned their attention to how audiences used the media to live out their fantasy lives and to seek out other gratifications, or even to inform and educate themselves about the world and its people. Thus media 'effects' were related to the needs and activities of audiences. The theory was largely concerned with the selection, reception and nature of response of audiences to the media, the assumption being that individual members in an audience made conscious and motivated selection of channels and programmes. It was also assumed that audiences made supplementary and compensatory uses of the mass media.

Cultural Cause

George Gerbner's dissatisfaction with effects research led him to evolve a sophisticated theory grounded on his longitudinal research on American television. He and his team undertook a content analysis of television programmes, looking at portrayals of gender, violence, the family, portrayal of minorities, and then matched these with actual situations, behaviours and attitudes in American society. Take the portrayal of crime, for instance. Gerbner concluded that there was a 'cultivation' effect or enculturation effect on audiences highly exposed to television. Audiences 'adopted' the perceptions and values which were consistently portrayed in different programme genres.

Gerbner and his team attempted 'to move beyond the analysis of effects on individual behaviour and to analyse communication systems at a social structural level.' Television was seen as the arm of the industrial and military establishment, an agent of social control.

Part of Technology : "The medium is the message", wrote Marshall McLuhan, setting the controversy over media effects on its head. No matter what the contents of programmes, he argued, people will watch television; it commands their attention as no other medium has. He warned like a doomsday prophet that "the electronic media are transforming every aspect of man's life and re-structuring civilization, not so much by the content of their messages, as by the nature itself of television, movies, computers and other media." Mass communications, therefore, are neither good nor bad, but rather mystical devices that possess powers to change the way mankind lives and thinks. For instance, Indian cities are already witness to some changes in eating, sleeping and socialising habits as a result of the introduction of television.

A rather different kind of effect on which no theory has yet been built is the impact of media among and within themselves. Mass communicators are known to review each other's work, and reporters carefully go through rival papers, and switch on to news programmes on the air. It is no surprise, therefore, that 'copycatting' in content and form has become a common phenomenon. Let a topic be introduced in one paper, and the others take it up with a vengeance. So when a 'health' programme proves popular on TV, every newspaper introduces a 'health' column.

Then there are the effects of new media upon the old, and vice versa. The formats of Doordarshan's newscasts and features have in fact been copied from All India Radio and magazines are all profusely illustrated because of the impact of television. Again, short stories first published in the papers or magazines, are turned into radio, TV and cinema scripts. All these inter-media and intramedia effects may be called "reflex effects" or "bandwagon effects."

Part Played by Education

Right from pre-Independence days, attempts have been made by both government and private groups to use the media for educational purposes. Dadasaheb Phalke, the pioneer of Indian cinema, made educational documentaries such as 'The growth of a Pea plant' and 'How to Make a Film' besides fictional films. Radio experiments in the use of radio for promoting literacy and education were conducted as early as the 1930s. Television was introduced into India by the Nehru Government with the primary aim of exploiting the medium for distance education. B.G. Verghese's Chattera experiment attempted to use the daily newspaper to educate urban Delhites about rural people and their problems.

The most ambitious attempt to exploit the mass media for education was of course, SITE (Satellite Instructional Television Experiment). It sought to educate rural people in six states of India about the need for family planning, improved agriculture, hygiene, nutrition and health care. Classroom-type instructions were also provided to school children.

Today, Doordarshan devotes at least ten per cent of its telecast time to educational or enrichment programmes for farmers, school children, youth and other groups. It has taken to promoting literacy on a nationwide scale. UGC's 'Countrywide classroom' and IGNOU's early morning transmissions are ambitious post-SITE attempts to use television for higher education.

Do media educate? How effective are the mass media in educating the people of our country? What are the 'effects' of media on 'education?' These are all loaded and difficult questions to which there can be no straight cut-and-dry answers. Literate and educated people benefit much more from educational media than the less literate and educated, unless the education-oriented programmes are specifically geared to the needs, interests and levels of specific groups. This is an essential condition of any educational programme on any medium to have some kind of 'effect.' Even before groups and regions can benefit from education through the print or the electronic media, they will need to become 'media literate.' Media literacy precedes or is simultaneous with the skill to learn from the media.

The folk media are perhaps much more effective in promoting the message of literacy than any of the mass media.

In Kerala, Maharashtra, Andhra Pradesh and other states, folk forms of the local regions have been utilised both by voluntary social action groups and by government-supported literacy campaigns. For example, in Maharashtra, literacy campaigns have used folk musical forms such as lavani, powada, gondhal, jagar and others.

During the campaign, cultural teams went out to the different villages on Kalajathas. The main thrust of the messages conveyed through song, dance and discussions was literacy. However, it was reported that other issues such as mother and child care, family planning, watershed management, the problem of alcoholism and dowry, small savings and agricultural development were also conveyed.

In some campaigns, the message of literacy was spread by relating the folk forms to local festivals: akshar kandlis and akshar rangoli at the time of Diwali and Akshar Ganpathi at the time of the popular festivals of Maharashtra. In the campaign at Sindhdurg, haldi-kumkum celebrations were widely used to mobilise women and to bring them together to discuss issues related to their everyday lives. However, in all these campaigns, there were few attempts to place literacy in the context of political, social and economic structures in the rural and urban areas. (for further details Cf. D. Saldanha: 'Cultural Communication in Literacy. Economic and Political Weekly, May 15, 1993, pp. 981-989).

It appears then that the media by themselves (whether modern or folk) do not promote literacy. Nor is commitment enough. The social structures obtaining at the grass-root need to be taken into account, as well as the infrastructure in the form of schools, teachers, volunteers, post-literacy facilities, and the caste and communal divides. A factor often overlooked is the time available to agricultural and industrial workers to respond in any meaningful way to literacy drives in the media.

Family's Role

The TV, cable and satellite 'invasion' of urban India is of great concern to parents and teachers. With so much time given to watching the small screen, parents are worried that little or no time will remain for conversation in the family, for family get-togethers and for family visits. However, parents must acknowledge that they too spend a lot of time with television, and that frequently they exercise no control on what their children watch and when. Further, parents frequently use television as a baby-sister or as an excuse for staying at home.

Except for Andal Narayanan's pioneering study on the Impact of Television on Viewers, and Neena Behl's close look at what happens to one Indian village when television is introduced in it, there are hardly any studies that take a hard critical look at what happens in the family when television enters the home and how it becomes part of the furniture after a few years. Multi-channel television often creates friction among siblings, or between parents and children, or even between parents themselves. But then TV also helps to bring a family closer especially when all members enjoy a popular programme together. It provides topics for conversation, for expressing opinions and for family discussions. A lot depends upon what the members of the family do with television. Since few Indian families can afford more than one TV set, gathering around the TV set is similar to the earlier practice of gathering round a fireplace.

The family, like any other social institution, is a power structure. The exercise of power in the home, in earlier times, was through the breadwinner, generally the man of the house. The remote control device now puts power in the hands that hold it. Ethnographic and focus group studies of the place of television in the lives of families clearly point to the remote control in most families being held by male rather than female members. However, in many Indian homes where the female is dominant, the remote control is invariably in the hands of the mother. In some families though, the remote control is in the hands of the children.

Without communication an individual could never become a human being; without mass communication an individual could never become part of modern society. Socialisation is a life-long active process, beginning on the day of one's birth. The child learns to socialise from the parents and the social groups he or she belongs to. As children grow up they come into contact with other social groups, but their basic loyalties are to their own primary and secondary groups which provide them their sets of attitudes, beliefs, and norms of behaviour. Children come under three kinds of social control: (1) tradition orientation-social control based on tradition; (2) inner orientation-social control achieved through standards, guidelines or values existing in each individual; and (3) external or other orientation-social control achieved by conformity to standards existing in other persons and groups.

The child of today comes into contact with groups other than those in school; for instance, through the mass media, which give him/her access to remote groups and their cultures. Besides, the mass media provide models of behaviour, and norms of living. The child begins to imitate them, particularly in cases where he or she is least integrated into the family or the peer group. Such children rely heavily on media advice and models; while others do not since their activities outside the home provide them greater stimuli and other role models.

But the socialisation effects of mass media cannot match the power of the home, the neighbourhood and the school where interpersonal relationships exist. In contrast, socialisation through the mass media is depersonalised and hence effective mainly in the peripheral areas of life. One would expect a national outlook to follow from a wide exposure to national news and social advertisements in the mass media. But communalism continues to hold out against all attempts at national integration through the media-so deep-rooted are our attitudes and beliefs. So also social evils like the dowry system, child marriages, caste conflicts and the like persist. The mass media are not a panacea for social or economic under-development as some governments are prone to believe.

In any study of media influence on children, or on the influence of children's interests and needs on the media, the age-group is an important variable. Other equally important variables are social class, religious and cultural background, linguistic background and community. It has been found from research in the West that the pre-operational child (aged 5 years and below), responds differently from the child belonging to the concrete operations stage (6 to 11 years) or to the formal operations stage (11 to 12 years). To illustrate, young children aged five and below see a series of separate and fragmentary incidents rather than the story of a film. They do not invariably recognise the identities of the principal character throughout the film, and they tend to believe implicitly what they see on TV to be real. And, interestingly, they sometimes read incidents into the plot from their own imaginations, or add incidents and events that they think should have occurred.

The 6 to 11 year old child, however, understands the story of a film, but still understands only the concrete physical behaviour of film performers. Only at the age of 10 or 11, does he usually understand the feelings and motivations and put himself in the shoes of a character.

The 11 to 12 year old comprehends films as efficiently as adults, and comes to realize the make-believe fantasy world of films. He also gradually begins to understand the emotional relationships in films, and to appreciate some and dislike other aspects of films. Besides, he can imagine hypothetically the sorts of relationships which may exist between film characters even if the relationships are not presented on the screen. Recent ethnographic and semiotic studies of children's interaction with television suggests that children make for a 'lively audience' and are highly discriminating and critical viewers.

Impact on Children

Children below the age of 16 comprise almost 40 per cent of the population of India. Yet barely five per cent of total telecast time is directly aimed at children; this is equally true of radio, fiction and documentary cinema, and the press. On television, programmes for children devote a lot of time to animation films and puppet shows. Several American animation series like 'Spiderman', 'Heman', and 'Mickey and Donald', have featured on Indian television. The advertisements that usually accompany them relate to toys and dolls. Interestingly, terrorist-related toys like 'G I Joe', 'Barbie' dolls, sold by India toy manufacturers like Funskool, an MRF-controlled company based in Goa, and Leo Toys of Blowplast company, are advertised regularly on children's programmes. Funskool is a collaborator of a subsidiary of Hasbro, the world's largest toy manufacturer, and the makers of 'G I Joe'; Leo Toys collaborates with Mattels, the second largest toy manufacturer in the United States. Mattel produced the TV series on 'He-man' to promote the sale of their toys.

It has set up a Barbie Friends Club, 'an interactive club where children could emulate the role model' The members of the club-over 12,000 of them between the ages of 6 and 12 years at a subscription fee of Rs. 95 each-write letters to Barbie and she writes back to them. It is claimed that Barbie receives over a hundred letters every day.

Should Doordarshan allow itself to become a commercial medium for the peddling of transnational manufacturers and their toys? The Joshi Committee warned against this 'cultural invasion', but Doordarshan has not heeded the warning. The Joshi Committee Report also observed that 'reviews of children's reaction to film and television in India have indicated that animation is not always successful with Indian child audiences. Unfamiliarity with the technique sometimes makes it difficult for Indian children to identify the characters and objects.' For Indian children to comprehend them it is necessary to keep the drawings in animation films simple and realistic and the message needs to be conveyed in a direct manner. It therefore urged that research-based software be produced so that programmes are appropriate in terms of the child's level of development as well as his or her life situation.

The comic strips that daily newspapers, Sunday newspapers, and magazines publish regularly for young readers are mostly 'syndicated' comics from the United States. Columns for children frequently include quizzes, contests and stories. Children's magazines like Chandamama (in different languages), Target, Quest, and Heights carry similar fare.

While there is a National Film Foundation for Children and Young People, and children's film festivals are organized sporadically, very little attention is in fact paid to the production of films for children on a regular basis. The Films Division, on the other hand, is the foremost producer of short animation films, either directly educational in nature, or telling popular stories from the Panchatantra or the wealth of Indian folk-tale tradition.

The Joshi Committee Report (1984) learned from its extensive analysis of television software that 'most of our children's programmes seem to have been designed for the upper-class child. This is somewhat paradoxical: the ultimate objective is to use television for education purposes, and it is the urban child who least needs additional educational inputs. Instead, television programmes should be directed primarily towards disadvantaged children in rural and urban areas.' The irony is that 'disadvantaged children' do not possess or have access to television receivers.

The Joshi Report also noted that children's programmes are among the most substandard of all programmes produced. Indeed, children's programmes are considered child's play; producers who are under-utilized at other work are allocated the children's programme section. Further, the time slotted for telecasting children's programmes is generally at the beginning of the evening's transmission, when most children should be playing outdoors.

Since children do not have any purchasing power, market researchers do not study children as television or radio audiences, or as readers. Except for SITE studies of children's response to educational programmes, and a few other studies, we have little significant research on children's use of, or interaction with, the mass media.

Female Role

The Joshi Committee Report observed in 1984 that Doordarshan is 'dominated by feature films and film-based programmes that exploit the female form to titillate and/or, through their socially insensitive approach, simply trivialize and debase the image of womanhood.' It therefore urged not only a reduction of the number of future films and film-based programmes on television but, more positively, "the incorporation of the 'women's dimension' in all programmes and "the need for a separate focus on and for women."

Other recommendations of the Joshi Committee Report included the following:

(1) The improvement of women's condition, status and image be defined as a major objective of Doordarshan.

(2) The formulation of clear guidelines regarding the positive portrayal of women on television, and a system of monitoring the implementation of these guidelines.

(3) The redefinition of the image and the promotion of the male 'ideal' as one who is carrying and willing to share in household, childcare and contraceptive responsibilities.

(4) The need for orientation courses for all Doordarshan policy makers, programming and production staff so that they are sensitised to social issues with particular reference to women's issues and their implications in society.

(5) The careful scrutiny (by a special committee) of all advertisements shown on television, to ensure that they do not portray women in derogatory and stereotyped ways.

(6) The need for a weekly programme on viewers' views, in which the audience, critics, commentators, women's organizations are called upon to analyse and evaluate the week's programmes.

(7) The involvement of Mahila Mandalas in the installation of community television sets, and in community viewing arrangements in rural areas.

Women's organizations across the country (such as AWAG in Ahmedabad, Vimochana in Bangalore, and the Committees on Portrayal of Women in the Media, in New Delhi and Mumbai), periodicals like Manushi and Stree, and Departments of Women's Studies in universities, have been active for a decade now in carrying out research on representations of women in the various mass media. Over a dozen serious studies, involving both quantitative and qualitative methodologies, have been conducted; the majority of them are available, however, only in mimeo.

Doordarshan's portrayal of women in its various programmes has been subjected to close critical analysis by a number of researchers. Two major studies are: Affirmation and Denial: Construction of Femininity on Indian Television by Prabha Krishnan and Anita Dighe (1990), and Vision Unveiled by Nandini Prasad (1994). The first study was conducted by Krishnan, Dighe and Rao in 1986. Programmes over a period of 15 days a sample of 30 news programmes, 30 special interest group programmes, 55 general enrichment programmes, 33 art and entertainment programmes, 27 fiction-oriented and cinema programmes, 186 commercials and two audience-contact programmes-a total sample of 363 items were scrutinized for women-related references. The largely quantitative analysis indicated certain definite trends:

In the first place, news related to women did not exceed 2.5 minutes out of the total 20 minutes. Women were news makers in less than ten per cent of the 30 news programmes telecast, mostly in the foreign news items that related to Margaret Thatcher and Corazon Aquino. Further, women invariably figured in the political news as wives, mothers, daughters of well-known men. They also appeared frequently as members of audiences and as victims of some calamity or accident. A significant number of women appeared as shoppers. In development-oriented news items, women featured as workers in tea plantations, sericulture poultry farming, etc., and as beneficiaries of welfare schemes. In women's programmes the focus was on the woman at home. The 'experts' in these programmes were men; in farmers' programmes all the experts were men; women, however, compared most children's programmes.

Where commercials were concerned, the life-styles promoted were largely elitist; the models in the commercials were overwhelmingly light-skinned. In voice-overs, male voices were presented as 'authoritative'; female voices as informative and 'seductive.' Women featured in all categories of commercials, but they were dominant in ads for foods, grooming and household items.

Prasad's content analysis of Doordarshan programmes was carried out in 1992, using a large sample of two and a half months of national news bulletins. The sample extended from October 1 to December 15, 1992, with every second day's bulletin comprising the sample, i.e. a total of 38 news bulletins. Prasad found that a mere 20 news items during the entire period related to women. Of the 20 news items, 5 related to social issues, 3 to mobilising public opinion on women's issues, and 11 to other women-related issues. Prasad's examination of the portrayal of women in Doordarshan's advertisements reveals that out of a total sample of 210 ads, 63 showed women in 'traditional' roles, 35 in a 'non-traditional' role, and 117 in a 'neutral manner.'

Descriptive analyses of the portrayal of women in popular television serials include those by Leela Rao, Jyoti Punwani and others.

Less than two per cent of broadcasting time on radio is devoted to programmes on or for women, yet over 25 per cent of radio advertising is directed at women, in the form of advertisements on cosmetics, food products, beverages and fabrics. The songs selected for broadcast on All India Radio and Vividh Bharati are 'by and large on religious themes or depicting themes of coy young women waiting to be married.' The plays convey the message of the ideal woman who is a housewife and mother. If she is employed, then surely she must be neglecting her home and children. Stereotypes of women are reinforced in songs, plays and commercial jingles.

An exhaustive study of the portrayal of women in Hindi and Gujarati films was conducted in 1976 by Ila Pathak and her colleagues at AWAG. Their analysis of 12 Hindi and six Gujarati films showed that the films emphasised young, beautiful and sexually attractive women; portrayed women in terms of their relationship to men; depicted women in traditional female occupations; and as overwhelmingly emotional, dependent, superstitious, and irrational beings. Besides, they stressed marriage as a goal for women, and offered a double standard of morality.

Dasgupta and Hedge did a quantitative analysis of 30 Hindi films available on video in a mid-Western city in the United States, with the objective of investigating how they dealt with 'mistreatment' of women. The analysis led them to conclude that mistreatment was not a central concern of any film; that mis-treatments (such as physical battering, assault, rape, homicide) occurred regularly when women step out of their traditional roles; and that mistreatment served the common function of returning straying women to their stereotypical and socially approved behaviour patterns. The recurrence of mis-treatments on the Hindi screen was, therefore, an established mechanism to monitor and perpetuate the patriarchal order. Another study by Vijaya Mulay revealed that women continue to be portrayed in traditional ways, and that in a few films, women beatings were popularized as a form of tanung and romancing. Madhu Kishwar, editor of Manushi, found that Films Division documentaries on family planning contained a strong sexist bias: they underscored the importance of sons over daughters, the responsibility of family planning as a woman's duty, and the general passive nature of women.

Studies of the print media have focused on the reporting of rape cases in the press ('as merely spicy news stories'), the presentation of women in women's sections of newspapers, general interest magazines and women's magazines. Ammu Joseph and Kalpana Sharma critiqued the news media's presentation of women's issues in their study, Whose News?

Ila Pathak's study of women's sections in the Gujarati dailies of Ahmedabad, for instance, found that there were hardiy any articles devoted to a serious discussion of women's problems at home or in society. Dasgupta's look at the Sunday editions of four English dailies found that articles on women were middle-class and urban-biased, and were restricted to a limited range of themes which did not take into account the political and economic realities of Indian women.

An analysis of fiction in three women's magazines and two general interest magazines concluded that they contained 'images and norms which should discourage female employment, particularly in higher-status occupations.'

Women's magazines have come in for a lot of criticism. Often, they are no more than a mixed bag of recipes, tips on beauty aids, romantic stories, features on women's issues, and discussions on gender problems, and of course women-oriented advertisements. Butalia found that, the advertisements, even in women's magazines, were sexist. Aminu Amin's 1982 study of 'Commercial Ads and the Great Health Robbery of Women and Children' showed how advertisers and manufacturers play on the susceptibility and vulnerability of women consumers and cheat them into buying food products, cosmetics, sanitary napkins, soaps and detergents that are positively harmful to the health of their families. The study also revealed that 'men in advertisements are fully clothed, appear confident and dignified' while the women are presented as glamorous but in traditional roles. Further, 'wares for men were sold for durability and economy; those for women for beauty and glamour.' Kalia's analysis of the language used in Indian school textbooks also concluded that it was clearly 'sexist.' Another analysis of the textbook series called Let's Learn English concluded that women were few in number when it come to central characters, and they were shown as either mothers or teachers.

Besides the question of 'representations', the focus of research has been the job opportunities for women, especially at decision-making levels, in the production, administration and technical departments of the various media. The most widely discussed is S.R. Joshi's study for UNESCO entitled Invisible Barriers: Women at Senior Levels. It analyses the status of women's employment at senior levels in Doordarshan. It found that women headed three out of 18 stations; that at the Delhi station 40 per cent of producers are women. Another important finding was that 'although overall employment figures were not available, 28 per cent of the producers at two other stations are women, with responsibility for determining the content of programmes'. Besides, one-third of the women at these levels are unmarried, compared to only one-tenth of the men. The women have fewer children, and are better educated though mostly in the arts, compared to the men, half of whom had gone for courses in science, engineering and commerce. According to the study, a large proportion of the women thought that there would be a change in programme content with an increase in the proportion of female employees programme quality would improve and a more balanced perspective would emerge.

But there are more women in senior positions in the government-owned radio and television than in the press which continues to be male-dominated. A 1987 study by the Women and Media Group, Bombay, discovered that women journalists are mainly on the staff of women's magazines; the women journalists in the daily newspapers and the news magazines also confine themselves to women-related issues and 'soft' news stories. Gita Aravamudan's study of the status of women journalists in Kerala, the state with the highest literacy in the land, found that most are employed by women's magazines, or hold desk jobs; dailies such as Malayala Manorama and Kerala Koumadi however, did not employ women as a matter of policy.

Recognising Audience

A largely neglected area in women-and-the-media studies has been audience research. Most of the audience research available has been conducted by market researchers where women are taken to be 'consumers'. The kind of research questions that need to be looked at are: How do women from different social classes 'read' the stereotypes in the various mass media and their genrès? Do they, for instance, swallow the stereotypical representations hook, line and sinker, or reject or even 're-read' them? Again, how are programmes for women on radio and television produced? Who takes the vital decisions on programme content? Does the very fact that women are producers necessarily add a women's dimension to the programme? Women film directors like Aparna Sen and Sai Paranjpe have sensitized us to women's issues, but so have Satyajit Ray, Kumar Shahani, Mani Kaul, Basu Chatterjee, and Shyam Benegal. Further, women-centred serials on Doordarshan (Rajani; It's A Woman's World, Kashmakesh. Chehre, Poornima, Rathachakra, Rathen Au Bhai Hain, Swayamsiddha, Basanti, Shanti, and several others) have attempted, some with greater success than others, to probe the woman/gender question through interesting narratives.

Further, several women have entered print and electronic journalism, but one wonders whether this alone has made any difference to professional values and news values which have been evolved and moulded by patriarchy, politics and the market. The core of professional journalism is still 'hard news'; 'soft news' which women reporters and feature-writers are generally asked to cover, is considered less important.

Factors Responsible for Consumerism : To most advertisers, people are not customers or even people but mere 'consumers.' Advertisers seek to entice target consumers to consume as much as possible, as frequently as possible, and with as much relish and envy or vanity as possible. It is not without significance that we are urged to buy and to consume wherever we are and whenever we switch on the radio, TV, cable or satellite TV, or read newspapers and magazines. Day in and day out we are bombarded with print and electronic messages promising us fun, frolic and happiness if we 'consume.' It does not matter whether we have the purchasing power to try out 'impulse products' like ice-creams, chocolates, candies, or soft drinks, but if we do not consume like the rest of the world we are likely to be left behind in the rat-race.

It is not only advertising that directly promotes consumption beyond one's means, but also 'sponsored' programmes and columns and supplements. The subtle messages of soap-operas, quiz and game shows (where expensive prizes are gifted by business and industrial houses), elite-oriented news and current affairs programmes, sports programmes, fashion shows, children's magazines and programmes, cartoon shows, 'advertorials' and almost every programme-all tell one persuasive story: consume or be damned. Advertisers like to believe that the consumer enjoys the freedom of choice. He is, after all, not compelled to buy. He must learn to live within his means. What is more, the consumer is not a moron; she is your wife!

The question that needs to be raised is: Do the mass media which thrive on advertising lead to excessive consumption in society, or is the other way around: Does an affluent and economically developed society or community persuade the mass media to turn consumerist? It is true that both manufacturing and service industries in developed economies spend more on advertising and media relations than those in developing economies. However, it is equally true that the world's biggest markets for consumer product as well as for consumer durable are in the less developed countries. Further, during the past decade or so, growth in advertising expenditure in Asian countries has been steadily rising, while it has been reduced in the United States and other western countries.

In sum, consumerism is a fall-out of an industrial society, especially a society that swears by the economic laws of the free market and a liberal democracy. The assumption of such a society is that an 'invisible hand' controls the forces that compete freely with one another, and that justice and equity is promoted by such competition. The reality is that in a so-called open and free market the law of the jungle prevails, and only the most aggressive survive. Public welfare and concern fall by the wayside. The Indian experience of 'privatization' and 'liberalization' during the post-Rajiv Gandhi years suggests that some 'regulation' is imperative if the public will is to be maintained.

Causes of Societal Nature

Over three thousand studies have been conducted during the past forty years in the United States alone that suggest that there is a 'correlation' between social aggression and the viewing of violence on the big and small screens. According to the American Psychological Association, by the time an average American child is ten or eleven years old, he/she would have seen 8,000 murders and 10,000 acts of violence on television.

Few studies on the subject have been conducted in India, and Indian children are not yet exposed to the excessive violence that American children are, at least on television. However, with the arrival of satellite television which is dominated by American films and television programmes, the Indian child is no doubt likely to be exposed to more and more violent fare. Of course, popular Indian films too have a surfeit of violence, much of it stylised, but some of it vivid and realistic, often bordering on the pornographic.

There have been cases of children and adults imitating on-screen violence and the modus operandi of gangsters, robbers and murderers. Such cases get prominent coverage in the press and other media. But all this does not lead one to the conclusion that cinema or television violence is the primary or even the secondary cause of violence in our society. At the most, screen violence may be one of the many contributory factors. More influential factors are poverty, frustration, unemployment, revenge, family clashes, urban decay, loss of self-esteem, a sense of failure in other words, a combination of sociological, psychological, economic and cultural factors. In any case, the 'correlations' that the American studies have found between screen violence and individual acts of violence do not mean that screen violence has 'caused' the violent behaviour. Statistical correlations, however significant, may point to an 'association' but hardly ever to a cause-and-effect relationship. What is of greater concern is the effect of 'desensitization' which could result from repeated exposure to scenes of violence in programmes, news and cartoons.

Exposure to violence constantly and on a daily basis can desensitize us to violence in real life: violence against women and children, for instance, will shock or move us much less than we ought to as human beings. Further, we might be convinced that violence is a part of society, and that it is normal, even glamorous to be aggressive and 'macho' in one's behaviour. It might lead us to believe that some groups (for instance, tribals, dalits and leftists) are naturally violent, and such stereotypes might endure.

Violence in the news and in comic strips is rarely talked about. While the portrayal of violence in the press and broadcast media is condoned because it is 'factual' and deals with real-life incidents, the caricatures of violent fights and clashes between heroes and villains are condoned because they are presented in a light and humorous manner. There has been hardly any study in India or elsewhere in Asia about the influence of such violent portrayals on society.

A recent study sponsored by AMIC, Singapore, of television violence in six Asian countries concluded that where American origin fare dominated, as in the Philippines and Thailand, the violent scenes were more numerous than in indigenous programmes, though this was not the case in Japanese television.

The violence on the Indian television screen was found to be mostly in the popular Hindi and regional language films. The Indian Institute of Mass Communication, New Delhi, undertook a study of television violence in 1996, using the Gerbner model of 'cultivation analysis.'

But violence is not related to crime alone. It must take into account state violence, like that of the police and the armed forces, or the violence of the law which does not bring the guilty to book, or which delays justice, or worse, punishes the innocent. Such violence too is sometimes the subject of cinema and television. The portrayal of such violence could help raise consciousness and thus lead to social reform (e.g. the film Ardh Satya, and the television serial, Tamas). Violence in the mass media is frequently associated with sex.

Indeed, rape or forced sex is the most violent crime that is often depicted graphically on the big and small screen. In recent years, a rape sequence has almost become obligatory in the popular film. Rape sequences are sometimes followed by scenes of blood and gore, since scores have to be settled and the rape avenged. Further, villains need to frequent night clubs where titillating cabarets are put on for their entertainment. The censors come down heavily on a few films, but the majority of popular films are 'passed' as okay for the entire family. Foreign television soap-operas, sitcoms, detective serials, music videos, and even talk shows and sports relays (especially those from the United States, Australia and Britain) have dollops of sex and violence, often verging on soft-core pornography. Doordarshan and Zee TV, in order to compete with STAR-TV, have begun imitating the fare on the satellite channels uplinked from Hong Kong, and other Asian cities.

4

The Evolution

Communication has played an important role in the development of human civilization. Computers have brought a revolution in the field of communication. Computer system improved communication facilities, which extend the power of computer beyond the computer room. Internet has linked every single field and every single part to each other. Information can be communicated from one place to another at very fast pace through internet with the help of computers. So, computer has become an important means of communication.

System of Data Communication : Data communication refers to the means and methods whereby data is transferred between processing locations. It is the link that permits people at different locations to have direct interaction with the central processing system. Nowadays, computers are quite used in transmission of data. Transferring data from one place to another is called 'data communication'. Data communication utilizes hardware, software and data communication techniques. Nowadays, data communication plays an important role in railways and airways reservation, ATM machine, weather forecasting etc. Data communication helps in transmitting data from one computer to another or from a computer to various parts like hard disk, printer etc. Internet has changed the entire scenario of data communication. Data communication is the combination of two words 'data' and 'communication'. By data we mean 'non-processed information' where as by communication we mean 'to transfer data and information from one place to another'. Data and information are different from each other. Information means processed data.

Components of Data Communication System

(1) Sender Computer

(2) Data Communication Device

(3) Medium or Channel of Communication

(4) Receiving Computer

Originating ——— ☎ ——— ☎ ——— Receiving

Computers	Computers
Data Communication Device	Data Communication Device
Digital Signals	Analog Signals Analog Signals

This computer is used to send the data.

These devices are connected to both sender and receiving computer. These devices convert digital signals to analog signals and analog signals to digital signals. Modem is such type of device.

Data is transferred from one place to another through these channels i.e. telephone lines, microwave channels, satellites etc.

These computers receive the data and display it on the screen or print it.

Transmission of Data : In this type of transmission every bit is transmitted in serial, one after another. So, this type of transmission requires only a wire to link the transmitting computer and the receiving computer. This is the most used technique for data transmission between two computers over long distance.

Under this each bit of the byte is transmitted separately on parallel path, so that all characters of a byte are transmitted simultaneously. One byte is send together. So, this requires more than one wire. One wire transmits single bit. It is used to transmit the data simultaneously to a device. Parallel transmission is used for short distances such as from the computer to the printer attached to it. It is much costlier than the serial transmission because of the large number of wires. It provides faster data transmission.

In this mode the characters are transmitted in a group and each block of code transmitted is preceded by a number of special signals called synchronization signals. There is a control character at the beginning and end of the bit chain. There is an equal interval between different characters. In this mode of transmission data transfer rate is very high.

Under this every character is transmitted separately. The signals in asynchronous transmission are sent in irregular time intervals. It is not suitable for transmission of larger data at regular intervals. The transmission from a mouse or to a printer is all asynchronous transmission. It is comparatively slower than the synchronous transmission. It is mostly used in microcomputer.

In analog transmission electromagnetic waves are transmitted. Electromagnetic waves are like sound waves which have electromagnetic properties. The transmission rate in analog transmission is expressed in frequency which is measured in Hertz. One Hertz means one cycle per second. The data is transmitted continuously under this method. Analog-transmission can be carried out through radio waves, Microwave and telephone lines etc.

In digital transmission electrical pulses are used as signals, which are in binary form. So the digital signals comprises of 0s and 1s called binary numbers. It transmits data in discrete form. The capacity of digital transmission is measured in bps-bits transmitted per second. Data transmission requires no data conversion under this method so it reduces the time required to send messages. In digital transmission there are fewer transmission errors than analog transmission.

Channels of Communication : Following channels are used to transfer data in LAN:

> The oldest and the least expensive type of cable used for LAN are the twisted pair cables. A twisted pair cable consists of two insulated copper wires wrapped around each other. The purpose of twisting the wires is to reduce the electrical interference from similar pairs. It has low transmission rate.

A coaxial cable consists of a stiff copper wire as the core material surrounded by an insulating material (generally PVC). There are two conductors in coaxial cable. One is the single wire in the center of the cable and other is a outer shield in the form of wire mesh with an insulator in between. The wire mesh is covered in a protective plastic cover. The construction and shielding provides a good combination of high bandwidth and excellent noise immunity.

This cable is made up of glass having thickness of about 50 microns i.e. the thickness of human hair. Data is transmitted in it in the form of light pulses, which makes the data transmission possible at a very high speed. These cablesare highly durable and offer excellent performance however they are very expensive.

It is used for transmitting 'sound'. It is quite economical technology but data security is quite low. Cellular phones use radio frequency.

To send data over thousands of miles companies use communication satellites. Satellite transmission can transmit both microwave signals and telephone signals to an earth station. Earth stations function as an antenna. It transmit and receive data from and to satellites. Communication satellites use transponders as transmission device. Most communication satellites are placed in geosynchronous orbit above the equator. The extreme length of transmission path also causes echo problems. That's why these are less used by the companies.

Rapid Growth

Data transmission speed is the speed at which data travel over a communication channel. The ray at which the data are transferred is known as *baud* rate. Baud rate means number of times per second the signals being transmitted changes. Baud rate is generally measured into bits per second (bps). Data transmission speed of modem which is used on personal computers is 56.4 kbps (Kilo bits per second). Larger computers transmit data at the speed of mbps (million bits per second).

The Set-up

Simplex : Under this technique data is transmitted in one direction only e.g. Radio and Television.

Sender Receiver

Half Duplex : It allows both way transmissions of data but data can be transmitted only in one direction at any point of time e.g. Wireless.

Sender Receiver

Full Duplex : It allows both way transmissions of the data at the same time

Sender Receiver

The View

Computer stores and transmits data only in the form of electronic pulses. Presence of electronic pulse is denoted by '1' and its absences is denoted by '0'. This is called binary arithmetic and the two digits '1' and '0' are called binary digits. Binary digits in short form are called 'bits'. So, bits are the basis of information generated by the computer. Words, numbers and symbols are made up of bits. Each character is a sequence of bits. Some standards regarding the bits have been developed in order to maintain the homogeneity between different computer systems. The following two standards have been developed for data communication-

ASCII (Americans Standard Code for Information Interchange)

EBCDIC (Extended Binary Coded Decimal Interchange Code)

ASCII stands for American Standard Code for Information Interchange. It is a seven-bit code, which was developed by ANSI (American National Standard Institution). The ASCII code uses seven bits to represent a character and the extended ASCII code uses eight bits to represent a character. ASCII code displays 128 characters e.g. small and capital letters, numbers, control characters etc. Nowadays, all personal computers use ASCII code.

Ebcdic stands for Extended Binary Coded Decimal Interchange Code. It was developed by IBM. Ebcdic is an eight-bit code, which displays 256 characters. This code is used in IBM mainframe and compatible computers.

Electromagnetic waves are broken down in a number of symmetrical waves having different frequencies. Bandwidth indicates the difference between upper and lower frequencies. It indicates the range of frequencies of signals that can be transmitted over the channel using electromagnetic waves. The data transmission at a particular time depends on the size of the bandwidth. Higher the bandwidth greater the volume of data that can be transmitted per unit of time. Channels are classified as narrow band, voice band and broad band on the basis of rate of data transmission. In narrow band data transmission rate is very low in comparison to broad band. Voice band are used in normal telephone lines.

In digital transmission the speed of transmission is expressed as bits per second (bps) which is called bit rate. Baud rate is also used for denoting the speed of transmission. Baud rate denotes the number of times the electromagnetic state of a data transmission line changes per second. The speed of the data transmission is also denoted as kbps (kilo bits per second) and mbps (mega bits per second).

This bandwidth is used to transmit small quantity of data. It is commonly used in Telex. The data transfer rate in this bandwidth is 45 to 300 bps.

Under this the data transfer takes place at the rate of 300 to 4800 bps. It is used for data transmission in telephone lines.

It is used to transmit high volume data, sound and video to far off places. Data transfer can take place at the rate of millions bits per second. Data transmission through microwave tower and satellite is broadband transmission. It is also called Wide-Band.

Protocols : Protocols are set of rules and standards, which govern the way the data are transmitted in a computer network. Communication Protocols tell us the serial order in which the signals are to be transmitted and also at what time the transmission will be considered complete. These protocols provide direction at the time of the data transmission. Many manufacturers are active in the field of computer hardware and software so it is important to maintain the homogeneity in protocols.

Only systems using the same protocols can communicate directly with one another. ISO (International Organization for Standard) has developed network protocols which is called open system interconnection (OSI) to make interconnection of different communication and computer systems compatible to each other. There are seven different interdependent layers in this model hence it is called layered protocol.

IEEE (Institute of Electrical and Electronics Engineers) has recommended three protocols for hardware levels, which are Ethernet, Token-bus and Token-ring. Different protocols are used for different purposes e.g. Tele typewriters use TTY protocols, Radio Broadcasting uses ALOHA while LAN uses IEEE protocols. CCITT (Consultative Committee for International Telephone and Telegraph) has developed X.25 protocol for physical connection between two different nodes. TCP/IP is an Internet protocol.

Functions of Protocols :

- Control on data transfer
- Error correction
- Re-transmission control
- Determine the data format

E-mail : E-mail stands for electronic mail. E-mail is the greatest gift of the Internet. It is the most modern and economical means of data communication. Under this the information is transferred from one computer to another through electronic media. It is also called 'Electronic Delivery System'.

Letters, short messages, multi media files can be send through e-mail from any corner of the world to any person at any time.

Advantages of E-mail :

- Message reaches the destination instantly.
- Acknowledgement of the message is ensured.
- User can read the message as per his own convenience.
- The received messages can be stored.
- It is quite economical.

The sender and receiver both must have the Internet connection.

Fax is a short form of facsimile machine. It scans the text and the pictures and transmits them through the telephone lines from one place to another. This machine digitizes the text or the picture after scanning them. Digitization means converting the text or the picture into the digital form ('0' or '1') which is again converted into analog signals by the modem. It sends the information to the modem of the receiving machine through the telephone lines.

Modem at the receiving end digitizes the information and the Fax machine prints it out. The optical scanner in the Fax machine performs the job of digitization.

Voice and Video Messaging : Voice messaging is a new communication approach similar to e-mail except that only audio message rather than text message can be processed through it. It is the easiest mode of communication. Under this method the sender speaks into a microphone rather than typing. Messages are sent through telephone lines.

Television is the best example of the video messaging. Through this two or more people staying at different places can see and communicate with each other. Through this one can talk to the person and view the happenings at far off places as well. Nowadays, the audio and video messages are obtained from the reporters by the news channels like CNN, BBC and the same is telecast to the millions of people via television. Video Conferencing is of two types:

Two people can be linked through point to point conferencing. Videophone is the best example of the Point to Point Conferencing.

Many users can be linked through conferencing with the help of multipoint bridge.

Online Services : Through this the business houses provides the various type of information to the customers through the telecommunication lines. The customers can receive the information regarding stock prices, news, events, features, and other important announcements. Online Services are different from the Bulletin Board Services as it provides different types of information where as Bulletin Board Services provides information relating to some particular subject. Online Services are also called Log On Services. As soon as the customer logs on to link himself to the service, he has to answer the questions displayed on the screen, which are related to the customer identity like name, password etc. You can access the services after ensuring your identity. Nowadays, many software are available through which the log-on is possible by touching just one Function Key. American Online (AOL), MSN, CompuServe are the main Online Services. Internet itself is an Online Service but it is not under the control of any one organization and its aim is also not to earn profit. The user receives the information instantly. The computer gets connected to the vast information, which can be put to use.

User Connection : In order to get connected to the Internet the computer user has to take the connection from ISP (Internet Service Provider). The connections are of following types :

A dial-up connection simply means that when you want to access the Internet, your modem dials the host computer and you are connected to the Internet. This is the most popular way to connect the user and the ISP. The user requires the telephone connection and the modem in addition to the computer. The connections can be of following types:

(a) TCP/IP Link - Dial-up Internet protocols links such as serial line Internet protocol (SLIP) and Point-to-Point protocol to make your computer a direct part of the Internet while you are on-line. One can run Internet applications like e-mail, file transfer protocol (FTP), Talent, Gopher etc. from his computer.

(b) Shell Connection /Account- Under this connection the user's computer does not directly connected to the Internet because the user's computer transmits the signals to the ISP, which is the host computer. User's computer functions only as a terminal. The user is bound to use a particular software, which the host computer provides. It is the cheapest connection. Graphics cannot be used in it, although the other facilities provided by the Dial-up Connection like E-mail, WWW, are available here also.

Dedicated Line- In this type of connection there is a cable to connect the user's computer and the ISP computer. Under this one line is always available independently to connect the user's computer and ISP computer. Local Area Network (LAN) can also be connected to the Internet by this connection. Both types of Internet connections- Shell and TCP/IP can be obtained on this type of line. One doesn't have to face the problem of connectivity here. It is mostly useful for organizations, which need to be connected to the Internet continuously. For this type of connection the user needs a terminal server, router and other equipments. It is more expensive than the dial-up connection.

In this type of connection the user can send the information directly through the satellite to the ISP Computer and can also obtain the information back. This type of connection is very expensive. For sending information to the Satellite, the Hub stations on earth are used. This Hub Station has a big antenna, which helps, in transmitting information between VSATs.

In this type of connection a user needs to have a cable TV connection to connect with the Internet. The facilities of the Internet can be used with the help of the cable. The ISP's in big cities in India has started giving such connections.

5

Rapid Growth

It is assumed that freedom struggle had been started since 1857. This struggle was fought between kings of states, Nawabs, Jamindars, Samants and Britishers of East India Company, who were ruling over this country. Because of several selfish policies adopted by East India Company, the existence of Indian rulers was in danger. To save themselves, Indian rulers took the help of Indian masses to fight against English people.

After conquering over the struggle for freedom by the Indians, East India Company was dissolved and since 1858, the Crown had started ruling over India. Sir A. O. Hume, a reformist Britisher, had founded Indian National Congress. The main objective of this Congress was to establish mutual relationship, creating faith between the crown government. Hume was not in the know that this Congress would have been the cause for removing the British rule from India.

To unite India, as a nation, the concept of Bharat Mata had emerged. To save Bharat Mata, it was obvious that the British should have to quit. Under British rule during 18th and 19th century, Indians had come in contact with British Education.

Since then, they have evolved a free sovereign concept for India. There was a spirit being developed for nation's safety and even a common man had started to think over nationalism and nation's safety. Britain tried to win over France but nationalism had been emerging in France in shape of John of Arc. In Europe, nationalism had been spreading after the division of Poland, French revolution and fight against imperialism of Napolian Bonapart, National Freedom movement had been started in Italy, Hangery and Germany. There was Unification in Italy and Germany, Sarkia, Montenegro, Rumania and Bulgaria got freedom. This current of freedom movement was being spread over Finland, Ireland, Cheekoslowakia, Poland, Egypt and India. Slowly and gradually all these nations had become free and emerged in form of independent sovereign. This nationalism and national spirit is the contribution of 18th century.

Before we discuss about the concept of education in free India, we must be acquainted with the concept of nation. Dr. Tara Chand stated- The struggle for independence was not narrowly limited for political emancipation. It was broadly an endeavour to reconstruct an old, static, collective society and to establish in its place a modern dynamic; organization for the promotion of such value as Liberty, Justice, Individualism, Humanism and Secularism. Rabindranath Tagor says- Hindu and Muslims constitute the two major communities of India. We must be prepared to show the sacrifice, the patience, the care and the self-restraint that are needed to unite them into a common political organisation.

The renaissance in India played an important role in developing nation system of education. It was the outcome of the ideas of political thinkers. Zacharia says- Renaissance movement produced striking religious and social reforms long before it issued in a movement for political emancipation.

Indian Nationalism was the outcome of the suppression by the Britishers. Indians wanted to be free from the clutches of British Government. Many struggles for independence movements were launched. Peoples and leaders made several sacrifices. Thousands of the people had been hanged to death, lacs of people were imprisoned.

Raja Ram Mohan Rai, Devendre Nath Thakur, Swami Vivekanand, Swami Dayanand, Lokmanya, B. G. Tilak, G. K. Gokhale, M. K. Gandhi, J. L. Nehru, M. N. Rai, J. P Narain and many others had launched movements for the spreading of national feelings. It was understood that only education could be helpful to inculcate the feelings of nationalism and patriotism in the country. Therefore, in northern India the Arya Samaj, founded by Swami Dayanand had started to establish DAV schools and colleges, Arya Pathshalas, girls schools all over Punjab and United Province (Now Haryana and Punjab, Uttar Pradesh). Similarly Swami Vivekanand spread the feelings of nationalism and humanity over the country.

Lokmanya Tilak gave a slogan- Swarajya is my birth right and I will take it. This slogan gave an impetus to the national movement, use of Indian articles and ignoring the foreign material and the national feeling emerged. National Education Institutions had been established. During First World War, Indian leaders gave help to Britishers with the hope that they might give us freedom. 1919 Two Houses were established- House of Commons and House of Lords, to satisfy Indians; but this was not an end.

Independence Movement

In South Africa, Mohan Das Karam Chand Gandhi, commonly known as Bapu or Father of Nation, had been emerging as a national leader. He came to India and established himself as national leader through his new ideas of Satya and Ahimsa. He started non-cooperation movement but he failed in his mission. He did not loose his temperament. In 1928, again, M. K. Gandhi regained leadership in Congress and a resolution for complete autonomy was passed. In 1930, the Civil Disobedience Movement was started. British government had been compelled before Indians and she had agreed to have talks with the leaders of the freedom movement. Gandhi-Irwin pact was the outcome of this movement.

During the World War Second, it was cleared that sooner or later British rule would have been ended. In 1942, Quit India movement had forced Britishers to leave India. But it was a bad luck for India that it was divided into two- India and Pakistan, but both were complete sovereign. India got freedom on 15th of August 1947 and this was the end of 200 years old British rule over India.

Perception for New India

The concept of national education had been evolved through the freedom movement launched from time to time. The pioneers of India were of the opinion that until the masses of India would have been educated there would not be any socio-political consciousness among them. Swami Vivekanand, Swami Dayanand, M. K. Gandhi, Aurobindo Ghosh and R. N. Tagore established various types of educational institutions for the development of national feeling among the children.

There was the need for the eradication of mass illiteracy from India. Therefore literacy movements were launched. Even ministers had to go to the villages along with role up boards, chalk and duster to teach the villagers.

M. K. Gandhi indicated the drawbacks of education run by Britishers:

(i) Education is related with the unjust government.

(ii) This education is based on foreign culture. There is no place for Indian culture in it.

(iii) The education, run by British Govt. stressed on the mental development. It does not give emphasis on hand and heart.

(iv) The medium of education is English, therefore reality is lost.

Considering the above defects of British education, M. K. Gandhi stated the following objectives of national movement :

(i) The gain of Sovereignty.

(ii) Use of Indigenous things.

(iii) Avoidance of British Goods.

(iv) Demand of National Education.

Even Mrs. Annie Besant had opposed the English shape of education and felt the need of national education. She said, nothing can more surely emasculate national life, nothing can more surely weaken national character, than allowing the education of the young to be controlled by foreign ideals.

Base of Structure

There was huge demand for national education and many institutions had been established to meet this demand and to achieve the following objectives.

1. *Indian Control :* In the words of Annie Besant- Indian education should be formulated, controlled and run by the Indians. Indian leaders had stressed on the education which should be free from the clutches of Britishers.
2. *Love for Motherland :* Annie Besant had rightly said that Indian education should stress on patriotism, sacrifice and love for motherland. It develops love, sympathy, sincerity and enhance the real feelings of nationalism.

3. *Ideals for Education* : Indian education should stress over spiritual, national, social development which gives energy to national freedom movement.
4. *Development of National Character* : Education must develop the national character, Annie Besant was of the opinion that there was no place for national education in British system of education.
5. *Opposition of British Ideals* : There was a coconscious among Indian leaders that the objectives of British education may be good for Britain but they were not good for India, therefore these objectives must be opposed.
6. *Emphasis on Indian Languages* : The education, given through the English medium, is incomplete, only education given through the medium of mother tongue achieves real objectives.
7. *Vocational Education* : To eradicate the unemployment from the country, some sort of vocational education must be provided to the student. For this, the use of indigenous things had been stressed.
8. *Western Knowledge* : It was also emphasised that proper knowledge of western thought, system, literature, science was given to Indians to keep pace with the world.

Indian education was the reaction against the rule of East India Company and the Crown. It got momentum after 1858. Even then George V expressed his views- It is my earnest desire that there must be a web of schools and colleges in India, from where the pioneers in the field of agriculture, industry and professions of life and loyal persons should come out. Therefore, British Govt. established many universities, colleges, technical institutes and inspired private sector to establish the various types of institutions.

As far as the achievements are concerned, done by Indians, Gurudass Banerjee organised a society for the expansion of National education which opened 51 High Schools in Bengal. In North India, Arya Samaj started to establish DAV institutions, Arya School. Similarly Ramkrishna Mission had also established several educational institutions. Movement for Buniyadi Education, run by M. K. Gandhi, gave birth to Sabarmati Ashram, Sewagram, Gujarat Vidyapeeth, Kashi Vidyapeeth, Hindu University, Gurukul Kangri, Shanti Niketan, Jamia-Millia and Bihar Vidyapeeth, etc. Thus parallel to British Govt. new nation systems had come into existence.

The movement of education in India took a significant turn from the fateful night of August 15,1947. Slaves had finally won independence and in the free air of independence, attention turned towards changes in education, formulation of an educational policy, and the needs of the country. In the early days of independence, India's educationists felt that it was not possible to find the right path without altering the structure of education.

In order to educate itself, society, has to resort to modernisation. It must make an effort to create a class of educated individuals, drawn from every part of society, whose beliefs and ambitions bear the deep imprint of Indianism. Such persons are needed to raise the educational level of the average citizen. In a democracy, the end is the individual himself. The major purpose of education is to grant the individual the maximum possible opportunities for the fullest development of his capabilities. Today, it can be said that India's destiny is being shaped in its classroom.

In this world of ours, founded upon science and technology, it is education alone which determines the level of prosperity, well-being and security of individuals. The success we achieve in the task of national reconstruction depends directly upon the qualities of our students emerging from our colleges and universities. Awakening a national consciousness should be an important objective of our school education. We must endeavour to achieve these objectives by bringing about a growth in knowledge based upon our cultural heritage, by indulging in its constant revaluation and by instilling the deepest faith in its future progress.

Today, education has undergone multifaceted growth and progress. In consequence, literacy has increased, but at the same time, the rapidly increasing population has also increased the problems of education. In the various spheres of education, many problems have assumed gigantic and frightening proportions. Although the Five-Year plans have made some progress in this direction, education has, on the whole, failed to satisfy the individual's needs.

Statutory Point of View

From one viewpoint, it is appropriate to treat the declarations of the Constitution as the starting point of education in free India. The Constitution states explicitly that education is a State subject. This has been made clear in entries 63, 64, 65 and 66 of Schedule 1, and the 25th entry of the Third Schedule.

The ideas expressed in the Constitution concerning education in free India are the following :

(1) *Free and Compulsory Education* : Articles 45 of Constitution states, "The state shall endeavour to provide within a period of ten years from the commencement of this Constitution for the free and compulsory education of all the children until they complete the age of 14 years."

In this statement, the term 'State' refers to the States subordinate to the Union government.

(2) *Education of Women* : According to Articles 15 (3) of the Constitution the State cannot be absolved of the responsibility of framing special scheme for the education of women and children. This section does not restrain the State in any way in making special provisions for women and children.

(3) *Religious Education* : Article 28 (1) of the Constitution lays down that religious education of any kind will not be imparted in any educational institution financed from the national treasury. However, according to Article 28 (2), any institution established by a trust or a religious body can impart religious education, eves though such an institution may be aided by the government.

It has also been made clear that, in such educational institutions, children cannot be forced to imbibe a religious education which runs counter to their own religion, without the permission of the parents. In this context, the Kothari Commission has also pointed out that in the new generation, social and moral conflicts are coming to the fore.

Western thinkers have come round to the view that there should be a balance between knowledge and skill, science and technology should be linked with morality and religion, research into knowledge of oneself should be encouraged, the meaning of life should be understood, the real truth should stand revealed and there should be an understanding of human relations. (Education Commission, p.19, para 14.7).

(4) *Union and State Lists* : In the Constitution, educational activities have been divided in the following manner- (1) According to the 62nd entry of the schedule- national libraries, national museums, the Imperial War Museum, Victoria Memorial, and historical places of national importance will be under the charge of the Union.

(2) According to entry 63, Benaras, Aligarh and Delhi universities will be under the control of the Union government. (3) The 64th entry of the Schedule points out that scientific and technical institutions of national importance, so declared by Parliament, will remain under the charge of the Union. (4) According to entries 65 and 66, the union government will have the responsibility for professional and technological institutions, research institutions, institutions for research into crime eradication, etc., as well as determining the standards of higher education and research. In the same way, Article 239 gives the Union the responsibility for education in all Union Territories A total of 66 subjects relating to education have been placed within the jurisdiction of the States. The 12th entry in this regard classifies that- the States will be responsible for libraries, museums, archeological institutions and memorials of national importance.

In addition to the above, the Constitution also contains a Concurrent list, which lists the following subjects:

(1) economic and social planning, (2) professional and technological training, (3) scientific research, (4) technological education, (5) the development and propagation of Hindi, (6) preservation of national art and culture, (7) preservation of Sanskrit literature, (8) education of disabled persons, (9) development of educational research, (10) protection of the cultural interests of minorities, (11) educational development of the scheduled castes; regions and classes, (12) national and emotional integration, (13) provision of scholarships to brilliant students, (14) continuous professional training, (15) establishment of central institutions and agencies, and (16) free and compulsory education for children upto the age of 14 years.

Commissions' Role

Board for Advice : In 1948, the Central Advisory Board held its 14th meeting, in which it reflected upon secondary education. It put forth the suggestion for the appointment of a Commission, whose main functions would be to (1) evaluate the existing secondary education in the country, and (2) give suggestions for the problems relating to it.

This suggestion was implemented when a committee was appointed under the Chairmanship of the then Advisor on educational matters, Dr. Tara Chand. Its report was considered in the 15th meeting of the Advisory Board, and in consequence, the government of India was requested to appoint a commission for determining the objectives and purposes, and suggesting solutions for the problems of basic, secondary and university education. This requirement was then reiterated in 1951.

University Education Commission

A University Education Commission was appointed in 1948 under the Chairmanship of Dr. Radhakrishnan. This Commission came forward with numerous significant suggestions for the improvement of education at the university level, and in consequence the following changes occurred : (1) emphasis was placed upon teacher education and training, (2) the curriculum was made comprehensive and diverse to accommodate the interests, abilities and talents of students, (3) research began to flourish, (4) religious and moral education came to be imparted, (5) importance was given to the three-language formula for solving the language problem, (6) many reforms in the system of examination were carried out. In addition, many steps for student welfare, education of women and related issues were taken.

Jurisdiction : The jurisdiction of the Commission was stated in the following words, "To report on Indian University

Education and suggest improvements and extensions that may be desirable to suit present and future requirements of the country. (Report of the U.E.C. Page 1.) This Commission stated the objective of university education in the following terms- it should seek to harmonise life and the various branches of knowledge. Hence it is essential that the subjects taught in the universities should bear a relationship to fife. They should comprehend all elements.

The Education Commission has laid stress upon formation of character. It clarifies that the objective of education is the achievement of justice, liberty, equality and brotherhood upon the foundations of a national discipline. Highlighting the importance of teachers, the Commission has declared that the success of the educational process depends upon the ability and character of the teacher. The most important aspect of any scheme for improvement of university education is the obtaining of able teachers. The Radhakrishnan Commission has reflected upon every possible way for improving the conditions of teachers. It has attached importance to raising the standards of teachers and the expansion of laboratories and libraries, etc.

The Commission has defined three objectives of the curriculum : (1) to provide general education, (2) to provide a liberal education, (3) to provide professional education.

To ensure this, greater importance is given to law and medicine, the commission has made some significant recommendations. It has also stressed the need to develop objective testing techniques. In connection with the we dare of students, the Commission has expressed the view that the prime functions of the university are imparting education to youth and searching for new truths. Students are not created for universities; instead universities are established for formation of the students' character. Hence, it is essential that the university should seek, by every conceivable means and ways, to bring about the integral physical, mental and spiritual development of the student's powers.

Throwing light on the importance of education of women, the Commission opines that without educated women, there can be no educated men or women. General education should not be confined to either men or women. Women, too, should get the opportunity to receive education because, it is only in this condition that knowledge can, with certainty, be transmitted to future generations.

Emphasizing the need for the setting up of rural universities, the Commission has stated that for the general progress of rural India, it is necessary to bring about a constant extension in skills, limits of training and its quality. In order to provide these, and to satisfy the need for educated citizens, it is necessary to adopt the technique of rural colleges and universities. Hence, work in this direction is very desirable.

Dr. Rajendra Prasad's opinion of this Commission was that the Commission had presented a very valuable document on the achievements of education in our universities, and that it had provided useful suggestions for the attainment of varied specialised skills.

Commissions of Other Types

A Secondary Education Commission was appointed in 1952–53 for the reorganisation of secondary education. Dr. Lakshmanswami Mudaliar was appointed its chairman. The recommendations of this Commission brought forth the following changes in education—

1. The Higher secondary programme was extended to 11 years.
2. Stress was laid on the establishment of multipurpose schools.
3. The curriculum was made comprehensive and varied.

4. Objective testing was given importance.

5. Schemes for welfare of teachers were proposed.

Jurisdiction : The sphere of operation of this Commission and the issues it was to examine were stated thus- 1. Evaluation of every aspect of secondary education in India and throwing light upon it. 2. Giving suggestions for the improvement and reorganisation of secondary education.

This Commission considered the defects of secondary education and determined its objectives in the light of the following needs-(1) development of qualities of character through education, propagation of nationalism and secularism, (2) increase in productive capacity so as to bring about an increase in national wealth. (3) Improvements in education.

Objectives of Education: (1) Development of democratic citizenship. (2) Training in the art of living. (3) Development of personality. (4) Supply of professional skills. (5) Training for leadership. (6) Propagation of love of country.

The Secondary Education Commission determined the period of education at 7 years, intended for children between 11 and 17 years of age. It was divided into two parts—(1) 3 years for middle education, and (2) 4 years of higher secondary education. Provision was also made for a three-years degree course.

The Commission considered it important that technical schools and other kinds of schools should be developed. It also provided for co-education. Its views on the study of languages were as follows-(1) Hindi has been given the rank of the national language by the Constitution. (2) After some time, Hindi was expected to become the language of exchange between the Centre and the States. (3) Hindi would become the practical language of the majority. (4) As the language of the government, Hindi would bring about a growth of national unity.

Similarly, the Commission put forth the following views on the subject of English- (1) English is popular in the country. (2) English will bring about political unity. (3) English has international importance. (4) English is necessary.

The Commission's views on Sanskrit were - (1) Sanskrit is the mother of Indian languages. (2) It has been responsible for the growth of the cultural and religious attitude. (3) Indian knowledge can be obtained only through knowledge of Sanskrit.

The Commission also gave many valuable suggestions concerning the curriculum. It divided this into two parts-the Core and the optional part. The Commission also advocated the nationalization of the text books. These should be cheap, and of good quality. The Commission has accepted formation of character as the basis of education. It has suggested that schools should have arrangements for consultancy and vocational guidance. It has also recommended physical or health education. In addition to improvements in examinations, it has suggested the proper maintenance of school records. It has also given importance to improving the conditions of teachers. The Commission has also reflected upon the economics of education, and pointed towards many important sources.

Under the Chairmanship of Dr. Daulat S. Kothari, a National Education Commission was set up in 1964. It put forward a national education scheme for the next 20 years. This Commission has given Indian education a new direction. The Commission has reflected upon the entire spectrum of education, from its objectives to its economic aspects, and in consequence, it has raised many illuminating questions for the country's educationists to reflect upon.

In the context of the establishment of this Commission, the Central government stated on July 14, 1964, that the Commission had been appointed to reflect upon and advise the government on educational policies, national standards of education, and the potential for development in every sphere of education. The prefatory statement throws light on-(1) Education and national ideals, (2) method of education, its structure and level, (3) the standard of the teacher, (4) teacher training, (5) enrolment and manpower, (6) equality in the opportunities for obtaining education, (7) the parameters of educational problems of schools, (8) method of education, direction or guidance, and evaluation, (9) school education, administration and inspection, (10) environment for higher education and programmes, (11) sovereignty of universities, (12) agricultural education, (13) professional, technical and engineering education, (14) scientific education and research, (15) adult education, (16) educational planning and administration, and (17) the economics of education.

With reference to the prospectus of this Commission, the contemporary minister for education, Sh. Muhammed Karim Chagla, said that the prospectus was a kind of Magna Carta for teachers. In it, thought had been given to national and social service, salaries of teachers, the three language formula, etc. This preface led to many important turning points in the sphere of education. Of these, the three language formula became a subject of considerable discussion.

Period of Success

Since independence, there has been a remarkable quantitative increase in the educational sphere. The number of schools has increased, and so have the students, but the objectives of education could not be achieved. Many new professional institutions came into existence, as did many new universities. There were many and varied experiments in education. The scales of pay of teachers underwent numerous revisions. There was progress in the sphere of women's education.

The new achievements in education can be enumerated thus:

1. The Centre has adopted democracy as a form of administration and way of life for the people.
2. It has reduced poverty through the means of education and thus brought about a general improvement in the level of the people..
3. Modernisation has been adopted in industry and agriculture.
4. Obedience to ancient Indian traditions has gone hand in hand with the acceptance of knowledge and science.
5. It has accepted a socialistic pattern of society.
6. Equality has been granted to the opportunities for education.
7. The rate of literacy has increased from 19 to 28 per cent.

In the context of this new age, we must accept that education is the basis of our consciousness, awareness of our society and our nation. According to Acharya Vinobha Bhave, revolution should be introduced into education, so as to bring about a synthesis between knowledge and action. It is the combination of knowledge and action which can be called education. In view of this, both physical and mental activities are essential for the individual. Every individual should possess the capacity for the complete and balanced development of both aspects. In spite of all these achievements, our educationists continued to feel that our educational structure suffered from some shortcomings.

In fact, the modern system of education was the contribution of British people. Missionaries played a vital role in emerging vast, successful and systematic shape of education. Nurrulah and Nionik say-To the missionaries, belong the honour of being pioneers in modern educational system of India.

East India Company was employed to perform all the state functions: executive, judicial, legislative and economic. Establishment of schools, Madarasas, Pathshalas, College, a current of education was shown all over the country.

Hunter Commission gave a shape to complete system of education. University Education Commission, Sadler Commission gave a concrete shape to higher education.

We conclude it in the words of Howell- Education in India under the British Government was first ignored, then violently and successfully opposed the conducted on a system now universally admitted to be erroneous and finally, placed on its present footing.

6

Planned Development

Seventh Five Year Plan (1985-90) gave much emphasis on the following aspects of education.

1. Eradication of illiteracy among the age group of 15-35 years upto 1990.
2. To achieve the objective of universal primary education.
3. To provide facilities in each district to develop qualitative improvement of education.
4. To make upto date the system of education to meet the challenges of science and technology education and to make it modernise.
5. To make wider arrangements for vocational education.
6. To reconstruct the system of education for the development of human resources.
7. To provide new shape to education to meet the challenges in 21st country.

During the plan period Rs. 6,382.65 crores were allotted, out of which centre had to share, 2, 388.64 and state was to share 3, 488.71 crores of rupees.

1. *The Prologue :* The large amount of social consciousness and political awakening which are seen in India, is due to the changing factors. These factors responsible for the socio-political and economic change are the outcome of industrial and technological progress and expansion of education Social consciousness and awakening for rights created the conditions by which India made her place among the powerful nations of the world.

National Planning Commission was appointed for the planned change in the country through Five Year Plans. Now. In the Seventh Plan the concept of education has been changed. Man is considered as resource for the development of the country. Therefore, a separate ministry of Human Resources was established and education put under it as a part of it.

Objectives of seventh plan were (i) production programme (ii) rural development (iii) increase in employment (iv) industrial employment (v) high rate of growth of industrial development (vi) development of transport, power etc. (vii) Technological development (viii) environment (ix) control over inflation (x) mass consciousness (xi) administrative reform (xii) basic priorities, i.e., food, work and productivity.

2. *The Background :* Human resources development has necessarily to be assigned a key role in any development strategy, particularly in a country with a large population. Trained and educated on sound lines, a large population can itself become an asset in accelerating economic growth and in ensuring social change in desired directions. Education develops basic skills and abilities and fosters a value system conducive to, and in support of, national development goals, both long-term and immediate. In a world where knowledge is increasing at an exponential rate, the task of education in the diffusion of new knowledge and, at the same time, in the preservation and promotion of what is basic to India's culture and ethos, is both complex and

> challenging. It is, therefore, appropriate that the commencement of the Seventh Plan coincides with a comprehensive review of the education policy.

The resolution on the National Policy on Education adopted in 1968 pointed out that the great leaders of the Indian freedom movement realised the fundamental role of education and, throughout the nation's struggle for independence, stressed the unique significance of education for national development. The Resolution further declared that the radical reconstruction of education as envisaged involved (i) a transformation of the system to relate it more closely to the life of the people; (ii) a continuous effort to expand educational opportunity; (iii) a sustained and intensive effort to raise the quality of education at all stages: (iv) an emphasis on the development of science and technology; and (v) the cultivation of moral and social values. According to the Resolution, the educational system must produce young men and women of character and ability, committed to national service and development.

There has been a great deal of accomplishment in the field of education since 1947. Any number which may be picked up as a parameter to define growth in education will show the magnitude of the massive quantitative expansion that has taken place (Annexure 1). The number of recognised institutions has increased from 2,31,000 in 1951 to an estimated 7,55,000 in 1984-85. The total enrolment over the same period in these institutions increased from 24 million to nearly 132 million. The national stock of educated manpower is estimated to have increased from less than 4 million to about 48 million at present, the annual increment to the stock now being of the order of 3.5 million. It is significant to note that facilities have not only increased but also diversified at all levels and in different subjects. The enrolment for postgraduate studies, for instance has grown from a mere 20,000 in 1951 to over 300,000 by 1984-85 while that in science subjects is estimated to have increased from 4,400 to about 73,000. Extensive facilities are available for education in a variety of branches of engineering and technology. The output of this system has contributed significantly to our achievements in areas like atomic energy and satellite communication and provides the trained manpower for our economic development.

The expansion of educational facilities has also helped to some extent in the correction of regional and other imbalances and in achieving progress towards equality of educational opportunity and social justice. The annual non-plan expenditure on education from the Central and State budgets has increased more than fifty times over the last 35 years, from Rs. 114 crores in 1950-51 to more than Rs. 6,000 crores in 1984-85.

Although the Indian education scene since independence has been characterised by massive quantitative expansion at all levels, it is still to undergo the kind of transformation envisaged in the National Policy. It is faced with a staggering backlog; the level of illiteracy is as high as 63 per cent to achieve universal elementary education, as enjoined by the Constitution. There will be need to enroll fifty million more children; vocationalisation of secondary education has yet to make headway there is very significant pressure on the higher educational system and a decline in the standards of quality. There is an urgent need for a new design for education. The Approach to the Seventh Plan has emphasised that one of the primary task is the harnessing of the country's abundant human resources and improving their capability for development with equity. It is recognised that programme for alleviation of poverty, reduction of social and economic inequalities and improving productivity can and should be integrated with educational development further, the strategies for educational programmes and training and their organisational designs should particularly focus on women, youth and economically weaker groups so that they can make increasing contribution to the socioeconomic development of the country.

3. *Sixth Plan Review* : The Sixth Plan provided, inter alia, for mass education through programmes of elementary education (formal and non-formal streams) and adult education. The Plan also envisaged increased bias towards practicals in secondary education, vocationalisation of higher secondary education and restructuring undergraduate courses with a vocational bias. Forging beneficial linkages between education, employment and development was another objective in the field of higher education.

An enrolment target of 18 million additional children was set for the Sixth Plan period under the formal system of elementary education. According to the available reports, the additional enrolment is likely to be nearly 22 million. Although the target has been exceeded on an all-India basis, there have been shortfalls in a few States, especially in regard to the enrolment of girls. Also, the enrolment ratio in 1984-85 was 92 per cent for primary and 53% for middle stages of education. For girls it was only 69 per cent and 38 per cent respectively. Some of the notable measures taken for the promotion of elementary education were : 'earn while you learn' scheme, mid-day meals for children, innovative curriculum renewal schemes, and special emphasis on appointment of women teachers. Funds available under National Rural Employment Programme (NREP) and Rural Landless Employment Guarantee Programme (RLEGP) were also utilised for construction of school buildings.

Under the programme of non-formal education although no specific targets were laid down, 8 million children were expected to be enrolled during Sixth Plan. This was an experimental programme under which diverse models were to be worked out to suit the area-specific or beneficiary-group specific requirement. It is estimated that over 3 million children would have been enrolled under this programme. Beside the non-formal education centres organised by State Governments, innovative and experimental projects were taken up by a number of voluntary and academic institutions. Syllabus and instructional material for use of learners enrolled in non-formal centres were developed following the integrated approach covering areas of health, hygiene, home science, agriculture, physics, chemistry, biology, history, geography and civics.

The position at the end of the Sixth Plan is that 80 per cent of the out-of-school children are in the nine States of Assam, Andhra Pradesh, Bihar, Jammu and Kashmir, Madhya Pradesh, Orissa, Rajasthan, Uttar Pradesh and West Bengal, but there is need in all States and Union Territories to improve the quality, relevance and effectiveness of the elementary education system, to improve enrolment and retention rates and to promote girls' education.

The Sixth Plan indicated the goal of reaching 100 per cent literacy in the age-group 15-35 years by 1990. While no definite physical target was laid down for the sixth plan, the adult education programme was to be developed on a large scale for the age-group 15-35 years to combat the problem of illiteracy among the productive segment of the population in general and, in particular, among the rural poor. The Central Government funded 386 rural functional literacy projects in the States besides giving assistance to 380 voluntary agencies and 49 universities for adult education programmes.

In additional there were programmes of the State Governments. It is estimated that 20 million adult illiterates would have been covered by these programmes during the Sixth Plan. Fifteen States Resource Centres provided the resource support to adult education centres in terms of curriculum formulation, preparation of teaching and learning material, development of methods and media, training of functionaries, monitoring and evaluation, and research and innovation. Development of learning materials for women and weaker sections was given special attention.

Enrolment in secondary and higher secondary levels has increased from about 10 million in 1979-80 to about 17 million in 1984-85. The 10 + 2 pattern of education has been adopted by 20 States and 9 Union Territories although it is yet to be fully implemented in some of these States. The National Council of Educational Research and Training, the State Councils of Educational Research and Training and the State Institutes of Education continued their efforts towards improvement in science and environmental education, value-orientation including national integration and curriculum reforms. Propagation of community singing in schools was launched as a national movement.

In the context of INSAT utilisation, State Institutes of Educational Technology (SIET) were set up in six States, namely, Andhra Pradesh, Bihar, Orissa, Gujarat, Maharashtra and Uttar Pradesh to produce educational television programmes. A Central Institute of Educational Technology (CIET) was set up for the production of programmes, training of personnel from the States as well as for providing guidance in the development of the programmes.

Vocationalisation of education at the higher secondary stage was one of the important reforms included in the Sixth Plan. This programme has made limited progress with an enrolment of about 55,000 students in vocational education, confined to nine States and three Union Territories where it has been introduced. Measures have been initiated to establish the necessary links combining vocationalisation, skill training, in-plant apprenticeship and placement in gainful employment as composite parts of an integrated effort to raise the level of utility of the programme, and its wider acceptance and success. The organisational requirements for the planning, implementation, supervision and evaluation of the integrated programme, along with the mechanism for effective coordination among the concerned agencies, are being assessed and defined.

Enrolment in higher education is estimated to have increased from 2.5 million in 1979-80 to 3.5 million in 1984-85. Efforts were made for the consolidation of existing institutions and to equip universities and colleges with essential facilities within the limited resources available. Other important programmes taken up during the Sixth Plan included restructuring of under-graduate courses, improvement in standards of teaching of sciences and the humanities, strengthening of postgraduate education and promotion of research within the university system. A one hour daily telecast on higher education was also initiated for the benefit of colleges. On the recommendation of the Science Advisory Committee to the Cabinet, a new scheme was introduced in 1983-84 for strengthening the infrastructure facilities for research and post-graduate education in science and technology within the university system.

During the Sixth Plan period, the major emphasis in technical education was on diversification and optimum utilisation of existing courses and institutional resources. Efforts were made to provide facilities in areas such as computer sciences, instrumentation, product development, maintenance engineering, bio-sciences, and material sciences. Forty-six selected polytechnics were assisted and supported to develop them into a network of "community polytechnics" which would help transfer and apply available technology with the object of modernising rural structures. New manpower training programmes were undertaken for emerging areas in technology such as micro-processor application, remote sensing, laser technology, atmospheric sciences, and energy sciences. Programmes of management, education,, particularly in the Institutes of Management were reviewed by an Expert Committee and on its recommendation, the establishment of a new Institute at Lucknow was taken in hand.

The Resolution on National Sports Policy was laid before Parliament in 1984 to serve as a policy frame for the Central and State Governments and all organisations connected with sports. The policy gives a new thrust to sports activities towards achieving excellence in as many areas of sports and games as possible and at the same time making "sports for all" a reality. The Eastern Regional Centre, Calcutta, of Netaji National Institute of Sports, Patiala (NIS) started functioning from 1983 providing additional training courses for coaches. The national coaching scheme now has an authorised cadre strength of 800 coaches. 25 Regional sports coaching centres have been developed in State capitals and district headquarters. Besides its regular training programme, NIS implemented on behalf of the Central Government programmes of National Sports Festivals for women, All India Rural Sports Tournament and Sports Talents Search Scholarship.

The Sports Authority of India was established in 1984 and undertook several sports activities in addition to maintaining and managing infra structure and other facilities created for ASIAD 1982. Sports Councils with the assistance of Central and State Governments have jointly undertaken programmes for improving and developing facilities for the promotion of sports and games. Specifically, assistance was given for development of playfields, construction of Stadia and swimming pools, construction of sports complexes, establishment and maintenance of rural sports centres, running annual coaching scheme and for purchase of sports equipment. The ceilings of financial assistance for these purposes were also enhanced. National Sports Federations were also told for organising coaching camps for preparing the Indian teams and competitors to participate in appropriate international competitions. Under the scheme of National Sports Organisation, financial assistance was provided for developing physical facilities for sports and games in colleges and universities, especially for developing playfields, and construction or gymnasia.

Youth programmes for student and non student youth were continued and expanded during the Sixth Plan. A National

Service Scheme originally launched in 1969-70 was a pilot scheme with 40,000 students, covered over six lakh students in the year 1984-85. The scheme enabled students to participate during their first degree studies in various programmes of social service and national development and provided them an opportunity to understand the conditions and problems of social environment. The activities undertaken by the students included environmental conservation, plantation of trees, cleaning of village ponds, construction of wells, health and family welfare programmes, family welfare education of rural women and sanitation drives in urban slums. They also undertook some production-oriented programmes. Nehru Yuvak Kendras set up to cater primarily to the needs of rural student and non student youth, organised several social service camps, slums clearance schemes and environmental awareness schemes as well as programmes for training of youth leadership. In the year 1984-85,120 youth leadership camps and 180 work camps were organised, involving 65,000 participants.

Programmes for preservation of monuments and sites of national importance were taken up on a priority basis. An expert group on archaeology carried out a professional study to prepare an overall plan of action. The number of archaeological circles which look after the preservation of monuments and sites of national importance was raised from 12 to 16. The number of excavation branches was also raised from three to five; Assistance was also provided to Indian National Trust for Art and Cultural Heritage (INTACH) for promoting the conservation and propagation of works of Indian art and culture. A large number of conservation programmes were taken up for repair and preservation of monuments and sites of national importance. The facilities at the National Museum, New Delhi, were further improved through taking up the first phase of its construction programmes.

The National Museum organised several aided tour and short-term in-service course. The Indian Museum, Calcutta, the Salar Jang Museum, Hyderabad, the National Gallery of Modern Art, New Delhi, the Nehru Memorial Museum and Library, the National Museum of Man and the National Archives were the other institutions whose programmes received support during the Sixth Plan. The National Council of Science Museums was also supported to undertake the task of popularising science and technology, among students in particular, through a wide range of programmes. The National Research Laboratory for Conservation of Cultural Property in Lucknow undertook a number of research programmes for technical studies with a view to improving conservation methods.

The Anthropological Survey of India was supported through funding of its several research projects on physical and cultural anthropology and allied disciplines. The Survey also undertook exploratory studies in the Himalayas, Narmada Valley and Coastal Andhra Pradesh.

Library programmes were another area of importance during the Sixth Plan. The construction programme at National Library, Calcutta, was taken up. The Raja Rammohan Roy Library Foundation which renders assistance to States and Union Territories for development of public libraries was further strengthened. Promotion and dissemination of culture was another major programme of the Department of Culture. The Sangeet Natak Akademi, the Sahitya Akademi and the Lalit Kala Akademi, besides the National School of Drama, undertook several programmes in this area. The Center for Cultural Resources and Training, New Delhi, organised a number of in-service training programmes for the benefit of teachers drawn from primary and high or higher secondary schools in different parts of the country. Financial assistance was also provided to dance, drama and theatre ensembles and to selected cultural organisations.

4. *Strategy and Thrust Areas in the Seventh Plan :* The Seventh Plan provides for reorientation of the education system

so as to prepare the country to meet the challenges of the next century. The main thrust areas in the Seventh. Plan would be: (i) achievement of universal elementary education; (ii) eradication of illiteracy in the age-group 15-35 years; (iii) vocationalisation and skill-training programmes at different levels of education; (iv) upgradation of standards and modernisation at all stages of education with effective links with the world of work and with special emphasis on science and environment and on value orientation; (v) provision of facilities for education of high quality and excellence in every district of the country and (vi) removal of obsolescence and modernisation of technical education.

The major strategies for achieving these objectives would include effective decentralised planning and organisational reforms, promotion of non-formal and open learning systems, adoption of low cost alternatives and optimum use of resources, forging of beneficial linkages with industry and development agencies, and mobilisation of community resources and societal involvement.

Basic Education

Overriding priority will be given to realising universalisation of elementary education for children in the age-group 6-14 years by 1990; this will continue to be part of the Minimum Needs Programme. The emphasis will shift from mere enrolment to retention of pupils in schools and to the attainment by them of basic elements of learning. The objective is sought to be achieved through a combination of formal and non-formal methods, focussing sharply on the needs of girls and of children belonging to the economically and socially weaker sections.

The enrolment at the elementary stage was estimated to have reached nearly 112 million by the end of the Sixth Plan period. For achieving the goal of universalisation by the end of the Seventh Plan, over 50 million children will have to be additionally enrolled. A projection of enrolment in full-time elementary schools is given in Table. Increasing enrolment in full-time schools beyond this level of 137 in classes I to VIII might not be feasible due to socio-economic reasons and other factors. Even to achieve this level effectively, sustained efforts will have to be made to reduce the number of dropouts.

Non-formal education would be the other important programme for the achievement of universalisation of elementary education as this can be useful to those who are not able or willing to attend full-time schools. The number of children to be covered by the non-formal programme is reckoned to be of the order of 25 million. Non-formal education in the Seventh Plan will, therefore, have to be expanded at a fast pace and made acceptable with a variety of forms to suit the varying needs of the target groups. Non-formal system should be made flexible and appropriately linked to the formal system. Adequate textual material with area-specific background and supplementary reading material would be developed and made available to students. Adequate teacher-training arrangements will be made for teachers participating in the non-formal system. For optimum use of resources, the schools, non-formal education centres and adult education centres should develop linkages and be educationally integrated with development programmes.

The enrolment projections in are indicative figures, worked out at the macro-level and disaggregated to the State level. Specific operational targets will require to be worked out by the State Governments concerned block-wise and village-wise through decentralised planning. Once such target was worked out for the catchment area of each school or a cluster of schools, it would be expected that the authorities responsible for the achievement of the target would adopt the most appropriate strategies of implementation and monitoring of progress.

Expansion of Elementary Stage Education

(Enrolment figures in million)

Sl. No.	*Classes/ Age Group*	*Likely enrolment (1984-85)*	*Projected enrolment (1989-90)*	*Additional enrolment (1985-90)*
1	2	3	4	5
I.	I-V (6-11)			
	Boys	51.20 (11748)	55 00 (110 00)	3.80
	Girls	34.17 (6920)	40 - 96 (8815)	6.79
	Total	85.37 (91.84)	95 - 96 (99 89)	10.59
II.	VI-VII (11-14)			
	Boys	17.46 (66.90)	25-12 (92.56)	7.66
	Girls	9.27 (38.19)	16. 55 (65.44)	7.28
	Total	6.73 (53 07)	41 .67 (79 46)	14.94
III.	I-VIII (6-14)			
	Boys	68-66 (90 96)	80 12 (104 24)	11.46
	Girls	43.44 (64.02)	57.51 (80.28)	14.07
	Grand Total	112.10 (78 21)	137.63 (92.60)	25.53

Note : Figures in parentheses indicate enrolment ratio relative to population in the corresponding age-group.

The role of the teacher is most crucial in achieving universal elementary education, especially in the motivation of children as well as their parents. 'They can play a leading role in improving the quality of primary education, bringing in environmental and health education and value orientation. In-service training of teachers thus becomes a programme of high priority. The training of teachers will include, apart from pedagogy, the use of mass media, science and technology, planning and curriculum design for local environment-based courses, mobilisation and use of community resources and other relevant subjects. There will also be special emphasis on teaching methods and other measures particularly required for first generation learners and for reducing the number of drop-outs. Teacher training institutions will be developed and strengthened accordingly.

Facilities will have to be created for the training of additional teachers required during the Seventh Plan period. There is as yet no infrastructure in the country for training of teachers in non-formal and early childhood education. Training of such teachers would have to be organised by suitably strengthening the existing teacher training centres.

Considering the numbers involved (over 2.5 million teachers), institutionalised in-service education of teachers will be difficult to organise not only due to the huge costs involved but also due to lack of facilities for training. It is, therefore, necessary to think of a variety of training arrangements. Among others, these would include

(a) In-service education by utilising the mass media, as was done during SITE;

(b) adoption of schools of lower levels of education by institutions of higher levels for upgrading of teacher competencies;

(c) despatch of teacher guidance notes by training schools;

(d) publication of bulletins informing teachers of new developments; and

(e) use correspondence course materials supported by occasional contact.

Drop-outs and non-attendance of children at the primary stage of education are due to poor school facilities, unrelated curriculum, poor methods of teaching and poverty. The reorientation of teacher training referred to above will help to a large extent in tackling these factors. In addition, suitable supportive programmes for the provision of incentives, the improvement of facilities, increasing community awareness, curricular reforms, adjusting of school timings, utilisation of local community resources and earn-while-you-learn scheme, etc., will be introduced or expanded selectively according to local requirements.

Enrolment of girls has been lagging behind despite special measures taken in the past towards' the end of the Sixth Plan some steps were taken to promote enrolment of girls and for providing non-formal education to them wherever necessary. In the Seventh Plan, the focus of effort will be on promotion of girls' education through appointment of women teachers, attachment of pre-school centres, provision of free uniforms and other incentives.

Special emphasis will be given to the enhancement of quality and efficiency of elementary education. The Seventh Plan will seek to provide specific funds for those programmes which will enhance the efficiency of the system. There is need to have a fresh look at the design and construction of school buildings as well as the text-books in use. Various projects like population education, environment and wild life education and curriculum renewal have helped in the preparation of suitable teaching-learning material and this material will be utilised.

Due to the difficult resource position and the magnitude of the task involved in the implementation of the programme of universalisation of the elementary education, optimal use should be made of the available infrastructure and funds. The Plan and non-Plan budget provision for elementary education and the existing teacher resources should be reviewed and redeployed on the basis of actual requirements and attendance in classes. Part-time teachers or helper-teachers on fixed salary, selected from among locally available educated men and women will be utilised to augment teaching resources and also improve relevance and cost-effectiveness of elementary education. Community support and financial contributions will be mobilised especially for clearing the backlog of physical facilities and school buildings. The construction of school buildings will be taken up also under the National Rural Employment Programme (NREP) and similar programmes.

Early childhood education is important both from the point of view of the personality development of the child and for inculcating in the children a healthy attitude to school-going to help increase their retention rate in schools. This programme will be dovetailed with nutrition, health care and social welfare as a package within the broad frame work of the programme of Integrated Child Development Service (ICDS). Voluntary efforts to undertake innovative experiments in respect of early childhood education will be supported.

The National Policy Resolution on Education recommends the placement of disabled children in regular schools. The scheme of integrated education of disabled children was started by the Ministry of Social Welfare as a Centrally-sponsored scheme where handicapped children were sought to be integrated in the normal school system with a view to promoting their psychological acceptance. The scheme is now being implemented by the Ministry of Education. One of the difficulties facing this scheme is the lack of trained teachers in special education. As such, during the Seventh Plan, greater emphasis will be laid on teacher training.

Education of Societal Nature

Eradication of adult illiteracy and the development of a programme of continuing adult education is a major thrust area in the Seventh Plan. The task of covering all the illiterates in the age-group 15-35 years by 1990 is a formidable one. As motivation of the learner is crucial for success and as the number to be covered is about 90 million, the strategy to achieve the goal can only be through a mass movement involving social institutions, voluntary organisations, students, teachers, employers and the community. This programme will also have to be linked effectively with various development programmes especially the Integrated Rural Development Programme (IRDP). Active participation of village panchayats, mahila mandals, community centres, etc., is essential. Employers will be required to impart necessary functional education to all their illiterate employees.

The programmes of Nehru Yuvak Kendras (NYK) and the national Service Scheme (NSS) will also focus on eradication of illiteracy. Programmes for motivating the learners by holding community meetings and through publicity, through posters, films, broadcasting, etc., will be implemented on an adequate scale and with sufficient intensity to create a conducive climate. A network of libraries and the development of literature for neo-literates will also be initiated as a follow-up programme to avoid lapse into illiteracy. Community participation in all literacy programmes will be an essential feature from village level upwards to give proper direction and orientation and lend effective support to this national programme.

Another aspect of education of adults relates to training in functional skills relevant to their respective economic activities. Programmes for this purpose will be strengthened and adequate resource support provided for organising technical and vocational skill-based courses for the benefit of adult learners through Shramik Vidyapeeths and other similar institutions. As a part of the post-literacy and follow-up services, short-duration condensed training courses will be organised for upgrading the skills of the neo-literates and for increasing their awareness of various social events. The existing programmes on rural functional literacy and State adult education programmes and various training programmes for adult learners will be consolidated and dovetailed in the new mass movement programmes of adult education. Citizenship education including adult education, will be a necessary part of the entire education system, and will be specially promoted.

Education at School Level

The demand for secondary education has been growing. The expansion and effectiveness of elementary education will provide a further impetus to this growth. The projected demand for additional facilities will, to some extent, be met by better utilisation of resources in the existing schools. Provision has been made for this purpose and for promoting distance learning techniques and open school system. Unplanned growth of high/higher secondary school will be checked. Norms for the establishment of secondary school will be evolved and strictly observed in order to avoid proliferation of economically non viable and educationally inefficient institutions. In expanding the facilities, special attention will be given to the needs of backward areas, of under-privileged sections of the population and of girls. Girls education will be free upto the higher secondary stage.

The teaching of science and mathematics at high/higher secondary stage of education will be strengthened and made universal. Efforts will be made to update and modernise science curricula, improve laboratories and libraries in schools and ensure the quality of science teachers through large-scale in service training programmes. Environment education will form an important aspect of science education.

The socially useful productive work (work experience) programme component seeks to highlight the link between work and education and to develop positive work ethics and work habits. The programme would allow for better utilisation and integration of community expertise in the teaching-learning process and the use of facilities available with local industry and development institutions. Besides, the support system for development, training, management and supervision available for vocationalisation programme will also be utilised for the programme of social useful productive work at the secondary stage. Semi courses/activities of pre-vocational character will also be introduced for more effective implementation of the programme.

In view of the importance of linking education with productivity, a major impetus was given in the Seventh Plan to vocationalisation of the higher secondary stage. Facilities for vocational education were suitably diversified to cover a large number of fields in agriculture, industry, trade and commerce and services. It was ensured that there was no duplication of courses between technical and vocational institutions and the schools. The skills imparted, were to be of adequate standard for securing gainful employment or self-employment. At the same time opportunities for pursuing higher general and professional education would be provided.

Vocational career courses in education institutions will be introduced in a flexible manner linked to emerging work opportunities. The current intake will be considerably increased by introducing vocational courses in many more institutions.

Based on the evaluation of the on giving scheme of vocationalisation, States are taking steps to re-organise and improve the programme. An Expert Committee has been set up to suggest ways and means of implementing an expanded programme of vocationalisation fully coordinated with the educational system and manpower needs of economic development. The report of this Committee will provide guidelines for further development.

The present wide reach of the media will be used for improving education, especially at the secondary stage. Facilities for production of the requisité audio-visual material including educational software for broadcasting and telecasting will be augmented substantially in the Seventh Plan. During the Sixth Plan, a small beginning was made in providing computer literacy to students in selected secondary schools, based on this experience, steps will be taken to extend the programme to cover different aspects of computer appreciation and application.

One of the essential conditions for continuous improvement in the quality of secondary education is an effective system of in-service training of teachers. The existing facilities were to be assessed, additional requirements identified and steps taken to meet them. The opportunity provided by the new communication technology will be explored for this purpose. Here again, special attention was to be paid to the development of requisite software. Training of personnel required for effective use of modern communication technology and computers in education was to be given very high priority. The NCERT which has already initiated programmes in this regard , would help the State build a network for this purpose.

Education has a crucial contribution to make towards promoting national integration, understanding and a sense of togetherness and harmony. There is, therefore, great need for an integrated and value oriented education with a national perspective. This programme should be so designed that its various threads can be woven into the curricular and co-curricular activities. Suitable revision of text books, strengthening of school libraries and training of teachers would be important from this point of view.

Education at University Level

The main emphasis in higher education will be on consolidation, improvement in standards and reforms in the system to make higher education more relevant to national needs and to forge forward and backward linkages of higher education with employment and economic development. Expansion of general higher education facilities will be carefully planned so as to take care of the need to provide larger access of weaker sections and first generation learners from backward areas. In doing so, emphasis will be laid on providing access to existing institutions through appropriate reservation, scholarships, provision of hostel facilities, etc. A network of facilities will be provided through open universities, correspondence courses and part-time education to meet social demand and the needs of continuing education.

The need and urgency for restructuring of undergraduate courses so as to bring in the necessary concern for relevance and use, application, orientation, flexibility and diversification is well recognised. The guidelines for restructuring of courses of study indicated by the University Grants Commission (UGC) provide for addition of groups of courses that may be relevant and useful according to local or regional needs. Extension activities will be developed as components within each subject/ discipline. Beneficial linkages will be developed between colleges and development institutions and programmes. Application oriented courses will be given due emphasis.

The Indira Gandhi National Open University, which has been established as a pace setting institution, will besides offering' courses in higher education based on the principles of the open learning system, be also responsible for training of personnel, production of programmes and development of material for utilisation through the electronic media. The National Open University will function as a nodal resource centre for coordination of programmes and development of models for distance education, documentation and dissemination of information and organisation of appropriate support programmes. Besides this, six centres of educational technology being developed by UGC would serve as regional centres for the production of software for educational technology and training of personnel engaged in the programme of distance education and correspondence courses for higher education.

In the area of post-graduate education and research, emphasis will be placed on promoting quality programmes, inter-disciplinary studies and on new emerging frontiers. Research within the university system will get due emphasis and be coordinated with national research efforts under the Science and Technology programme. The programme of strengthening infrastructure facilities for research in science and technology and of postgraduate education within the university system which has started on the recommendation of the Science Advisory Committee to the Cabinet, will be further developed.

Training of teachers in higher education is another area which needs special attention in the Seventh Plan. The faculty improvement programmes will be designed to impart knowledge of new methods and techniques of teaching, learning and evaluation, to develop a national value system, and to prepare the teachers for the task of restructuring undergraduate courses.

Many of the reforms initiated earlier, such as autonomous colleges and examination reform, seem to have faced obstacles and delays in the process of implementation. The Seventh Plan will give high priority to the speedy implementation of various reforms already initiated and to the modernisation of university administration.

Besides concerted efforts to increase the enrolment of Scheduled Castes/Scheduled Tribes students, the most significant programmes for these students will consist of remedial teaching, preparatory training and special coaching. These programmes will be implemented on a large scale by institutions with sizeable student population drawn from the Scheduled Castes and Scheduled Tribes and other weaker sections. These institutions will be strengthened to impart a better quality of education. The scope of these programmes will also be enlarged to include training for employment, coaching for competitive examinations for recruitment to various services and adult and continuing education programmes.

Streams of Vocational Nature

In the context of the rapid modernisation of the economy envisaged in the near future and given the Seventh Plan objective of improvement in productivity, technical education has to play a leading role. The main emphasis in the field of technical education during the Seventh Plan period was on the following :

(i) Consolidation of infrastructure and facilities already created;

(ii) Optimum utilisation of the existing facilities with attention to cost effectiveness;

(iii) Identification of critical areas with a view to strengthening the facilities in the fields where weaknesses exist in the system at present;

(iv) Creation of infrastructure in new areas of emerging technology vital for the development of the country and provision of necessary facilities for education, training and research in those fields;

(v) Improvement of quality and standards of technical education;

(vi) Removal of obsolescence;

(vii) Modernisation of engineering laboratories and workshops in the technical education institutions;

(viii) Effective management of the overall system of technical education for an optimum return on investments made;

(ix) Innovative measures to improve existing facilities to provide low-cost alternatives to achieve various goals and objectives laid down in the Plan; and

(x) Institutional linkages between technical education on the one hand and rural development and other development sectors, on the other.

To achieve these objectives there would be a balanced development of institutions of technical education at all levels. The Indian Institutes of Technology which have been set up as pace setting institutions, would be further developed as advance centres of excellence. The Institutes have already initiated research work in a number of new areas. An expert committee has been set up to look into the requirements of these Institutes in the context of the challenges ahead. The regional and other engineering colleges would also be developed further particularly with a view to their modernization and to making their courses relevant to the emerging requirements. The upgradation of standards and modernisation of polytechnics will also be accorded a high priority. A major task in the Seventh Plan will be the removal of obsolescence in equipment and revision of courses in all technical education institutions, many of which were drawn up more than two decades ago. The All India Council for Technical Education has recommended that it is necessary also to restructure polytechnic education with a view to:

(a) improving the standard and contents of technical courses;

(b) providing a lateral entry to the vocational stream from 10 + 2 stage;

(c) restoring the balance in the employment pattern of engineering graduates and diploma holders; and

(d) providing multi-point entry to the various courses.

Besides the improvement on these lines, polytechnic education for women was to be given greater attention to meet their special requirements. Further as a result of reorganisation of school education in the 10 + 2 system and with vocationalisation becoming the major thrust in it, the polytechnics will play a significant role in the promotion and development of vocational education, particularly in engineering and allied trades. Besides modernising polytechnics and removing obsolescence in courses and equipment, special attention will be paid to emerging technologies and computerisation. Development of interaction between the technical institutions and industry will be taken up. Removal of regional imbalances would be another major objective in the development of technical education at all levels.

The faculty in the technical institutions have to keep themselves abreast of the latest knowledge and advances taking place elsewhere in the world and also have to be in constant touch with industry. A number of schemes have already been instituted under the quality improvement programme including M. Tech. and Ph.D. courses, short-term and mid-term courses and industrial training for engineering college and polytechnic teachers. However, these arrangements need considerable strengthening. Special attention will be paid to the problems of staff training and retraining and to continuing education for staff, including those of the polytechnics, to facilitate academic and professional advancement.

A reliable manpower information system is a pre-requisite to planning in the field of technical education. A national manpower information system is being developed for storage, updating, retrieval and analysis of manpower information to assist in technical education planning. It has at present

17 nodal centres and is coordinated by the Technical Education Division of the Department of Education with the assistance of the lead centre located at the Institute of Applied Manpower Research. The manpower information system will be considerably strengthened and integrated with the planning of technical education.

Besides general improvements, polytechnics will be assisted to undertake extension services for the benefit of the community. The programme of community polytechnics, already initiated in the earlier Plans, will be expanded in the Seventh Plan to cover as many polytechnics as possible.

Curriculum changes need to be introduced periodically in the light of emerging trends in technology. This will require more effective collaborative linkages with industry and research and development establishments and agencies. The allocations provided from budgetary funds for technical education have to be supplemented by contributions from user industries and organisations, which will be facilitated when closer collaborative arrangements are established.

Disciplines of Technical Sides

Considerable emphasis will be laid on the improvement of the quality of teaching science and technology at all levels of education. At school level NCERT at the centre and SCERT s/SIEs in States will provide training to teachers on all aspects of science and technology including design, development and production of science kits and strengthen science laboratories of secondary schools. A National Science Centre will be established for displaying experimental models and projects.

The quality of higher science and technology education has to match the best in the world. In this connection, university departments and colleges will be selected for providing special assistance to bring about improvements in science education.

Modernisation of laboratories in Indian Institutes of Technology, Regional Engineering Colleges and other institutions of technical education will be accorded priority for providing research in' technology. An International Centre for Science and Technology Education will be established. This will operate through a network of existing institutions and serve as a resource centre for cooperative research, and will also disseminate ideas, methods and materials to bring about basic improvement and modernisation in Science and Technology education. The total estimated outlay for S & T component in the education sector will be of the order of Rs.180 crores, including Rs. 35 crores for the programmes recommended by the Science Advisory Committee to the Cabinet.

Respect for Heritage : The present examination-oriented system has distorted the very character of education and has converted it into a mere system of certification to regulate the flow of manpower to the labour market. The dominance of the examination system over the educational processes has led not only to the wrong type of learning, but has also led to many attendant malpractices. Examination reforms to remedy the present malaise would be given the utmost priority. At the same time, the employing sector should be helped to devise its own selection procedures, lay down academic qualifications, prepare assessment tests and evaluation systems in keeping with job content and the ability and skill for performance of the tasks attached to a job.

The Seventh Plan provides for the continuation and limited expansion of on going programmes relating to scholarships, development of languages, book promotion, educational planning and administration as well as to effective monitoring, particularly of elementary (including non-formal) and adult education.

The existing schemes of scholarships will be reviewed and,

if necessary, re-oriented to help talented students to develop their full potential. The Central Government schemes of national scholarships including that for talented children from rural areas will continue in the Seventh Plan. Financial assistance by itself is not adequate for the development of talented children, especially from the poorer sections of society and from backward areas. Their access to, and placement in, good academic institutions is equally necessary. Placements in residential schools will be particularly helpful and a scheme for this purpose is already in operation.

To provide good quality modern education with Indian values to talented children, particularly from the rural areas, it is proposed to set up 432 model secondary schools, one in each district, during the Seventh Five Year Plan. These schools will offer a common core curriculum, ensuring comparability in standards and promoting National Integration and National Values. They will bring together students from different parts of the country, providing opportunities to talented children to fully develop their potential. Admission to these schools will be through a test conducted at tehsil/block level, in which the best performers from every primary school in the district will be eligible to appear. The test would be designed by the NCERT, and it will be associated in conducting and evaluating the test. Residential facilities will be provided in these schools. An autonomous organisation, registered under the Registration of Societies Act, will be set up for establishing and running these schools.

Languages' Role

The development of languages is of basic importance for all educational development programmes. The activities and programmes undertaken in the field of languages comprise: (i) promotion of Hindi (as envisaged under Article 351 of the Constitution); (ii) promotion of modern Indian Languages (as provided in National Policy of Education); (iii) promotion of

English and other foreign languages; and (iv) promotion of Sanskrit and other classical languages such as Arabic and Persian. Other languages for which the Centre has special responsibility, like Urdu and Sindhi, have also received attention. These activities will be further developed in the Seventh Plan, with special attention being paid for raising the standards of language competency, spoken as well as written.

The capabilities of existing institutions will be strengthened, particularly, with a view to enabling them to undertake a much larger programme of in-service training, publication of textual and other materials, production of software for transmission through radio and television and to work at the grass-roots level. A selective approach will be adopted in respect of publications, so as to ensure that materials of good quality become available and are widely disseminated. Instead of entrusting publication of dictionaries, terminologies, text-books, etc., exclusively to governmental agencies, it is proposed to involve creative scholars, university departments and literary organisation with publication activities. Voluntary organisations working for the development and promotion of various languages will be supported, particularly, for undertaking innovative and experimental projects the experience from which will assist in more effective teaching and learning of languages, whether by formal or informal methods.

In Sanskrit, emphasis will be given to activities which will ensure preservation of Shastric and Vedic traditions in oral and written forms, preservation, editing and cataloguing of rare manuscripts, publication of rare and out-of-print books, and training of teachers. It is proposed to assist selected institutions for audio and video taping of recitations of various sakhas which for want of continuing training of scholars in the oral tradition, are becoming extinct. Support will be provided for interdisciplinary research, particularly with a view to identifying the scientific and technical advancement that had taken place in the past and has been recorded in various Sanskrit texts.

The programmes being undertaken for the development of modern Indian languages, including Urdu and Sindhi and also classical languages, in Arabic and Persian will be continued and additional support provided to increase their coverage.

In Art & Culture the main thrust in the Seventh Five Year Plan would be on the development of culture in all aspects, with emphasis on dissemination, and on the promotion and development of regional cultures and building up of a sense of oneness and underlying unity and cohesiveness of Indians. This would require the involvement of the masses in cultural activities. In order to achieve these objectives, the programmes of the Seventh Plan would include:

(i) Zonal Cultural Centres being set up at different regions of the country. The essential thrust of the creative development efforts of these zonal centres would be to bring about awareness and participation at the grass root level, cutting across-territorial/linguistic boundaries.

(ii) The existing activities of various cultural organisations for dissemination of culture would be stepped up on a wide scale with adequate financial inputs.

(iii) Introduction of a cultural component into the educational system at different levels. The Departments of Education and Cultural Affairs would work together in close coordination for inter-linking education and culture through appropriate programmes.

(iv) Cultural inputs would be integrated in youth activities, rural development activities, domestic tourism, etc.

(v) For the dissemination of culture to the masses, the mass media would be utilised.

(vi) Besides the national cultural organisations, the State agencies would also strengthen their programmes. The Central and State agencies would work with greater coordination towards this objective.

It is proposed to set up seven zonal cultural centres which while developing the unique cultural identities of various areas in the states would also stress and explore their cultural kinship in relation to the totality of India's composite culture, highlighting the essential unity in diversity of the Indian cultural heritage. The Centres would provide facilities for creative development of arts; with special emphasis on folk arts as also the revival of vanishing arts.

The traditional fairs and festivals which provide the continuing link with the rich traditions of the past would be supported through the State agencies and Zonal Cultural Centres. Appropriate programmes would be taken up to provide exposure to youth to the cultural diversity of the country to raise their awareness of the rich heritage that exists in the country.

Preservation, documentation and conservation of our rich and varied cultural heritage would continue to receive priority in the Seventh Plan. This would mean greater attention to the development of archaeology, museums, archives, manuscript libraries, Buddhist/Tibetan studies, and to folk-lore and oral traditions. It is recognised that strands of cultural heritage run through a wide range of development sectors and programmes. These need to be identified and demonstrated as diverse aspects of our rich traditions. Art forms and cultural institutions provide a powerful medium to foster national integration as well as national development. Necessary co-ordination links will be established and cooperative programmes will be undertaken for this purpose.

Greater emphasis will be laid on strengthening of arts through institutions, such as the Academies. Assistance would continue to be provided to voluntary organisations engaged in the promotion of art and culture. Library systems would be strengthened throughout the country with special attention to improving the facilities in the National level institutions.

Some of the rich art forms existing are in the realm of tribal and folk art. The development of folk and tribal arts, especially those which are facing extinction such as the folk art of the Himalayan regions, threatened ecologically as also culturally, would be supported through assistance to voluntary organisations engaged in these fields and areas.

In the field of anthropology, new projects have been identified to study the people of India and promote dissemination of culture. The Rashtriya Manav Sangrahalaya which is expected to be completed in the Seventh Plan, would recreate the history of human evolution, the evolution of culture and the range of living cultures in India.

The Indira Gandhi National Centre for Art will be set up at New Delhi as a resource centre and data base for the arts. It will also develop a major informatics library of cultural materials. The National Theatre will also be established on the same premises to support and project activities particularly in the field of visual arts, including folk and tribal arts.

Arrangements for Games

According to the 1981 census, 220 million or about 30 per cent of our population is in the age-group of 15-34 years, with 73 per cent living in the rural areas. The majority of them do not have the benefit of formal education the problems of youth, therefore have to be identified, with existing programmes being strengthened and new programmes devised to involve their participation and development. The two existing programmes of National Service Scheme (NSS) and Nehru Yuvak Kendras (NYKs) have proved useful in promoting the involvement of youth, both student and non-student, and urban and rural, and in creating awareness among them of nationally accepted objectives and motivating them to work towards their fulfilment. Both these programmes will be further developed and expanded in the Seventh Plan. The strength of the NSS will be raised from six hundred and ten thousand at the end of the Sixth Plan to one million at the end of the Seventh Plan. Activities of Nehru Yuvak Kendras will be expanded to cover all the districts in the country and will also be diversified.

The organisational structure of the Yuvak Kendras will also be revamped to impart greater flexibility in the development of programmes for youth, their speedier execution and closer monitoring. The aim will be to make the Kendras effective by ensuring coordinating links between youth and the various agencies of Government and public sector in the national development effort. Programmes of scouting and guiding, mountaineering and adventure, Commonwealth youth programmes and International Youth Exchange Delegations, and National Service Volunteer Schemes will be continued.

A major step will be taken during the Seventh Plan to translate into action the newly adopted Resolution on National Sports Policy, by giving high priority to the development of infra structure and facilities for sports and games at grass-root levels and developing the potential of our human resources both in the rural and urban areas. Efforts will be made to raise national standards in games and sports. Programmes for spotting and nurturing potential sports talent through coaching, training and nutrition required for helping the talented to realise their highest level would be continued. Present schemes like Rural Sports Tournaments, Women's Sports Festivals, National Talent Search Scholarships, grants to National Federations and State Sports Councils, etc., will be expanded. The activities of the Netaji Subhash National Institute of Sports, Patiala will be intensified and its coverage enlarged. The Sports Authority of India will be assisted to pursue its main objective of promotion and broad-basing of sports in the country and creation of health consciousness among citizens through appropriate and meaningful schemes.

Fiscal Viewpoint : The Seventh Plan outlay for education is of the order of Rs. 6383 crores of which the States sector outlay is Rs. 3994 crores. The sub-sectoral distribution is given in Annexure 2.

The provision for education is mainly in the States' sector. The Centre will play a coordinating role and provide leadership and guidance for new and innovative programmes. Out of the total non-plan budget estimates of education in 1983-84, amounting to Rs. 5229 crores, nearly 91 per cent was in the States Sector. Nearly 87 per cent of the total national expenditure on education is incurred on non-Plan side. In view of the constraints on resources for education, the structure and pattern of utilisation of Plan and non-Plan funds needs to be reviewed, to ensure the optimal use of funds in relation to the goals of the Seventh Plan. It is proposed to adopt low cost designs and devices for effecting economy and for reducing unit costs. Besides, non-budgetary resources have to be tapped and substantial resources mobilised from the community especially for replenishing and augmenting physical facilities in educational institutions.

It is also necessary to emphasise the non-monetary inputs in educational development, i.e., better planning, advanced technologies and practices, careful block level and institutional planning, and school mapping; better systems of supervision and administration; monitoring and evaluation a good information system; dedicated efforts by teachers, students and educational administrators; intensive utilisation of existing resources and facilities; and above all, commitment and active involvement of the local community. Educational research and training and planning and administration of education needs to be streamlined. The State level capabilities particularly require to be built up under the leadership of the National Council of

Educational Research and Training and National Institute of Educational Planning and Administration.

ANNEXURE 1

Educational Development From 1950-51 to 1984-85

S. No.	Item	Year 1 0-51 (Actual)	1960-61 (Actual)	1970-71 (Actual)	1980—81 (Actual)	1984-85 (Actual)
1	2	3	4	5	6	7
1.	Institutions (Number)					
(i)	Primary	2,09,611	3.30,399	4,08,378	4,85,538	5,50,000*
(ii)	Middle	13,596	49,663	90,621	1,16,447	1,40,000*
(iii)	High/Higher Secondary	7,288	17,257	36,738	51,594	60,000*
(iv)	College					
	(a) Art, Science & Commerce	548	1,161	2,587	3,393	3,500*
	(b) Professional	147	381	1,017	1,382	1,500*
	(c) Universities and Deemed Universities	28	44	93	123	135
2.	Enrolment by Stages (in '000)					
(i)	Primary (1-V Classes)	19,155 (42-6)	34,994 (62-4)	57,045 (76-4)	72,688 (83- 1)	85,377 (9184)
(ii)	Middle (VI-VII Classes)	3,120 (12-7)	6,705 (22-5)	13,315 (34-2)	19,846 (40'0)	26,729 (5307)
(iii)	High/Higher Secondary/ Intermediate	1,481	3,483	7,167	11,281	16,800*
(iv)	University-end Above (1st Degree)	174	557	1,956	2,752	3,442*

Contd....

S. No.	Item	1 0-51 (Actual)	1960-61 (Actual)	Year 1970-71 (Actual)	1980—81 (Actual)	1984-85 (Actual)
1	2	3	4	5	6	7
3.	Expenditure (Rs. in scores)					
	Total	114	344	1,118	3,746	6,000
	Plan	20	90	115	520	800
	Non-Plan Estimates	94	254	1,003	3,226	5,200

Source: (i) For School Education sir Expenditure—Ministry of Education & Planning commission.

(ii) For Higher Education IOC Reports.

Notes: Figures in parentheses indicate Gross Enrolment Ratio, as percentage of the total population in each category.

ANNEXURE 2

Major Heads of Education (7th Plan Outlay in Crores)

Sl.	Heads	Centre	States	U T.	Total
1.	General Education (of which MNP Component)	1518.64	2863.18	393.48	4775.30
	(a) Elementary Education	100 00	154905	181-40	183045
	(b) Adult Education	130 00	227.66	2.34	36000
	Total outlay on MNP Component	(230.00)	(1776.71)	(183.74)	(2190.45)
2.	Technical Education	220.00	388.12	73.67	681.79
3.	Art & Culture	350.00	114.86	17.26	482.12
4.	Sports & Youth Services	300.00	122.55	20.88	443.43
5.	Grand Total	2388.64	3488.71	505.30	6382.65

Education Meant for All

It is now universally acknowledged that the goal of Plan efforts is human development, of which human resource development is a necessary prerequisite. Education is the catalytic factor, which leads to human resource development comprising better health and nutrition, improved socio-economic opportunities and more congenial and beneficial natural environment for all. There is already enough evidence in India to show that high literacy rates, especially high female literacy rates, are associated with low rates of population growth, infant mortality and maternal mortality besides a higher rate of life expectancy.

Although the country has not so far achieved the goals of universalisation of elementary education (UEE) and eradication of adult illiteracy. (EAI), the 1991 census results reveal a literacy rate of over 52 per cent, with a higher rate of growth for female literacy. This is highly encouraging and the country can hope to achieve the broader goal of 'Education for All' (EFA) which has incidentally received international recognition at the world conference on EFA held at Jomtien in March, 1990. The commitment of the Government to the National Policy on Education (NPE), implemented from 1986-87 onwards and reviewed in 1990, has been reaffirmed with revised formulation in respect of a few paras, placed before the Parliament on 7.5. 1992. On the eve of Eighth Plan, therefore, the country is poised to make a real breakthrough in achieving its long-cherished educational goals as well as in supporting the drive for higher rate of economic growth.

The Assessment : The development of education in terms of institutions and enrolment from 1984-85 onwards is indicated in the Table.

Fundamental Education

The Seventh Plan gave overriding priority for the realisation of the objective of UEE by 1990. It was estimated that for achieving the goal, over 5 crore additional children would have to be enrolled. By 1991-92, however, about 2.53 crores were actually enrolled in the formal system and even after taking account of 0.72 crores in the non-formal system, the target could not be achieved. At the end of 1991-92, the gross enrolment at the primary and upper-primary stages is likely to have reached 10.09 crores and 3.44 crores respectively. The details of enrolment at the elementary stage are given in the following table.

Enrolment in Elementary Education: Additional and Cumulative Achievement During 1985-92

(Figures in Crores)

Sl. No.	*System/Stage*	*7th Plan (1985-90) Addnl. Achivmt.*	*Annual Plans (1990-91 & 1991-92 Addnl. Achivmt.*	*Cumulative Enrolment at the end of 1991-92*
1.	Formal:	1 - 95	0 - 58	13 - 53
	(a) Primary	1 - 34	0 - 36	10 - 09
	(b) Upper Primary	0 - 61	0 - 22	3 - 44
2.	Non-formal:	0-61	0-08	0-72
	Total	2-59	0-66	1425

The latest data show that in 1990-91, the gross enrolment ratio (GER) had reached 101.03 per cent at the primary stage and 60.4 per cent at the upper primary stage. Considering that the number of overage and underage children in the GER data was in the range of 16-23 per cent and the dropout rate for primary stage in 1987-88 was 46.97 per cent and for elementary stage as a whole 62.29 per cent, we are clearly far away from the goal of universal enrolment and retention, much less achievement.

The strategies of the Seventh Plan underwent a change in the middle of the Plan period with the adoption of the NPE in 1986. The new thrust in elementary education emphasized the aspects of (i) universal enrolment and universal retention, and (ii) substantial improvement in the quality of education. As part of implementation of NPE, the new scheme of Operation Blackboard (OB) was launched. Besides, the scheme of Non-Formal Education (NFE) was revised and a number of schemes for teacher education were also taken up. By March, 1992, the scheme of OB covered about 80 per cent of the blocks and 49 experimental, innovative NFE projects were sanctioned. There were 27.342 NFE centres run by 419 voluntary agencies and there were 2.72 lakh State run NFE centres.

Teaching the Teachers

In 1987-88, a Centrally-Sponsored Scheme (CSS) for restructuring arid reorganisation of teacher education was started, which included Mass Orientation of School Teachers (MOST), strengthening of Secondary Teacher Education Institutions (STEIs), State Councils of Educational Research and Training (SCERT), setting up of District Institutes of Education and Training (DIETs) and establishment and strengthening of Institutes of Advanced Studies in Education (LASE) in Universities. Between 1987-88 and 1991-92,12.96 lakh teachers were covered under the scheme of MOST and Central assistance was extended to set up 287 DIETs, 25 STEIs and 12 IASEs. The scheme of strengthening SCERTs did not, however, make headway.

Education at Societal Level : The NPE and the Programme Of Action (POA) envisaged that the Adult Education Programme (AEP) would cover 4 crore illiterates by 1990 and another 6 crores by 1995. With the launching of the National Literacy Mission (NLM) in 1988, the targets were reformulated and strategies recast. Accordingly, 3 crore illiterates were expected to be covered by 1990 and 5 crores by 1995. While Rural Functional Literacy Programme (RFLP), the post-literacy the teaching-learning process were modified, new strategies like area-specific and time-bound approach to achieve 100 per cent total literacy (TL), massive participation of non-governmental organisations (NGOs) and students and effective utilisation of traditional and folk theatre forms in literacy work were evolved. By 1991-92, the post-literacy programme was institutionalised in the form of 32,000 Jan Shikshan Nilayams (JSN). Apart from the introduction of Improved Pace and Content of Learning (IPCL) method, which reduced the duration of learning from 500 to 200 hours, technology demonstration programmes were initiated in 42 selected districts.

The scheme of Shramik Vidyapeeths (SVs) was reviewed, suggesting a need for expansion. The number of State Resources Centres (SRCs) increased from 19 to 20. A National Institute of Adult Education (NIAE) was set up in January 1991 to augment the technical and academic resources support to adult education and to undertake quality research and evaluation studies.

Area-specific and time-bound mass campaigns for TL first launched in Kottayam town and Ernakulam district in Kerala in 1989 with the active participation of students and voluntary agencies have been extended to other districts. By March 1992, twenty-five districts had achieved total literacy (in the sense of 85 per cent literacy) and TL campaigns were at different - stages of progress in 80 districts in Andhra Pradesh, Bihar, Gujarat, Haryana, Himachal Pradesh, Karnataka, Madhya Pradesh, Maharashtra, Orissa, Punjab, Rajasthan, Uttar Pradesh and West Bengal covering over 3 crore illiterates with the help of about 30 lakh volunteers.

Education at School Level : As part of NPE, new CSS for vocationalisation of higher secondary stage, improvement of science education and environment orientation to school education were started. The new Central schemes of Navodaya Vidyalayas (NVs) and National Open School (NOS) were also initiated. The existing schemes of Integrated Education,

Educational Technology and Computer Literacy Studies (CLASS) Project were strengthened.

By the end of 1991-92, about 8.7 per cent of the higher secondary students (5.85 lakhs) would have been diverted to vocational stream. The Open School affiliated to Central Board of Secondary Education (CBSE) was converted into an autonomous NOS in 1989 and by 1991-92, the total enrolment was in the neighbourhood of 1.50 lakhs. Under the CLASS Project, 2598 schools were equipped with computers, with 60 institutes providing resource support to these schools. As many as 275 NVs designed to provide good quality school education to talented rural children have been established in 29 States/Union Territories. As on March 31,1991, there were 64 ,517 students in the NVs and the pass percentage of the first batch, which took Class X examination was 95.77. The National Council of Educational Research and Training (NCERT) brought out the National Curriculum Framework for all stages of education and undertook a massive revision of text books for classes I-XII on the basis of the revised syllabi designed as per the framework.

7

Systematic Scheming

The outcome of the past three decades is before us. We are passing through a period of change in generations. The children of yesterday are the citizens of today, and they wish to bear the burden of the nation on their shoulders, but on observing their attitudes, conduct and bearing, one feels hesitant and suspicious about handing over the reigns of the nation to them, though this will be inevitable. However, some burning questions stare us in the face.

If the nation's reigns are given to the present generation, what will become of our nation? Will the values and attitudes of our public men lack our national characteristics? Will the process of national reconstruction continue at its present leisurely pace? All these questions relate to different aspects of life, but there is a common answer to them all-that, we have treated education as a means to selfish attainment. We have not given priority to education. In the absence of desirable plan, the results of education have not produced any long-term results. Because of aimless education, the younger generation has lost sense of direction. The result is that the youth of today is dissatisfied, despairing and doubtful. He wants to do something, but he does not know what he should do. For all this, it is necessary that we initiate plans for improvement of schools.

Schemes at the Beginning

According to the Kothari Commission, in India the problem of educational planning means simply that we need to evolve a national policy in the educational sphere while, according to our Constitution, education is a state subject, and consequently, educational officials at various levels take decisions on all of its varied aspects. The task before us is not simple, and we also do not have much experience to guide us. Hence, we will have to evolve our own techniques, and change, modify and improve them as we go along'.

The following are the elements of a comprehensive educational plan which have to be improved in order to overcome the problems that arise in the educational sphere-

1. Creation of literature in the modern Indian languages, which is necessary for making these languages the medium of instruction at the university level.
2. Educational Research
3. Preparation of text-books for schools and help-materials for teaching and study.
4. Improvements in the system of examination.
5. Arrangements for the in-service training of teachers and officials of the education department.
6. Improvements in the methods of supervision.
7. Increase in the contact with guardians and the local community.
8. Provision of progressive schemes for brilliant students and programmes of special assistance to backward students.

The Obstacles

The results of education can be good only if educational planning is successful. In our country, educational planning faces the following obstacles :

1. Excessive emphasis upon enrolment and expenditure.
2. Decentralisation of efforts.
3. Indifference towards accepting clearly defined paths of action.
4. Absence of adequate evaluation and research.
5. Failure to initiate programmes of superior quality.
6. Weakness of the educational planning mechanism.

The Planning Commission's Working Group on education has identified the following causes of the failure of planning:

1. Administration of the police kind, obsolete methods, inadequate resources, increased responsibilities of development, and untrained, incapable and inadequate staff.
2. Lack of attraction for trained individuals ; tradition of making appointments from above ; absence of any system of in-service training ; excessive emphasis upon individual and financial administration. There is need for a revolutionary change in the nature and structure of the states department of education. Instead of functioning as groups of individuals concerned with grants, statistics, financial permission, transfers, appointments, study of complaints, etc.,-these groups have to become organisations of educationists which possess the imagination to visualise the objectives of educational reconstruction, which are sensitive enough to recognise quickly the needs and demands of people immediately, which can prepare satisfactory plans for reconstruction and implement them successfully, which

can fulfil the roles of friends, philosophers and guides for the teachers as well as students and their guardians. However, so far, no effective steps are being taken in this direction.

3. The entire society is responsible for making the educational plan successful. Till the present, there is no effective system for establishing contact between teachers, students, guardians educational administrators and the rest of society, though the existence of such a system is a prime necessity.
4. Co-operation and harmony with other governmental departments and non-governmental agencies is weak and ineffective.
5. Proper utilisation of resources is hindered because of lack of resources, lack of extension schemes, delays in obtaining financial clearance, changes in the proposed amounts 'Or corrupt activities.
6. Political pressures are often seen working powerfully in the appointment and transfer of teachers, setting up of new institutions and location of schools. The same pressures also influence and modify approved schemes.
7. Wherever-suitable leadership has been found lacking, democratic decentralisation has led either to the obstruction of educational schemes or a complete and destructive change in their very nature. Local influences and force often create problems for the teachers.
8. The thought that goes into making a budget or preparing in a plan is the equivalent of a kind of evaluation. Evaluation is made from time to time. The discussion in the organisations of teachers, the press and the legislative assemblies are also forms of evaluation. But, hardly any efforts have been made so far towards introducing a systematic and formal mode

of evaluation by individuals directly involved in education.

In view of these factors, the Working Group felt constrained to say that comprehensive educational plans, keeping in view every aspect of education, should be prepared. The existing situation is that the states' departments of education thrust the responsibility for planning on certain officials, who then prepare plans and programmes without getting into touch with anyone. Specialists, teachers, organisations of teachers, or educational officials of the district level make no contribution to such plans. Besides, these plans are full of statistics about goals of appointments and expenses, while other much more important aspects of education are completely neglected. Whatever little is done at the higher levels, without making any effort to find out the views of individuals working in education at the grass-roots.

Detailed schemes and blue-prints are also required for the successful implementation of a plan. No attention is paid to this fact. The Working Group's view is that educational programmes should be treated in the same way in which projects concerning irrigation, industry or power are treated. We should see not merely the clarity of objectives; we must also seek to ensure the achievement of these objectives by considering the time division, need for preparatory work, materials expenditure needed for creating the necessary skills and motivation and administrative requirements, and then try to harmonise them with the time available and conditions existing. At present, there is a complete absence of such projects.

It seems that detailed thinking does not go into the preparing of plans by the education ministry and the Planning Commission, and after plans are once prepared, re-thinking occurs only after a year has passed. Assessments are hardly ever made. Besides, the various agencies looking after education also lack coordination among themselves. At the national level, various ministries, such as food, agriculture, labour, social welfare, home, etc., are also involved in educational planning. Similar agencies exist in the states also, but the co-ordination among them is quite weak.

The Suggestions

It is true that education is the state's responsibility, but it cannot be denied that the nation has an equal responsibility as well as stake in the success of education. Hence, the states and the centre should be regarded as equal partners in education. There are three main agencies of education- (i) the central government, (ii) the state governments, and (iii) local bodies and voluntary organisations. Besides, it is evident that (a) school education involves the partnership of the local government and the state government, and (b) higher education is conducted through the partnership of the state and central governments. A balance can be struck between complete centralisation or decentralisation after these truths are recognised and accepted.

The Working Group has offered the following suggestions for making educational planning successful:

1. *Preparation of Comprehensive Educational Plans :* Allocation of resources is all that is actually being done in the name of formulating plans. A comprehensive educational plan is inclusive of the existing situation in education, the objectives, of education, the steps to be taken for achieving these objects, all programmes, those which involve no expenditure or those for which expenditure has to be reduced, etc.
2. *Basis of the Process of Planning :* The second necessary reform relates to giving the planning process a wider basis and decentralising it, as well as bringing about co-ordination between the institution, district, state and centre. This will produce a wide range of advantages.

3. *Introduction of Institutional Plans* : The basic principle of this new technique will be institutional plans, i.e., plans prepared by the schools themselves. At the school level, plans have to be formulated by considering what can be done within the available resources or by adding a little to them. Good schools in particular should work in this direction.

Work can be started in the states on the basis of the following suggestions:

1. An essential condition for granting recognition and aid should be that each school should prepare a five-year plan, as well as annual plans, for its own development.
2. These plans should also become the basis of inspection.
3. The department of educational should provide some guidelines in the preparation of the school's plan which should be clearly in consonance with the state's policy on education.
4. The principals of institutions should prepare plans according to the directives of the department.
5. The state educational institution should train principals as well as inspectors.
6. Long-term plans will run concurrently with the state's five-year plans. Schools will re-open at the fixed time, though students will attend school a week latter. During this period, the teachers will consider every aspect of teaching and prepare plans for the forthcoming session.
7. Inspectors should receive detailed information about plans and evaluation well in advance.
8. Inspectors often compel schools to adopt many schemes simultaneously. For this, it is essential that the schemes should be limited in range, and they should be completed before others are taken up.

9. All the related agencies-teachers, students, society, guardians, principal, the management committee, etc., should participate in the preparation of the plan.

We should remember that education is a never ending or inexhaustible source of personal satisfaction. It is related directly to the nation's social and economic development. If education is systematically initiated at every level, and if it is intimately related to national programme, the pace of social and economic development increases.

Programming in Systematic Style : While reflecting upon institutional planning, we are faced with the following questions- (1) What are your objectives? (2) Is our purpose to work for the achievement of new objectives (3) Do we want to bring about a change in individuals? (4) Is it our purpose to replace the old patterns with fresh ones? These questions imply that our thinking on the issue should be clear. The function of institutional planning is to keep an institution occupied in the search for the best possible results in the existing social environment.

In the context of formulating a plan with clear objectives for any institution, it is necessary to reflect upon the existing circumstances. One cannot turn away from the realities of life and society. We must overlook the fact that our universities are tradition bound and that they have to work according to the directives of the department of education.

It is the department which formulates the curriculum and also issues orders about its implementation. Thus, if we can still think of an imaginative plan for a particular institution, despite the existence of these circumstances, it must necessarily be appreciated.

In order to prepare an educational plan for a single institution, it is necessary to consider the following bases:

1. Achievement of the best possible results in the given social and physical environment.
2. Reform and progress in technique, materials, resources, etc.
3. Making the best use of the talents of the students and teachers.
4. Generating a suitable atmosphere for the development of creativity.
5. Recognition of innate powers, their use, encouragement of efforts and leadership.
6. Encouraging mutual co-operation without injuring freedom of thought and action.
7. Achieving the maximum utilisation of building, laboratories, libraries and other resources.
8. Practising self-service and self-achievement.

The Working Group of the Planning Commission has suggested the following means of bringing success to the plans of schools:

1. The states' departments of education will have to begin to think a new in order to recognise or identify good schools and grant them greater aid as well as freedom, to guide the weaker schools towards improvement, and also to encourage competitiveness, creativity and experimentation amongst teachers and students. Instead of uniformity and rigidity, it will be necessary to adopt an approach which is dynamic and flexible.
2. The schools themselves should try to secure the means needed for their development. The best steps in this direction would be (i) the co-operation of local officials, guardians and the local community, (ii) a change in the method of giving grants in order to encourage superiority, and (iii) establishment of experimental schools and autonomous colleges.

3. It is necessary to initiate co-operation and mutual dialogue between schools and colleges, instead of allowing them to throw allegations at each other. School complexes can be of tremendous advantage in this sphere.
4. Transfers of teachers in government schools should be reduced to a minimum. Organising committees or boards of governors should be created, and in these the teachers should have an important voice, so that their commitment should be to the institution, and not merely to their cadre. Such a situation does not exist in private institutions, and hence they should make efforts to attract the best teachers towards themselves.
5. Teachers have necessarily to shoulder the leadership in the formulation and implementation of institutional plans. Among primary schools, there exists the peculiar problem of single-teacher institutions. For such cases, all institutions within a radius of three to five miles will treat the higher secondary school as the centre, and function as a school complex, and their institutional plan will also be a collective one. From the viewpoint of organisation, each complex should be treated as a unit. At the secondary school level, the form of principals will work to achieve co-operation from the nearest college or university and to ensure mutual co-operation. A complex can also be created by linking a college or even a department of a university with a group of secondary schools.
6. Transfers can help each other in the framing and implementation of plans even through the method of Panel Inspection. The panel can consist of some selected teachers and principals who can give the benefit of their experience and knowledge to other institutions, apart from their own, by giving a little extra time.

7. Colleges will, in general, not have much difficulty in preparing their own plans, but they can seek the guidance of the university. The universities, too, will frame their own plans. For this purpose, in keeping with the suggestions of the Education Commission, they will create their own 'academic planning boards.'

Institutional planning operates at three levels- (1) District, (2) State and (3) National.

1. *District level Plans* : Accepting the district as the fundamental unit of planning, development and administration, work is to be initiated in some districts in the next year itself. It is to be introduced in every district by the end of the sixth five year plan. Today, the expenditure on education in a single district is more than the total expenditure in India in 1882. The educational plan of a district should comprehend all educational activity below the level of university education-preprimary, primary, secondary and vocational. Towns with a population of a lakh or more can also have their separate plans, in which the municipal boards should also offer co-operation.
2. *State level Plans* : Plans at the state level have to become the centre of gravity of the entire planning process, and for this purpose, it is essential that every state department of education must have a powerful and effective planning wing. For the near future, the following programmes have been suggested for immediate implementation: (i) Evaluation of the development from independence till the present, (ii) formulation of a long term plan for fifteen or twenty years, publication of a white paper on the subject, and giving it a final shape in the light of the suggestions received, (iii) framing of an education Act.
3. *National Plans* : At the national level, the government of India has suggested the formulation of a national

educational policy which should be reviewed every five years. National plans will be based on this national policy. Their main elements will be the following: (i) the synthesizing element of framing a national plan based on all state-plans, (ii) co-ordinated action on the national plan by the centre as well as the states, (iii) central programmes to be implemented either by constitutional directives or the assent of the states. It will be the Centre's responsibility to produce a plan which does away with regional differences, which is balanced, and which is suited for a long term period For this purpose, special national programmes within the overall national plan will have to be evolved.

4. *The Dual Process of Plan Formulation* : Planning has to be done both from above and from below. It is necessary to have two time-tables in the planning process. For example, guidelines and hints about the temporary allocation of resources will flow from the central government to the state government, from the state government to the district level officials and institutions. In the reverse process, the institutions will prepare their own plans in the light of the information given. They will indicate the plans they can implement with the given resources, and what they may be able to do if more resources are made available, etc.

5. *Contribution of Teachers* : Teachers are expected to co-operate intimately and effectively in educational plans. Theoretically, this does not appear to be an unusual idea, but in effect, it has been implemented so far because of the following four factors: (i) The government has never shown any interest in this, and in fact the government has never understood either this problem or its importance. (ii) We have, as yet, never seen even a dream of any institutional organisation which makes it possible for teachers to participate in the formulation

and implementation of educational plan. (iii) There are so many differences among the various categories of teachers that the whole profession has been weakened, and consequently the teacher's capacity to contribute to educational planning is almost destroyed. (iv) Teachers are also lacking in specialisation and leadership, besides which they have adopted an attitude of indifference towards the problems of education planning. These four difficulties have to be overcome in order to benefit education by raising the status of teachers, which can be done by giving them the leadership in educational planning and development.

For this, the following suggestions have been offered:

(a) School-planning should be introduced in every school.

(b) At the district level, there should be an advisory board council of teachers on which every teacher organisation of the district should have representation. It should be consulted in every matter pertaining to educational planning and development.

(c) Similar advisory boards should also be created at the, state level, and these should be called joint teachers' councils.

(d) The central ministry of education should establish a national committee of teachers on which every teacher organisation of the national level should be represented. In planning and development matters, this committee should be consulted, as is to be done at the district and state levels.

(e) The government should declare, without any reservations and conditions, that it wishes to hand over the leadership in matters of educational planning to the teachers, and, that the responsibility for helping in this work and collecting the necessary resources will fall upon the department of education. Such a declaration will influence the attitudes of departmental officials as well as teachers and lead to the creation of a suitable environment which is essential for the success of this entire programme.

(f) Efforts must be made to win the co-operation of the teachers in administrative activities relating to the school as well as other matters.

(g) The teachers themselves should develop an interest in planning. It is unfortunate that teachers have neglected this important aspect of their vocation. Teachers organisations have shown no interest in the past three five-year plans and three annual plans. They have not indulged in any profound criticism or analysis, though it is expected of them that they would not only subject the government's plans to criticism, but also offer a parallel plan of their own, so that the people may have an opportunity for a comparative study. It is obvious that teachers will have to give up this indifference, and the sooner it is done, the better.

(h) Teachers will also have to develop the necessary skills for planning; both individuals and in groups, through their organisations. Of course, it is true that this will happen only when the plan for decentralisation outlined earlier is implemented and teachers are asked to cooperate.

(i) If teachers of all categories unite and form a single, organised community, their contribution to educational administration can become more effective. For this, the first thing necessary is a change of attitude. At present, the teaching profession is divided into a number of discrete units which, it appears, visit their own classrooms individually without ever entering into a working relationship. It is obvious that there is no place for such an alienated outworn attitude in the new India that we dream of, a country with a social system based on equality, freedom, justice and the dignity of the individual. The community of teachers is one, and all within it are fundamentally equal. Everyone will have to strive to generate the spirit of brotherhood, and create opportunities which may encourage a spirit of unity and foster it.

(j) In order to generate a commitment among the teachers for the institutions in which they teach, it is essential for them to have an effective voice in its administration. Suitable efforts for this will have to be made in private as well as governmental institutions.

6. *Training* : It is necessary to train all individuals concerned with the formulation and implementation of plans. Besides, some selected individuals must also be specially trained for formulating and implementing certain specialised projects. A detailed document should be prepared for each scheme, showing the objectives, period of work, finance, individuals involved, description of resources, arrangements for co-ordination, a detailed time division plan, made of evaluation, preparatory work, etc. This task is undoubtedly difficult, and the specialists available will also be few. Hence, the Asian Educational Planning and Administration Institution can be entrusted with providing help in this sphere.

7. *Eradication of the Stress on Money* : Every effort should be made to get rid of the stress on money in educational

plans. If we imagine that surplus funds will help us to end every conceivable problem in education, the idea only indicates our naivette. After spending substantial amounts of money we have succeeded in expanding the general system of education and in creating new institutions, better scales of pay for teachers, more teaching, putting up more buildings, and expansion of resources. However, those improvements which were not related with finance have met with limited success only. We have almost completely failed in the growth of adult literacy or in preventing wastages and stagnation in primary education. The enrolment at the university and secondary level has not decreased. No noticeable progress in the schemes for qualitative improvement has been noted. For all these activities, what is needed is more and better human resources, not more money. In the sphere of human efforts, our work has been unsatisfactory. In a rich country, the emphasis upon money may not mean a serious loss, but in a poor country like ours, this lavishness is intolerable. We can achieve success in our objectives if we adopt the following major programmes along with our other schemes:-

1. *Cost Consciousness :* The money invested should not exceed the profit gained.
2. *Intensive Use of Available Resources :* Efforts should be made to derive the maximum profits from the existing investments, instead of seeking avenues for fresh investments.
3. *Research on Inexpensive Techniques :* Science should pay attention to this field.
4. *Selective Technique :* Instead of taking up numerous schemes simultaneously some selected schemes should be chosen on the basis of priorities.

5. *Human Efforts* : The vicious circle- lack of education in a poor country itself becoming the cause of further poverty should be broken through enthusiastic and dedicated human effort.

8. *Priorities* : It is necessary to determine priorities at the national, state and local levels. Today, there is a tendency to think of everything in terms of the national level. Instead of this attitude, it would be better if, at the national level, priority is given only to some subjects of truly national importance. These can be treated as national schemes. In teaching, production of books and teaching of science can be treated as national schemes for the sixth plan. On these issues, the Centre should finalise decisions after consultation with the states. But once a decision has been taken, the states will compulsorily have to act upon them in the most potent and effective manner possible.

On most of the remaining issues, the states themselves must take their own decisions, and in accordance with local needs, determine the priorities. For instance, at the secondary level, the question of an educational fee can be taken up. There is no need to seek uniformity at the national level in such matters.

In many other matters, such as facilities in schools and non-teacher costs, priorities will have to be fixed at the local level, in consonance with local needs and the clearly defined rights and authority of the school or local body, which should also have the necessary freedom to take decisions. There is no need to expect absolute uniformity in all districts. In some matters, freedom must be given even to the schools.

Neither is there any need to accept complete uniformity and conformity in all schools of the same category. A system based on co-ordinated and rationally determined priorities separately determined, at the national, state and local levels will be far better than the prevailing system in which, so far, many decisions have been taken, even in matters of regional and national importance, without the least attention to local needs. Such a system has led to the complete obstruction of any tendency to take the initiative and bring improvements. What is needed is relatively better coordination and harmony between all the agencies, departments and ministries concerned with education, rather than any attempt to foist an unnecessary uniformity.

The Setup

For the proper implementation of educational programmes, it is necessary to bring about improvements in educational administration on the basis of well-defined priorities. At present, the education department focuses its attention only upon maintaining organisational administration, with the result that the duty of developmental administration is not fulfilled at all. For this latter purpose, the departments of education should have full knowledge of educational programmes in all the states of our own country as well as the programmes initiated in foreign countries. Besides they should give suitable importance to all such programmes in their own educational planning, keeping in view the needs, aspirations and ambitions of the people of their region. Such a developmental administration will possess the following characteristics:-

1. Developmental administration accords equal importance to the twin aspects of quantitative and qualitative improvement in education. It makes continuously modifiable and improved schemes for the future, evaluates the experiences of the past and present, and simultaneously provides the administrators with ever increasing opportunities for increasing their professional skills.

2. The existing organisational administration soon becomes involved in its own web of ever-expanding rules and regulations, -by laying excessive stress upon control. It is thus unable to spare a thought to progress or development. In contrast, developmental administration gives importance to the independence of teachers and institutions, expansion in extension services and guidance, experimentation, initiative and creativity, and encourages all of them.
3. Organisational administration is suitable for a static or slowly progressing society, because it always sticks to uniformity and insists on obedience to rules. On the other hand, developmental administration concerns itself with the development of the individual in a rapidly changing society, and for this purpose, it does not hesitate to modify its own policy, if this is necessitated by circumstances.
4. Another drawback of organisational administration is that it creates the two classes of teachers and administrators, with greater benefits invariably flowing to the latter. This discrimination invariably has an adverse impact both upon the teacher and the teaching process, as well as development of education. In contrast, developmental administration invariably aims at healthy relations between the two classes so that both of them are able to fulfil their respective duties without coming into conflict with each other.
5. Developmental administration is completely democratic and decentralised. As is the case of organisational administration, it has no place for the centralisation of power or the creation of a bureaucratic approach. Every individual, at every level, has the right to make rules, to work accordingly and to evaluate his activities.

Having been accustomed to organisational administration for almost centuries it now appears difficult to adopt developmental administration. Even today, our administration spends almost the whole of its time in the appointment of workers, their transfers, promotions and investigation into anonymous complaints and allegations. Whatever time does remain is spent in sorting out financial complications.

The consequence of this is that the department soon loses all touch with society, and it turns into an isolated tower standing in a waste land. In order to introduce developmental administration, we will first have to overcome these drawbacks. The suggestions for the improvement of educational administration are based on our assumption that the central and state governments are faced with the major task of making the objectives of education determined by the governments themselves.

The outstanding purpose or aim of educational administration is improvements in educational services. This should be done at the state and central levels. It was with this in view that the suggestion for an Indian Educational Service was mooted, but, for a variety of reasons' it was never implemented. Hence, it has become necessary to think of some other means of achieving the necessary goal. In this connection, the following measures are suggested:-

1. An educational advisory service should be established. A service of this kind, associated with the ministry of education, suffers from many drawbacks, the main one being that its members are out of touch with existing realities, since they never have an opportunity to work in the practical field. The following programmes can be adopted for overcoming this weakness.

   (a) All the posts under the government of India requiring educational expertise as well as such voluntary organisations such as the Central Schools Organisation should be combined under this. If possible, the states desirous of joining the unit may be allowed to do so.

(b) Some posts in the central ministry of education should be reserved for officials nominated by the state governments. In exchange, some officials of the central ministry should be appointed in the states' departments of education. This policy will benefit both the Centre and the states. Officials from the central ministry will get an opportunity to increase their knowledge and experience about the actual conditions existing in the states, and also to make their own attitudes more liberal, while the states will benefit from the diverse and wide experience of the central government's educationists.

(c) The officials of the states' departments of education, principals of schools, vice-chancellors of universities and famous educationists should be appointed to the posts of additional educational advisors. Such appointments should be made only for five years, though they may be extended for another 5 years under exceptional circumstances.

2. For the improvement of the states' departments of education, the following steps can be considered :

(i) The scales of pay of their officials should be improved.

(ii) The number of posts of inspectors should be increased to the extent necessary.

(iii) It is generally seen that the department fills the senior posts in the department by promoting junior officials. Even if direct recruitment is adopted for some posts, priority is still given to promotion of juniors. Consequently, fresh and enthusiastic individuals do not get any opportunity and the qualitative development of education suffers a setback.

(iv) The posts from the level of district education officer to the level of the director of education (where special qualifications and abilities are needed for framing policies and setting down rules) should be filled through offers of five-year contracts to able individuals working in schools, colleges and universities, though few such posts may be reserved for promoted individuals. Those employed on contract may be allowed to extent their contract for another five years, but only if their work in eminently satisfactory in the initial period.

Educational institutions should possess facilities whereby individuals with marked administrative talent may be enables to take up administrative jobs. On the other hand, administrative officials interested in teaching should be allowed opportunities for appointment in schools, colleges and universities.

The second very significant programme far important is the provision of in-service education for educational administrators. This is even more important in view of the fact that the condition of the states' departments of education is truly pitiable at present. For this, the following steps have been suggested:

1. Each administrator or inspector should be required, on being first appointed, to complete a course of training, whose period and subject should be in accord with the posts held by the individual.
2. Education of this kind should have two purposes-one, to acquaint the officials from time to time with the

state's educational policies, and two ; to get an opportunity to study improvements in education in India and abroad and to assess them in the light of the conditions in their own state. These officials should participate in conferences or seminars or workshops for at least a week twice a year. Such conferences should be organised, at the district or regional level, by the district officials, for the non-gazetted staff, while for the gazetted staff, they should be organised by the director of education.

3. Each department should regularly publish a newspaper or letter of the highest quality in order to acquaint its officials with the latest government policies as well as the least thinking in the educational sphere by leading educationists.
4. It is essential to have provisions for granting leave to those officials who wish to improve their knowledge or enter specialised studies at regular intervals. Six months leave can be granted after every six years for such purposes. In the past, India did have a system of further studies'. Similar schemes should now be evolved and adopted.
5. Officials of one state should be sent to other states for studying particular problem.
6. The ministry of education, the NCERT, and the Asian Educational Planning and Administration Institute should prepare a programme for in-service training, since such a programme can bring to the participants the knowledge, experience and guidance of experts and scholars in this field. The states' departments of education should allow their officials to participate in such programmes freely.
7. Both at the national and state levels, there should be arrangements by which officials of other departments

concerned with education and its problems can be kept in touch with latest ideas, and also be given training.

The Kothari Education Commission had suggested the establishment of a National College for the training of educational administrators. This is a very valuable suggestion, and it should be accepted and implemented in the present plan-period. Giving opportunities for improving professional qualifications is a good idea, but not all individuals are able to benefit from them. Hence, for encouragement, they should also be given incentives, such as promotions or increase in pay. In view of the existing circumstances, it is essential that, within the next one or two years, massive programmes for the reorientation of our educational administrators should be taken up. In all such programmes organised at the national, regional or local level, the states and the Centre should co-operate with each other.

Schemes of Different Nature

The third programme for the improvement of educational administration concerns the proper organisation of developmental work regarding schools and workers. For the last twenty years, our attention has been focused upon the quantitative expansion of education, but the time is now ripe for concentrating upon its qualitative improvement. Many elements are important for this, for instance - the abilities of teachers, their devotion to duty, the commitment and motivation of students, an atmosphere conducive to truth and hard work, provision of facilities, a developed curriculum, dynamic methods of teaching and evaluation, research, good supervision and guidance work, and a favourable social climate.

However, solving the problems of educational administration depends upon two factors- (1) school organisation, and (2) supervision and guidance.

Before 1947, educational authorities were compelled to bear two burdens, those of administration as well as introduction of programmes of qualitative improvement. But after 1950, the work load of administrative activities upon these officers increased to such an extent that they had almost no time to spare for programme of qualitative improvement. Even as early as 15 years ago, it was felt that there was need for establishing special agencies to carry out developmental programmes.

It was with this in view that such institutions as the Central Text-book Research Bureau, the Central Educational and Vocational Guidance Bureau, the National Audiovisual Education Institution, the National Basic Education Institute, the National Institute of Primary Education, Directorate for Extension Programmes in Secondary Education, Central English and Hindi Institutes, etc., were established. In a similar fashion, in the states, too, state education institutes audio-visual education institutes, educational and, vocational guidance institutes, evaluation organisations, state science teaching institutes, and the English institute, etc., came to be established.

It is beyond doubt that these agencies have succeeded in those states in which due attention was given to these two conditions, one, the department of education appointed its own highly qualified staff in these institutions, two, these officials were able to win the co-operation of all administrators in education for the fulfilment of their goal and the implementation of their ideas.

On the basis of past experience, the following suggestions can be offered for bringing about qualitative improvement:-

1. In the organisation of the above institutions, those professionally skilled individuals should be appointed who can understand the problems of school education, seek solutions to them and guide the teachers.

2. So far, universities have remained completely cut off from schools. Now, they should offer their co-operation for the improvement of school education through research, improved curricula, search for new and better methods of teaching and evaluation, teacher training, preparation of superior text-books, etc.
3. At the national level, too, there should be an ideal institution capable of working for the improvement of education. At present, the NCERT is performing this function, but it is necessary to make its efforts more fruitful in a shorter time frame.
4. In the states, too, there is the need to establish such institutions as - state secondary education board, teacher training board, text-books improvement centre, curriculum research institute, vocational guidance institute, etc.
5. At the district level, there should be strong organisation under the direction for the district education officer, and the principals of all training colleges in the district should offer him their co-operation.

The following points should be kept in view in order to make the working of institutions more effective:

(a) In these institutions, only the most capable and highly qualified officials should be appointed, with suitable attractive scales of pay.

(b) These institutions should co-ordinate and harmonise their activities with each other. For example, the NCERT should associate itself with the state educational institution, departments of universities and district level organisations while district level organisation should devote itself to the assistance and supervision of schools, teachers and school organisations.

(c) The functioning of these institutions should be regarded as an inalienable part of the working of the ministry of education and department of education.

If a system of the kind outlined above is introduced, there is little reason to doubt that classroom teaching and research level activities of the highest order will be linked with each other in a single chain. All the problems of education will be tackled as soon as they arise, and new and superior programmes will be formulated and implemented promptly.

Awakening and Vigilance

Although various suggestions have been given for making supervision and guidance of schools more effective-and these include formation and implementation of institutional plans, reorganisation of the department of education, adoption of the school complex scheme, introduction of panel inspection, etc., it is equally important to raise the standard of inspection through the proper training of the inspecting staff. For this, the first step is to increase the number of inspectors, because at present, each inspecting officer has the responsibility for inspecting the working of between 22 and 246 institutions, (an average of 51), and between 94 and 1091 teachers (an average of 197).

The second step is the appointment of specialist officials, in addition to the general inspection staff, and the former should be capable not only of evaluating the teacher's teaching work but also of guiding him. These specialists should be of two kinds-one, those who pay complete attention to the teaching in specific subjects, such as mathematics, science, English, etc., two, those who possess specific qualifications in such fields as programming, physical education, improvement of examination system, construction of courses, etc. These specialists should be entrusted, not merely with the routine inspection of schools, but with the task of providing in-service training and guidance.

Initially, specialist inspectors should be appointed for particular subjects in some selected districts. A panel of between 3 and 5 such inspectors should work at the regional level.

The fourth programme for the improvement in administration is the modification and modernisation of the department's method of working, which, at present, is in a deplorable state. For this purpose, the measures outlined below should be adopted:

1. The National College, whose establishment has been recommended by the Kothari Commission, should provide opportunities for research into educational administration. In addition it should study the following subjects and offer its suggestions-rules pertaining to admission to educational institutions of particular classes, provision of financial grants to institutions, selection of teachers, evaluation of teaching work, determining the internal and external techniques of evaluation, adoption of a convenient method for payment of teachers salaries, preparation of text-books and their acceptance, and analysis of the work of official concerned with inspection and supervision.
2. The department of education in each state should have a wing for the study of organisation and working, and it should offer its suggestions for administrative reforms from time to time.
3. In the annual conferences of educational administrators of various levels, information about departmental policies and programmes should be given, but in addition, they should also be made aware of the changes introduced. Their views on these changes should be invited and discussions initiated.
4. Excessive and unnecessary staff should not be appointed, but at the same time, care should be taken

to see that important officials do not waste their time and energies in routine and minor works.

5. Delays in work and inconveniences are occasioned by an irrational division of authority. Hence, as far as possible, more and more administrative and financial responsibility should be shifted to district level officials. The directorate of education should concern itself mainly with co-ordinating their efforts, formulating policies, and ascertaining whether the authority delegated to them is being properly utilised or not.

In this context, it is to be noted that improvements in departmental working require officials with open minds and hearts. When the organisation suggested above it introduced, it is hoped that these administrators will be able to develop the right attitudes.

The fifth step towards the improvement in administration lies in introducing flexibility and dynamism in administration. The problems of India's education are very complex, and the diversities and variety in the country's economic and social conditions have obviated the possibility of finding a single solution for them all, under all conditions. Even this diversity can be converted into a virtue if the method of working is dynamic and flexible. What will happen in such a situation is that varied experiments will be carried out in different situations and contexts, and with their help, solutions will be found quickly and inexpensively. This important principle can best be illustrated through some examples:

1. Under the present educational system, all the colleges and schools in the state have a common curriculum, and whatever changes are introduced usually produce destructive results in certain plans. The reason for this is that those who formulate the curriculum invariably keep their vision fixed upon the weaker and backward students. In consequence, the brilliant students and

enthusiastic institutions are never benefited. Besides, the rigid curriculum makes it impossible to exploit the institutional advantages that some institutions may have over others. Hence, it is essential that, in a state, more than one, or at least two curricula-one generalist and the other specialised, must be introduced.

2. The second rigid constraint in the existing system is that the child makes his choice of subjects in class 9, at the age of 14, and then remain tied to this choice for the future. This kind of responsibility, thrust upon the immature child, is as harmful in the long run as the institution of child marriage proved to be. Besides, deciding upon groups of subjects is also counter-productive. In this context, we should be more liberal and the student should be given more freedom in his choice of subjects.
3. Efforts at making secondary education development oriented and reducing the enrolment in research at the university level have both failed. Hence, a plan should be prepared in which the curricula for the first degree synthesizes a number of vocational studies. Later on, specialised education in those vocations should be provided, to the extent of allowing the candidate to obtain his Ph.D. degree in the subject, if he so wishes.
4. No less important is flexibility and variability in the methods of teaching and evaluation. The existing fixed methods, a fixed curriculum and a definite system of education may satisfy the average teacher and the average student. But teachers with creative minds, if prevented from working outside the guidelines fixed by the department, will be completely stultified.
5. There should be flexibility even in the sphere of education. At present, an excessive expansion in secondary and higher secondary education in certain

regions has led to increased unemployment while on the other hand in some regions, these levels of education have been introduced quite recently. In the future, expansion of education should be limited only to the underdeveloped regions only. Besides, those subjects should be encouraged for study which have remained neglected so far.

6. There should be a practical and flexible approach towards the medium of education. So long as regional languages remain incapable of shouldering the burden English should be retained as the medium of education, in order to maintain standards.
7. The current fashion is to give financial grants upon certain fixed principles to all educational institutions, with the result that the superior as well as the inferior institution obtain under the same rules and conditions. This policy of uniformity should be modified so as to make provisions for additional grants to the better and more progressive institutions.

It is of course true that it is as difficult and problematic to implement a flexible and dynamic method of education as it is easy and convenient to implement a rigid and uniform system of education. But, in modern society, we just cannot make progress without a flexible and dynamic system. In fact, we must now grant freedom to every student, every teacher and every institution. This is a difficult task, but it is not impossible. In order to make it possible two aspects must be strengthened-the teacher, and the administrator.

Way of Assessing

The need for a continuous evaluation of programmes is self-evident. In fact, planning, implementation and evaluation are mutually correlated functions. They help in overcoming the obstacles that arise during implementation. Besides, they also help in finding solutions to the problems that remain. Unfortunately, we have not laid sufficient stress upon evaluation and research, as yet. We suggest that in the next few years, special emphasis should be laid upon evaluation and educational research.

There are three modes of evaluation, which will have to be adopted simultaneously and continuously:

1. One simple form of evaluation is that, in which each teacher, administrative official of the department and educational institution will have to become involved. In the context of school planning and implementation, the institution should itself periodically evaluate its own progress. Similarly, teachers and administrators should also evaluate their own work. The state as well as the central governments should also evaluate their programmes from time to time to discover whether their policies are being promptly, effective and economically implemented or not.

2. There is need for the evaluation of the programmes and schemes adopted by district level organisations, central government and the state governments. Realistically, periodical evaluation should be necessarily provided for in every important programme. This provision should provide a clear statement of the aims of evaluation, its process, agency and period. Briefly stated, just as teaching and evaluation are inseparably related, in the same way policy formulation and evaluation should also be regarded as inseparable.

3. There are certain aspects of planning which must be evaluated at the highest level. For' instance, there is the very important question how does education contribute to national development, or what contribution can it make? Equally important are the questions of the use of manpower, the need for it, and the opportunities for

planning its utilisation. In addition, there is the problem of standards in education. In connection with brilliant students at the various levels of education as well as in different kinds of institutions, it is necessary to discover the extent to which they achieve the desired standard. It should be the duty of the Ministry of Education and the Planning Commission to encourage research into this aspect. Famous departments of universities can be beneficially associated with these programmes of evaluation.

Development—Organised Manner : The administrative problem of universities are no less complex neither are they in any less need of attention. In this connection, the recommendations and suggestions of the Education Commission should be implemented. We suggest that the Indian branch of the Asian Institute of Educational Planning and Administration, with the cooperation of the University Grants Commission, should take into its hands the work of research into this aspect, and also prepare programmes for the proper, training at the university level. It is also our suggestion that the Planning Commission should establish a working group, under the guidance of the Asian Institute, for a detailed study of these problems, and on the basis of its findings, it should also promptly take definite and concrete steps for the improvement of university administration.

The Directives

It is desirable that specific programmes concerning educational planning, administration and evaluation should be evolved on the basis of priority in the present plan period. In the last 20 years, the states' departments of education have not expanded at the same rate as that at which facilities have expanded. For instance, in 1946-47, only 3.2% of the total expenditure on education was expanded upon supervision and inspection, although at least 5% should have been spent.

In 1965-66, this expenditure increased by 6 times, but during this period, the expenditure on education had risen from Rs. 50 crores to Rs. 600 crores, with the result that the percentage spent upon inspection and supervision fell to only 1.9.

This tendency of spending less and less on educational administration has continued over the years, and in the last three, plan periods, it has become even more marked. In the states' plans, no money is at all allocated for administration and inspection in the first place, and even when some provisions are made, deductions are made in it, whenever there is any need to reduce expenditure. The outcome of this short-sighted policy is that although a small amount of administrative expenditure is saved, a much larger sum is wasted on education because of the lack of proper administration, and inspection.

Different Schemes

It is most sadding to note that there is very little awareness of the great, harm that has been caused to educational administration. In many matters, the quality of administration has deteriorated sharply, while in many others, administration has completely vanished. For instance -

1. The director of education is usually so completely occupied by his work in the office that he is unable to undertake regular tours of schools, as he did in the past. He is also unable to establish close relationships with district officials, and thus, he is unable to stimulate or direct them fruitfully. Regional officials also suffer from similar handicaps.
2. The result is that even district officials are often unable to inspect schools for long stretches of time.
3. Many very important responsibilities have been thrust upon the departments of education, but they have failed to evolve an efficient machinery for implementing their

schemes. For instance, text-books have been nationalised, but there is no efficient machinery to oversee the production of text-books of the desired quality or standard. Consequently, in some places, the district inspector has been converted into a mere bookseller, while at other places, he wastes two-thirds of his time in paying the salaries of teachers.

The Assessment : Not only is it necessary to reverse this flow, it is essential to achieve this promptly. Hence, it is suggested that, for the purpose of improving and strengthening educational administration, 5 per cent of the educational budget should be earmarked, on a priority basis, for educational planning, administration and evaluation, and this should also include research and the training of educational administrators, principals, as well as the in-service training of teachers.

Plans of Other Nature

1. Instead of allocating funds for a few selected schemes, complete educational plans should be formulated.
2. Well co-ordinated and harmonised plans should be framed at the district, state and national levels in order to meet the need for a decentralised approach to educational planning.
3. Institutional plans will provide the basis for this novel process of educational planning.
4. The district should be regarded as the basic unit of educational planning, administration and development. From the very next year, district plans should be initiated for purposes of guidance, and these should be adopted within a five-year period.
5. State plans must be made the basis of the entire process of educational planning.
6. It is the responsibility of the Central Government to adopt and maintain a balanced viewpoint and foresight

regarding education development as well as the eradication of regional imbalances among states in the matter of education. From this viewpoint, specific programmes should be included in the national plan. Planning should have a dual aspect-planning from above, and planning from below.

7. It is necessary to involve teachers, intimately and effectively in the formulation and implementation of educational planning.
8. All individuals concerned with educational planning and implementation should be given suitable training.
9. In preparing plans for educational development, the technique of preparing projects should be adopted.
10. The tendency towards heavy investments and negligence of costs in educational development programmes should be curbed; instead, programmes more in keeping with the conditions of a developing country should be prepared.
11. Priorities at the district, state and national level should be clearly defined for effective educational planning.
12. There is an acute need to establish co-ordination and harmony between the various agencies concerned with educational planning. The states and the centre, too, should co-ordinate and harmonise their activities in plan formulation and implementation.
13. For improvement in the implementation of educational plans, it is essential that the existing organisational administration should be immediately replaced by developmental administration.
14. Under the new concept of developmental administ-ration, there will be great need for re-organisation in the state and central educational services.

15. Programmes for the in-service training of educational administrators should be given a high priority.
16. Giving the highest priority to the Education Commission's suggestion for the establishment of a national college for training such administrators, we recommend that this should be established immediately and developed fully within the five-year plan period.
17. There is need to encourage departmental officials to increase their professional competence.
18. In addition to developing programmes for in-service training, it is also necessary to adopt a programme to complement such training. In this the administrative officials at every level should be acquainted with the complex problems of educational reorganisation.
19. If educational administration is to be improved, proper provisions of institutions and able individuals for the supervision of programmes for qualitative improvement must be made. These should include the NCERT at the national level, state educational institutes at the state level, and other institutions and school complexes at the district level.
20. Effort must be made for providing better supervision and guidance to schools.; For this, wherever necessary, the staff for inspection must be increased and subject-inspectors appointed.
21. Departmental working, which is unsuitable for developmental administration must be improved quickly.
22. The mode of working of departments of education should be dynamic and flexible.
23. In the forthcoming years, due emphasis should be placed upon evaluation and educational research. In these fields, some determined progress must be made.

24. The Indian branch of the Asian Institute for Educational Planning and Administration, with the co-operation of the University Grants Commission, should conduct research into the problems of university administration, and also introduce programmes for the suitable training of university teachers.
25. Priority must be given in the present plan to schemes for reforms in educational planning, administration and evaluation. For this, 5 per cent of the expenditure on education should be set apart for this purpose.
26. It is our suggestion that a sum of Rs. 26 crores should be provided for developmental schemes relating to educational planning, administration and evaluation.

8

The Organisation

The rapid development of industrialisation gave rise to new technologies which were instrumental in bringing about a change in the process of communication. The process of communication was fast and receipts of communication and the feedback were ensured. Mass Media and Communication technologies have become integral parts of our life and our society.

Functioning Methods

Media are used to add new information to human knowledge and keep on upgrading it. Ignorance can not be eradicated without adequate information supply. The overall development is directly related to education. Media enable the spread of education through conventional as well as unconventional methods. The desire to have access to media increases the level of education and knowledge among the population.

Increase in media use increases the level of education. Thus, people's demand for education has given rise to the need for greater access to informations which has further boosted the media hardware production causing an unprecedented growth in the economy. This, in turn, has stimulated the expansion of communications industry including media industries.

The mass media has monopolised the leisure industry. Transactional media giants have started invading the continents via the sky, using satellite slots. The competition for audience attention has become fierce.

Mass media have also played a leading role in shaping, guiding and reflecting the public opinion. These functions of media help to establish democracy. Use of media in a democratic polity creates critical awareness among the people. The media may not be able to perform these functions unless the access to them is ensured to a large section of our population.

Access to media means access to facts and documents which help one acquire information and knowledge. In comparison with individuals, media have more access to sources of information due to their reach and institutional character. Media power makes access easy.

Media access is important in the political sphere. Access to media is access to public opinion, so essential to protect and preserve democratic institutions. It is advantageous to both the leaders and masses. Leaders can address masses depending upon their convenience. They reach widely dispersed masses simultaneously through the electronic media in particular.

Free Press

As technological innovations improved, as the spread and reach of the press expanded, attention was focused on diffusion of information upholding the right of the public to the freedom of information. Originally, the freedom of information meant the people's right to information. In simple words, it was the right to know whatever affected the individuals themselves. New information technology has posed new dangers to the freedom of media person as well as media consumers. In theory, everybody enjoys the right to freedom of expression, but the huge capital needed for investment in new media of mass communication, has negated the whole concept since only the very-well-to-do, the elite can afford to launch the media ventures.

India is a classic example of communication contradictions. Certain media are allowed in the private sector while others are controlled by the Government. Newspapers in India have traditionally uphold the freedom of press. In India, with a low literacy level, the influences of print media are limited to the urban centres. Further, most Indian newspapers being privately owned, are supposed to guarantee free and unbiased reporting. Several defects have been identified. Most of the largely circulated newspapers are owned by big business and industrial houses, and thus political interests take precedence over any other human interests. A study conducted by the IIPA, Delhi, revealed that out of 54 dailies selected, 27 newspapers were owned either partially or totally by business and industrial houses and controlled about 50 per cent of the total circulation. For the purpose of unbiased and objective performance, delinking the ownership of newspapers from large industrial houses was suggested.

However, inspite of all this, the Indian Press enjoys credibility with reading audiences. Public opinion is reflected either in the editorials or letters to the editor published in newspapers. But, with 85% of the population totally unexposed to the press and its accessibility limited to just the elite, it is questionable how accessibility to the media can be a criteria for its high credibility. Further, how can editorials or letters to the editor from the literate few, constitute feedback of the entire nation.

Government controlled electronic media are anathema to the very concept of an open society. Frequent political interference has eroded the credibility of both AIR and Doordarshan. Added to this, bureaucratisation has affected professional aspects of their functioning. These two powerful media can cross the barriers of illiteracy and their reach is the reason why political authorities keep a stranglehold on them.

A community is an assembly of people in an identified geographical area. A community's development hinges on effective communication. The increased use of local media makes communication a vital input of every community development programme. Community participation in media programmes accentuates free flow of information. Consequently, the democratic process acquires more meaning and relevance. Community participation in mass media can be both at the level of decision-making and management.

The mass media are very important component of society. Their use in a developing country like India is considered most crucial in the challenge to mobilize people for development activities. Therefore, there must be a communication policy. The policy should give direction to the programmes which are channeled through various mass media networks.

Problems of Grave Nature

The mass media systems may fail to perform their functions when unplanned use of such technology creates problems. For instance communication resources can be concentrated in a few centres alone. The mass media may be misused by the owners to exercise their power, or the media content may be manipulated to give as a result of the communicators biases. All these problems forced the formulation of a viable communication policy. If the policy itself becomes outdated in the face of technological developments, it will have to be suitably changed.

Traditionally, communications research in India has shown a remarkable orientation towards social problems. Studies on propaganda techniques, attitude change, effects of mass media, personal influence, diffusion of innovations, flow of information, media uses and gratifications and the economics of communication have been motivated by practical problems faced in society. These studies focus on the need to understand the role of communication in those problems and the desire to apply the knowledge gained from research to solve them.

In spite of a great deal of empirical research, no systematic knowledge about the nature, frequency and origin of communication problems in India is available. However, the situation is changing now. Demands are being made for improving existing regulations, resource allocation principles, institutional arrangements, and defining the rights and responsibilities of professional communicators, commercial communication organisations and the bureaucracies. A communication policy must give importance to these issues. The policy, in effect, is built on the body of knowledge developed by research.

Press View : A Policy is a set of principles, rules and guidelines to help in the tackling of problems which may be faced by a society in any particular field. A communication policy is formulated in response to the challenges of new communication technologies. We can define communication policy as action-oriented principles, outlining objectives and means of achieving objectives, focusing on what needs to be done and what is to be avoided in dealing with current and anticipated communication problems in society. The policies are formulated on authoritative guidelines.

Given the centrality of communication in modern society, one should rightly expect that communication policy would have a distinct and independent role to play. It would take into account the problems that crop up when using communication in varied activities. Communication policy should be based on an understanding of the totality of communication problems. Such a policy should aim at achieving society's goals and expectations regarding the applications of communication.

The priorities according to which the developed and the developing countries formulate their policies differ, sometimes even contradict each other. The technologically advanced countries like USA and Japan are concerned with mobilizing world markets for their communication goals and services. The developing countries like India, on the other hand, are concerned with building and expanding their communication systems with indigenous and appropriate technology. One major objective of their policy is to eliminate the vestings of colonial dependency. A major thrust area of communication policy of developing countries is the implementation of viable alternatives to the one-way flow of information into their societies. Most of the developing countries are busy waging a constant battle against poverty, malnutrition, illiteracy and indebtness. Thus, communication development receives scarce priority in their national objectives.

The mass media can be tools of cultural enrichment, national cohesion and advancement. The media policy makers in India first have to bridge the gap between ground realities and ideal situations. Certain paradoxes exist in the field of communication which need to be considered by policy makers. Some of these realities are elucidated here:

(a) Whereas there is an urgent demand to realise the right to equal access to information, there is a widening of the information gap between the richer and the poorer sections of society.

(b) There is misappropriation of the mass media for commercial and political purchases, when the need of the hour is to apply the media to the task of propagating culture, education, information and leisure time entertainment.

(c) There is predominant use of media to impose foreign values.

(d) In India, by and large, the communicators don't desire to find out the reactions of the audience to their programmes.

(e) The increase in the number of channels is not matched by any corresponding increase in the standard of programming.

(f) While communication satellites remove the barriers to information and education across the national boundaries all over the world, the same technology pave the way for cultural imperialism and new communication colonialism.

The Doordarshan has always suffered from the dichotomy between policy pronouncements and the continuous drift and departure from them in actual practice. In developing and democratic country like India, access to television and the social benefit accruing from it, is a crucial test of the social relevance of such an expensive medium. The importance of utilising TV is not just for the idle entertainment of the elite but for the uplift of the poor. But in effect and in actual practice, the purchase of a TV set is seen as wholesale investment in entertainment which obviates the bother and expense of going to an auditorium or a stadium.

From inception, broadcasting in India has been looked upon as a public service for the promotion of social objectives. The concept of advertisements for the promotion of consumer goods was also considered incompatible with the prevailing philosophy of the "socialistic pattern of society". In a developing country like India, radio and TV should be viewed as a national resource for the uplift of the masses. It is only through a strong media network that the eight kind of information and education can be imparted to the people. But the media in our country, like elsewhere in the world, have buckled under the pressure of commercial interests. Mindless entertainment with little or no educative value defeats the very purpose of building up a strong media network.

The press in a democratic country plays a vital role in creating, moulding and reflecting public opinion. It is a fundamental institution of our society. Though the press in India is free, it suffers from many ills. There are a few in-built handicaps such as vast geographical area, illiteracy, poverty, multiplicity of languages and absence of adequate communication facilities. Some other bottlenecks exist like:

(a) the linking of ownership of newspapers with other industrial or commercial enterprises.

(b) limited newspaper ownership with closely held share interest.

(c) Urban-oriented expansion of newspapers leaving the vast country side population untouched.

(d) inadequate and expensive newsprint.

(e) the lack of local advertisement support.

Man's greatest invention is language. The invention of the script has helped mankind to preserve human thoughts and learning. It has helped society to conquer both space and time. An important product of the script was the book. The books helped older civilisations like the Chinese and the Indian civilizations to preserve heritage. Books spread ideas which set people thinking, as a prelude to individual and group action. For this reason, they met opposition from guardians of political and religious doctrines.

Plato argued that wise men alone could rule and the state would control education. For Machiavelli, the security of the state was supreme. Hegel regarded state as embodiment of morality. John Milton (1608-1674) in Areopagitica gave a solid reason for the freedom of the Press. In his essay on liberty

(1859) John Stuart Mill (1806-1873) proclaimed that liberty was the right of the individual.

Today freedom of expression and speech are internationally reorganised rights. The league of nations made the first organised attempt at the international level to proclaim rights of speech and expression by launching a series of conferences. In just a few years of its birth, the United Nations approved the UN Declaration of Freedom of Information (1946) and the Universal Declaration of Human Rights (1948).

With the gaining of independence, freedom of speech and expression were recognised as fundamental rights and were included in the Indian Constitution. They are provided in the Article 19(1) of our constitution. Article 19(2) provides reasonable restrictions on freedom of expression.

In U.S.A., freedom of the press was very clearly recognised for the first time in the Virginia Bill of Rights in 1776. Unlike U.S.A., Britain has no written constitution. But it has been the fountain of all philosophy concerning freedom of speech, expression and the press, as John Milton did most of his work in Britain. The rights of free speech, expression and the press are in a constant process of evolution.

In general press freedom means freedom, unless specifically prohibited by law, together, print and publish information and to set up technologies in pursuit of such objectives, to claim and gain access to information. In practice, freedom of the press means freedom of the owner of a newspaper. Journalists enjoy only that much freedom as is given to them by the owner of their newspaper/magazine.

From the beginning, freedom of the press was sought and obtained on the ground that it was a prerequisite to democracy. The press demand freedom because of the functions they discharge for the benefit of the society. In today's context, freedom of the press is only an extension of the citizen's right to freedom of speech and expression. It is the press alone which can thwart the attempts of any government to deny this right to the citizen. Today, the press, the electronic media, wherever they operate privately, have information-gathering networks spread all over the world. They are the eyes and ears of the people everywhere.

In connection with the limitation, the very first thing is that the right of the freedom of the press is only an extension of the citizen's right to freedom of speech and expression. Therefore, all those laws imposing restrictions on this right of the citizen apply to the press too. It has no special privilege that the citizens do not enjoy in this area. In all western societies and in India, the constitutions as well as the general laws of the countries, set the limits for the exercise of freedom of the press. It goes without saying that with regard to freedom, the press is not on any higher footing than the ordinary citizen. Since the press is also a business and an industry, all those laws which apply to business and industry, also apply to newspaper organizations.

The theory of responsibility is simple that everyone is responsible for the consequences of his actions. 'No Rights without responsibilities'. Therefore, freedom of the press is also linked with responsibilities.' At least, the freedom should not be abused.

When we say that somebody is responsible, we mean that he has a duty to do something, when we say someone is accountable, we mean that if he fails to do what his duty is, he is accountable to some person or institution. Thus, the right to freedom of speech and expression carries with it, a duty not to disturb public peace. If he so disturbs it he is accountable to the state for such breach of responsibility. Since media circulates information for the consumption of members of the society, it is natural that they should be responsible in the dissemination of the information. With every increase in the power of media, this responsibility towards the society also increases.

Editors and others often say that they have a right to inform the public. These are self-imposed responsibilities. These arise from an unwritten understanding between the media and society. On the basis of the responsibility of the media to inform the public, media have fought for and gained the right to free speech and expression.

But state has also imposed some obligations on media like not to publish anything that leads to, or has a tendency to lead to, a breakdown of public order. These are responsibilities imposed in addition to, and sometimes in contrast to, self-imposed responsibilities.

Role of Government : The First Press Commission was appointed in 1952, because after independence the role of the press was changing. It was fast turning from a mission to' business. The commission founded that there was a great deal of scurrilous writing often directed against communities or groups, of indecency and vulgarity and personal attacks on individuals. It felt that the best way of maintaining professional standards of journalism would be to bring into existence a body of people principally connected with the industry whose responsibility it would be to arbitrate on doubtful points and to ensure the punishment of anyone guilty of infraction of good journalistic behaviour. Second Press Commission was appointed in 1978 and it wanted the press to be neither a mindless adversary nor an unquestioning ally. It wanted the press to play a responsible role in the development process. From the role that the two commissions recommended for the press, we can summarise the responsibilities of the Press thus:

— Help the country in its development process both by making constructive suggestions as well as criticism of delays and distortions in the development process.

— Give the widest possible access to people, reflecting the pluralistic composition of Indian society.

— Maintain internal stability and safeguard external security.

— Prevent and deflate social conflict.

Complaints are heard throughout the world that a section of the press functions without regard to its responsibilities to the society. There is a vast area not covered by any legal regime. Media ethics apply mostly to cases not specifically concerned by law.

The Second Press Commission observed that one of the functions entrusted to the Press council was the building up of a code of conduct for newspapers, news agencies and journalists in accordance with high standards of journalism. The second Press Commission lists a number of codes drafted in India, the USA and Britain have through the years. The All-India Newspaper Editors' Conference formulated a Code of Ethics and a Charter for Editors in 1953. The National Union of Journalists (1981), the All India Small and Medium Newspapers Association (1975) had all drafted similar codes. But the Editors Guild of India refused to draft any code arguing that responsible people do not need such a formal code.

The second Press Commission said that it would not be desirable to draw up a Code of Ethics for newspapers. The Code of Ethics (1953) of All India Newspaper Editors' Conference asks journalists to serve and guard public interest, to be alive to fundamental human and social rights, to observe restraint in reports dealing with tensions leading to or likely to lead to public disorder, to assume responsibility for all information published, to respect confidence, not to exploit their status for non-journalistic purposes, not to allow personal interest to influence professional conduct, to correct inaccurate information, not to demand or accept bribe. The National Union of Journalists' Declaration of 1981 is also largely on similar lines.

The idea of an Ombudsman is of Swedish origin. In Sweden the Press Ombudsman at the national level is appointed by all the newspaper organizations together. Ombudsman generally means an intermediary, investigating complaints by private citizens against government officials or agencies. However, at present private or voluntary organizations are also having Ombudsmen to decide public complaints made against themselves or their members. In India, the Lok Ayuktas in some states are Ombudsmen.

Although this concept first originated in Sweden, but it was first adopted by the Press in USA.

The world's first Press Council took its birth in Sweden in 1916. In USA, a Press Council (National News Council) worked for 11 years and today there are nearly 50 Press Councils all over the world. The Press Council of India was set up on July 4, 1966 and Justice J.R. Mudholkar, was its chairman. It consisted of 25 members who were editors, working journalists, proprietors etc. In 1970, news agencies were also put under its jurisdiction. The council has powers to levy a graded fee on newspapers and news agencies to meet its expenditure and to reduce its dependence on government's financial support.

The countries of North and South are separated by an enormous gap in their respective communication capacities. The developed countries continue to exercise considerable political, economic and technological control on information flows. Nearly 80 per cent of the information disseminated in the world originates from five largest transnational news agencies as told before. About 15 great media corporations dominate the production of the radio sets, television sets and printing equipment; ten of these corporations belong to the U.S.A. Due to our dependence on the media delivery systems of the West, we also become dependent on the West.

Self-reliance in news and information distribution, both in disseminating news to the outside world or in getting news and information from various places in the world, for internal consumption, is essential for the following reasons:

(a) To provide the media a national identity and personality.

(b) To facilitate the analyses of the world events not from the perspective of the West but from the national perspective.

(c) To foster better understanding among the developing countries, which is far more essential now than ever before.

(d) To prevent the unwarranted entry of foreign and alien ideas, cultures and life-styles, that always tend to contribute to shaping public opinion in favour of foreign countries, particularly of the West.

(e) To provide an objective account of the news and developments that were considered newsworthy by the indigenous media.

As per the directives of the UNESCO to establish a news pool or consortium of news agencies, the 'pool' of news agencies of the non-aligned countries was formally launched in July, 1976 at the New Delhi Conference of Information Ministers and Representations of the news agencies of the non-aligned countries. The objective of the pool is to expand the mutual exchange of information among the non-aligned countries in a spirit of collective self-reliance.

The Non-Aligned News Pool is not a transnational news agency, but a system of exchange of agency information, based on co-operation and co-ordination among individual news agencies taking part in these activities. The Pool is not based on any formal membership. The Pool has no single directing centre, nor does it have its own budget.

Many of the developing countries do not have an extensive and elaborate telecommunication network. For some, high tariffs are major barriers. Optimum information exchange depend on the level of development of communication systems in the individual non-aligned countries.

A few year ago, about 85% of the news items received by PTI from the Pool partners were spiked. The reasons for this were given as delay in news reception, poor quality, low news value, or propaganda material.

The lack of proper training among the non-aligned journalists and their inability to match the professional standards of the journalists of the transnational news-agencies, are the reasons for the poor quality of material put out by the Non-Aligned News Agencies Pool.

In many of the non-aligned countries, the news agencies are under the strict control of the governments. The first casualty of such a solution is the objectivity of the news and information put out by their agencies.

The editors of private-owned newspapers in the democratic countries like India, either are not convinced of the need for such an inter-regional co-operation or they do not respect the news coverage of several agencies, which are participants of the pool.

While there has been a continuous effort to establish alternative news and information distribution systems in the world, the recent global changes have had a deep impact on the information scene.

The West has been for a long time using the concept of 'Freedom of Information' as an ideological weapon, and successfully deploying it to deflect the 3rd World from its pursuit of a new world information and communication order.

In the matter of broadcasting, the Western powers insist upon the 'open skies' policy, which they claim to be consistent with the principle of freedom of information. On the face of things, this seems a plausible argument. Open skies, seems to connote a situation of an unfettered information exchange of knowledge flowing freely across the national boundaries. On the contrary, the same western countries, show a complete disinclination towards free trade by imposing heavy tariffs to protect their own products.

These developments call for a greater unity among the 3rd World countries to come out of the dependence and dominance in the field of information, and promote self-reliance. The existing world information order provides an opportunity to the richer nations to use the scarce global natural resources, and exclude the poor nations from using the same. An attempt is made through the on going GATT talks to impose stronger forms of monopoly control over the content of information flows.

World Standard : The developing nations campaigned for a 'new order' in the field of international information and communication, which would facilitate a 'free and balanced flow' of information capable of breaking through the stereotypes created and nurtured for over 50 years by the western media empires. The new order, they maintained, would create a new international information climate that would foster a closer and better understanding among nations and individuals. The most important step in this direction was the launching of the Non-Aligned News Agencies Pool, in 1975. The 'free flow' concept was amended to 'free-and balanced flow', when a declaration on the role of the media in the promotion of international understanding and peace was approved by the UNESCO in 1978. 'The right to know' was transformed into 'the right to communicate'.

The non-aligned nations coined the phrase, New International Information Order (NIIO). The MacBride Commission broadened the sphere by substituting the term 'world' for 'international' and incorporating 'communication' along with 'information'. Since then the phrase the 'New World Information and Communication Order (NWICO) has been widely used.

A major factor that helped the growth of US agencies was the wireless transmission technology, which reversed the world communication imbalance to the overall advantage of the American interest. Another factor was a general realization in the US of the advantages that world communication control bestowed on foreign trade and commerce. Following such realizations, ideas on unrestricted How of communication between nations began to crystallize in the US.

The following overlapping and mutually complementing factors are at the base of the demand for a new order in the field of information:

(1) The emergence of new nations following the dissolution of the colonial empires after World War II.

(2) The asymmetrical economic relationship between the new nations and the western industrialized nations which, while strengthening the latters' wealth and power, perpetuated the new nations' dependency, not merely economic but political and cultural as well.

(3) The coming together of the new nations under the umbrella of non-alignment in the wake of aggressive bloc-building by the US and the USSR.

(4) The new nation's realization that their under-development was related to their dependence on rich nations followed by a firm resolve to assertive actions to correct imbalances in world trade and commerce, and cultural exchanges.

(5) Their gaining in strength in international organization, such as the UN and the UNESCO. Four stages can easily be identified in the history of the NWICO. The

first stage (1973-76) marked the evolution of a new order. The second stage (1976-79) saw the accumulation of data and empirical evidence to give credence to the new order demand. The third stage followed the publication of the MacBride report in 1980. The fourth stage is the period following the adoption of the NWICO Resolution in the UNESCO.

Generally, the evolution of the new order concept is credited to the NAM. Much of the credit for the enlarging communication agenda of the UNESCO in the 1970s goes to the Non-Alignd Movement, which saw communication, at least in the early 70s, as a means to an end, the end being economic development of the poor nations.

The Algiers Summit of the non-aligned countries, held in 1973, is a major landmark, in the history of NWICO, for it was here that communication concerns were addressed directly in more than one paper in the context of their economic development programmes.

The 19th UNESCO General Conference adopted a resolution inviting the Director General to undertake a review of the problems of communication in modern society. Director General constituted a 16 member commission for the study of communication problems.

The 20th UNESCO general conference, held in 1978 was marked by a spirit of compromise. The new Mass Media Declaration (MMD) text now retitled as 'Declaration on Fundamental Principles Governing the contribution of the Mass Media in strengthening Peace and International Understanding and in combating was Propaganda, Racialism and Apartheid' was approved.

The 21st general conference of the UNESCO, held in 1980, accepted the MacBride report and unanimously adopted Resolution outlining the basic character and content of the

NWICO. The establishment of the NWICO depended upon five major factors—(1) the will of the developed and developing countries to bring about changes in all areas of communication within their respective regions; (2) Co-operation between the developed and developing nations for removing all obstacles to a two-way and balanced flow of news and information among nations; (3) sharing of communication resources, including technologies, for countering monopoly of the international news flow by a few; (4) cooperation among the developing countries to correct imbalances with their own regions by increasing horizontal flows and (5) Co-operation between the media-rich and media-poor for mobilization of resources to strengthen communication infrastructure in the latter's region.

The 21st General Conference of the UNESCO approved the establishment of a news agency, the International Programme for the Development of Communication (IPDC) within the framework of the UNESCO to reduce the gap between the developed and developing countries by strengthening infrastructure and services through international cooperation and assistance. The objectives of the IPDC cover all facts of communication development.

The withdrawal of the US on December 31, 1984, and Britain and Singapore a year later, from the UNESCO, was not a deterrent to the objectives of the NWICO. Today, the evolving goals of the NWICO rest with not just the UNESCO, but a large number of international organizations such as the Organization for Economic Co-operation and Development (OECD), the International Telecommunications Union (ITU), the IPDC and the Third World and its organizations for moving the aim of the NWICO to a higher plain. The IPDC has done its best to help develop communication capabilities of the media-poor regions. Between the second session in 1982 and the seventh session held in January 1986, it had allocated US$ 9.74 million for some communication projects in the developing countries.

Those included 3 regional news agency projects Pan Africa News Agency (PANA), the Agencia Latino American De Servcios Especiales do Information (ALA SEI) and the Asia-Pacific News Network (ANN) and 14 national news agency projects in different 3rd World countries. These agencies and news exchange arrangements operating within the developing countries, no matter how inadequate they are, indicate that the NWICO has set itself on its evolutionary path. But there is more to be achieved.

Imbalances in the flow of news and information at international level have not ceased to exist. The one-way flow is still very much in evidence. Most of the news flowing through the transnational agencies into the developing regions concerns the developing world. The agencies continue to view the developing world's events and issues from their own perspectives. As a result, news everywhere is seen through the prisms of the West, the developed world. The Western media giants continue to set the world's news agenda.

The developed countries should be more open to redress the ever-increasing asymmetrical economic relations between them and the poor countries. This calls for hastening the pace for the establishment of the NIEO as it is linked with the NWICO. The developed world could make available resources for communication specific projects in the poor regions of the world. New technologies needed to be viewed as resources for the benefit of the mankind, and not as a new tool for exploitation of the disadvantaged.

Steps are needed to establish a balance in the information flow by devoting more space and lime to news and issues concerning the developing countries. The developed countries should join hands with the developing countries in making the telecommunications tariffs more suitable for a better use of existing systems.

The developing world, on the other hand, needs to formulate communication policies, without which the media development would get hampered. The press must make conscious efforts to free itself from the attitudes fostered by the Western news criteria.

The free flow of information is a Western concept, by which almost all western countries rationalise the operation of their media and information agencies. The term means that any person or persons and any organization or organisations can own and operate any media or information agency, gather any information, and disseminate the same, if they so desire, to any target audience, wherever and whenever they want. The concept is basic to the history, culture and life of the liberal capitalist western society. Any challenge to this concept is rejected on grounds that it is undemocratic, inhuman and even uncivilized.

The philosophy of free flow resulted in the consolidation of the centres of information gathering and dissemination in the western countries. The socialist and the 3rd World countries could see that they were not represented objectively in the western media. Significant happenings in their countries were paid scant attention and whatever done, those were only half truths coloured by the Western perceptions. Slowly, this situation got concretised, and the leaders of the 3rd World countries endured the situation as they were unable to take steps to change the situation. The 3rd World countries had no infrastructure or active network to make a difference.

There is imbalance in the flow of information between the developed West and the developing 3rd World countries, which can not have any say on the mechanism of gathering information as they do not own and control the technology of the giant information agencies of the West. Moreover, the 3rd World countries, knowing fully well that the information disseminated from these agencies doesn't represent all the truths about them. The imbalance is in terms of volume of information, flowing into the 3rd World countries, when compared to the volume of information flowing out from them.

The root of the problem goes back to the late 1950s and 1960s, when the concept of 'Development Communication' was born. The communication specialists thought that what the West achieved in centuries, the 3rd World could achieve the same in a matter of decades if aided by the mass media. Two eminent western scholars-Daniel Lerner and Wilbur Schramm-were in the forefront to suggest this theory. Their theories were tried in many 3rd World countries..

It was assumed that mass media used for creating a stable and sustainable democratic nation and implementing programmes to uplift the living conditions of the common man in society would transform the developing societies into modern, vibrant and stable societies. However, a decade later, it was found that most of the social problems remained unsolved. Instead more problems.were created.

The western media organizations focused the negative developments of the developing society. In such a situation, an American author, Herbert Schiller articulated something very new. He said that the free flow of communication was essentially meant to safeguard the economical growth of the West. And any attempt to regulate the flow of information beyond borders is seen as a threat to the western economies. Thus, it is termed as interference with the basic human right. Hence, the concept of 'imbalance' is an economic issue, and the international flow of information is just another fact of this issue.

Although the flow is still imbalance, exchanges of TV programmes, specially educational programmes, are quite frequent. More western programmes are seen on the TV screens of the 3rd World countries. Despite the large scale changes brought about by technology, imbalance persists in the media and coverage of the development west vis-a-vis the developing countries of the 3rd World.

Organisational Structure

Although the government doesn't own a majority of the newspapers and magazines, yet it is the government that remains at the helm of affairs in matters such as newsprint allocation, Registration of newspapers and periodicals, conduct of research and collection and maintenance of exhaustive reference and archive material.

PIB is the central agency of the Government of India for the dissemination of information on government policies, decisions, programmes, initiatives and activities. It puts out this information to daily newspapers, periodicals, news agencies and All India Radio and Doordarshan. The PIB has its headquarters in Delhi. The Bureau in Delhi consists of information officers attached to different ministeries and departments of the Government of India. It also has the job of evaluating public reaction and accordingly renders advice to the Government of India on its information policy.

This is the largest publishing house in the public sector. It is the media unit of Ministry of Information and Broadcasting. Earlier it was known as Foreign Branch of the Bureau of Public Information and was renamed in December 1944. It has many wings to oversee the production of print material. These are Editorial Wing, Production and Art Wing, Business Wing, Administration Wing and Employment News Wing. Employment News Wing brings out the weekly Employment News and Rozgar Samachar. The Publication Division also publishes Kurukshetra, Aajkal, Bal Bharati, Yojana, Mass Media in India etc.

This is an agency that conducts research and provides reference information on a variety of subjects. Compilation work is carried out by the documentation and catalogue section of the library. There is a separate wing that specifically collects and maintains newspaper cuttings.

A Reference Annual is published every year by the division. The National Documentation centre on mass communication, set up as a part of the division in 1976, documents and indexes news items and information about the mass media.

The Photo Division comes under the administrative purview of the Ministry of Information and Broadcasting. It documents the socio-economic progress and cultural activities of the country through photographs. The photographic prints of major events in the news are distributed to the media through the Press Information Bureau. It has its head office in New Delhi, with regional offices at Mumbai, Kolkata, Chennai. It also has a photo unit at Guwahati.

The Press Council of India is a quasi-judicial body, constituted by an Act of Parliament. It has 28 members headed by a Chairman, who has traditionally been a sitting or retired judge of the Supreme Court. Twenty members are press personnel, five are members of parliament and one each nominated by the University Grants Commission, Sahitya Academy and Bar Council of India. It hears complaints by the Press and against the Press regarding freedom of the Press.

It was established in 1948 under the Imperial Library Act, 1948. It is situated in Kolkata and has more than 20 lakh volumes in its custody, excluding the maps, manuscripts, official documents and books received as gifts or in exchange schemes. It is a subordinate department under the Ministry of Human Resources Development, Department of Culture, Government of India. The special feature of this Library is that it organizes exhibitions, lectures and seminars at the national and international levels. It is headed by a Director in addition to a librarian.

We have already dealt with the growth and evolution of PCI. Here we will look into the principles, structure and function of the Press Council.

The guiding principle of the Press Council is that if any section of the Press violates the tenets of journalistic ethics, whether written or unwritten, the Press itself should take appropriate action against it rather than the authorities punishing newspapers. The PCI was first set up in 1966 under the Act of 1965, and was abolished after the proclamation of emergency in 1975. However it again came into being in 1979. The council comprises a chairman and 28 other members. Until now, only former Supreme Court judges have been selected for the chairmanship of the council. 13 members are nominated from among working journalists including six editors and seven other working journalists. Not less than three editors and four other working journalists should be from newspapers in Indian languages. Out of the six owners or managers of newspapers, two each should be from small, medium and big categories of newspapers. One person is nominated from among the managers of news agencies.

The term of the chairman and of the council is three years. While the members retire on the expiry of the term of the council, the chairman may continue in office until a new incumbent is nominated, but not for more than six months beyond the three year term. A retiring member can be re-nominated for not more than one term. That is a person can be a member of the Press Council for maximum period of six years. Three person having special knowledge in respect of education and Science, law and literature and culture are nominated, one each by UGC, the Bar Council of India, and the Sahitya Academy. The PCI has very wide functions in furtherance of its dual objectives of preserving Press freedom and maintaining and improving standards of print journals. But it does not deal with the electronic media.

It has also been vested with powers of a civil court. It can summon and examine witness, require the discovery and inspect documents, receive evidence on affidavits, issue commissions for examining witnesses or documents, or any other matter which may be prescribed. The council holds open inquiries on complaints received both against newspapers and news agencies, journalists as well as authorities, individuals, associations or groups of people and on the basis of its inquiries the council declares its adjudications.

The Working Journalists and other Newspaper Employees and Miscellaneous Provisions Act. 1955, is a welfare measure meant to regulate conditions of service of the people employed in the newspaper industry.

Its provisions relate mainly to (a) special provisions in respect of certain cases of retrenchment, (b) payment of gratuity, (c) hours of work, (d) leave, (e) fixation of revision of rates of wages, (f) enforcement of the recommendations of the wage fixation machinery i.e. wage boards and wage tribunals, (g) employees' Provident fund and (h) recovery of money due from the employer.

A work of literature, drama, music or art is an intellectual property. It must be protected from illegal copying or reproducing. The Copyright Act 1957 accords this problem. Copyright has been held to be a right which a person acquires in a work which is the result of his intellectual labour. The primary function of the copyright law is to protect from annexation by other people the fruits of a man's work, labour or skill.

News Agencies of Various Types

It is an agency of the U.N. All UN Member states have a right to belong to it. UNESCO has been concerned both with the development of the media and also the problems such a development brings with it. It is always alert to find out how the media and development work in the 3rd World countries. For UNESCO, it is necessary to understand that the purpose of the organisation is to contribute to peace and security by promoting collaboration among nations through education, science and culture. It also realised that only a few of the developing countries had any newspapers and more so, news agencies, which could provide the media with news.

The role of UNESCO became more significant in the context of the demand by many developing countries for a better deal from the developed countries. The first step in this direction was a call for the establishment of a New International Economic Order (NIEO) and was realised that NIEO can not be independent from socio-cultural factors, apart from political and economic factors. The 5th conference of the Heads of State of the Non-Aligned Countries (1976) and the 19th General Conference of UNESCO crystallised the idea of a New International Information and Communication Order (NIICO).

ITU was founded in Paris in 1865, as the International Telegraphic Union to co-ordinate and monitor the development of the telegraph, which was a new invention. With the development of other systems, the name was changed to International Telecommunications Union.

In 1947 ITU entered into an agreement with the United Nations and thus became a specialised agency for telecommunications. The ITU secretariat is in Geneva and works at various levels. The main functions of ITU are to :

(a) allocate frequencies to avoid interference

(b) co-ordinate efforts to eliminate interference

(c) foster the creation of telecommunication in newly independent developing countries

(d) promote safety measures

(e) undertake studies in the area of telecommunications.

Although ITU performs a very technical function, it is an important agency that is central to communication development.

In addition to UNESCO and ITU, there are other UN organisations whose activities have a bearing on communications developments. Regional intergovernmental organisations, such as Council of Europe. European Economic Community, Organisation of American States, Organization for African Units, South Asian Association for Regional Cooperation and Association of South East Asian Nations are active in the Communication field.

The essence of any interregional cooperation in the field of information is to bring about a new sense of common destiny, and unite news agencies operating under different levels of development. The fundamental problem in the inter-regional news networks and co-operation is that the participating news agencies in the network being, essentially, domestic agencies are geared to serve purely national needs in their news coverage.

Another area is about the issue of relevance. Most of them are editorially ill-equipped to produce copy for the consumption of the other agencies in the region. They are mostly irrelevant to each others, needs.

In most of the networks, almost all agencies are in principle, committed to producing a regional file containing news reports and features, especially prepared for the consumption of the readers outside their national frontiers. However, the tendency that persists is to move copy originally written for domestic readership for the network transmission without necessary rewriting. A great deal of information may be missing in such reports for the readers abroad, or much more than necessary is included. But, criticism on several agencies, which are part of such networks are a large majority of reports transmitted in these networks are hard news, which rarely attract the attention of the editors in other countries.

Another criticism is that they do not make amendments and changes in the news reports, keeping in view the requirements of the readers abroad.

Information can be defined as facts about an event, a place, a person, or whatever is communicated, by a person or persons to another person or persons. Mere facts do not generate knowledge. The human minds in interaction with facts produce knowledge. This knowledge has helped and is helping the human race generation after generation. Knowledge is wealth and when this wealth is used properly, it brings power.

Foreign News Agencies

There are hundreds of agencies, which are in the business of supplying information to the mass media. These agencies are referred to as news agencies, feature services, and syndicates. The impact of these agencies on what we read and see is quite significant.

A news agency generally deals with news coverage. It combines spot coverage with interpretation of the important political and economic events. Although its emphasis is limited, the news agency plays a very important role in shaping public opinion on crucial national and international affairs. The news agency doesn't deal directly with the public. It works through the intermediary of the other means of mass communication, namely the press, radio and television. For a majority of the news media, the news agencies are a major source of news supply. The two leading news agencies in India are United News of India (UNI) and Press Trust of India (PTI), which have contractual agreements with these global news agencies. Certain studies reveal that there are about 1200 news agencies operating in the world. However, the five transnational agencies, Reuters, Agence France Presse (AFP), Associated Press (AP), and United Press International (UPQ and Telegrafnoi Agentsvo Sovetskavo Soyusa (TASS) put out around 35 million words per day, and claim to provide nine-tenths of the total foreign news output of the World Media. Other major agencies are Deutsche Press Agenteur (DPA) of Germany, Kyodo of Japan and Xinhua of China.

Various Agencies

This news agency takes its name after its founder, Paul Julius Reuter. Around 1850, he set up a carrier pigeon service. Initially his services were confined to commercial information. His first major breakthrough came in 1859, when he sent a dispatch for shadowing a war in Italy. Since then the agency has expanded. Reuters supplies news to its media clients such as other news agencies, newspapers, the radio & television stations. Under its present form of ownership Reuters claim that it can ensure that no particular group or faction can have control. Consequently, it hopes to preserve its integrity and freedom from bias.

The impetus to provide speedy transmission of news was given by the telegraph invented by Samuel F.B. Morse, in 1844. The telegraph enables many small town newspapers in the US to get their news. The meeting of the leading New York publishers was held in this context in 1848. Although a decision was made to start a news agency, the name, Associated Press, was not used till about 1860. Associated Press took a concrete form in 1900 as a modern news gather association. The struggle by AP to establish its base and the restrictions the rivals placed on it is often cited as a case that is reflective of many 3rd World countries wanting to break the monopoly of the 'big five', which ironically includes AP.

AP with its wide communications network using advanced technology has bureaus in more than 100 countries. Its 5000 plus correspondents and a host of stringers cater to about 1300 newspapers, 3400 broadcasters in the US and 1000 private subscribers.

The growth of AP spurred the rise of competitors. Edward Willis Scripps formed the United Press Association in 1907. Scripps started two regional news services to cater to his own newspapers. At the same time, there was another association the Publisher's Press Association formed in 1898 by the Non-

AP newspapers. In 1907. Scripps merged his United Press Association with the PPA to form United Press Association. A major set back occurred in 1918. It sent a report that the war had ended, and later it turned out to be false. Its credibility suffered. But slowly it recovered. The backgrounds and personal accounts enabled UPA to score over AP. Parallel to these developments emerged a third press association, the International News Service (INS). It faced severe competition from AP. Although, it was emerging as a major service, by 1956, it decided to merge with AP in 1958 to form United Press International. UPI claims to have an overseas electronic strength of about 200 journalists overseas distributed in Europe, Latin America, Asia and Australia. Its broadcast related services are considered to be a specialisation.

AFP, founded in 1835, has the maximum representation on its board of directors. Although AFP is described as an unsubsidiscd autonomous organisation, in effect, the French government and various agencies under its control subscribed to AFP, and provided good support. AFP is regarded as one of the major global news agencies. It has more than 10,000 newspapers and 70 agencies as its subscribers. Its operations are in more than 150 countries with a network of 110 foreign bureaus.

Often it was customary to exclude TASS from the 'globals' as the transnational news agencies are called. However, in terms of influence, impact and coverage, TASS was in no way different from the other agencies.

TASS began on the foundation of what was known as the Petrograd Telegraph Agency, in 1917. It supplied news through a network of correspondents in all regional and territorial centres. TASS has approximately 20,000 subscribers both domestic and foreign.

The work of TASS was complemented by another information agency, Novosti Press Agency (APN), established in 1961 by the Union of Soviet Journalists, the Union of Soviet writers. TASS and APN merged to form anew Russian information agency called ITAR-Information Telegraph Agency of Russia.

The International broadcasting by different countries are aimed at serving their people settled in other countries, and also to propogate the policies of the respective countries.

BBC occupies a central place in terms of its international reach and influence. Now through satellites, millions have the benefit of watching the BBC-TV. BBC is a central institution in the broadcasting system of the United Kingdom. In 1922, several radio manufacturers established the BBC. In 1926 it became a public corporation. BBC draws international news from its correspondents. The operations are not commercial, and finance is provided in the form of a special grant approved by the British Parliament. Consequently, the Government is directly involved in the international broadcasting system.

The External Services Department has responsibility for international broadcasting. The scape, nature and character of BBC External Services was affected during the Falkland crisis. It was also the target of criticism during the Iranian Revolution and the Gulf war. However, contemporary developments indicate that international broadcasting is here to stay.

Another country which has systematically used and realised the potential of the radio and television in international affairs is U.S.A. During the World War II, two government organisations, the Office of War Information and the Council of Inter-American Affairs were responsible for international broadcasts during the period. The programming titled Voice of America was done on a contractual basis by the private US broadcast corporations. And when US. Information Agency (USIA) was established in 1953, VOA became one of its divisions. Apart from VOA, there is a separate television service of the

USIA. Through satellite networking, it also arranges for direct telecasts.

It is a London based international TV news film agency owned by a consortium of the BBC, Reuters, Canadian Broadcasting Corporation, Australian Broadcasting Corporation and New Zealand TV. It is related to the international broadcasting service in the supply of audio-visual material. The service has over 170 subscribers in 95 countries.

Structural Foundations : The degree of formal organization given to the media information service depends to some extent on the size of your organization or, for a consultancy, on the size of the fee paid by the client. Some large organizations have specially designated press officers working within a press office which, though coming under the surveillance of the public relations department, is separate from it. Other organizations designate a press officer within the PR office and others simply expect all the PR staff to act as press officers as the need arises.

It probably does not matter what title is held by the people who will be dealing with media enquiries, but what does matter is that they should be reasonably au fait with the company and its products. The lack of even basic knowledge is probably a fault encountered more when dealing with a consultancy than with in-house PROs. If the query is of a complicated or technical nature it is quite acceptable to pass it on to the expert. And you really should have price lists and stockists handy.

As well as having a good working knowledge of the subject with which you are dealing, you, as an efficient PRO, should also have at your fingertips the names and telephone numbers of people within the organization who are competent to speak to the media on specialist subjects, and this list should include others apart from the brand managers and marketing department personnel. It is annoying to a journalist who is working on a story to be told that the PRO will ring back with the relevant numbers and then not to get them for another two or three days.

If the queries coming into the public relations or press office are short questions they can usually be answered on the spot, but quite often they will be in the form of a general request for information on a specific topic and it could be that your organization has in its files material which could be sent out. Do make sure that all this material is filed in such a way that it is easy to find and is related to any photographic or other reference. Some information services are organized in such detail that they have a grandiose title such as 'The Barbed Wire Information Bureau', information sheets and a direct telephone line. However, such a detailed service is usually organized primarily for the consumer rather than for the media, though answering press queries will be part of its function.

If you do have a fairly sophisticated information service it is easy to think that you have all the answers to hand, but this may not be the case. So when taking down details of media enquiries don't just record them: listen, be constructive and ask questions. If you know what the story or feature is to be about and the angle from which the producer or journalist is approaching it you will be able to be more helpful. There may be a booklet on the subject, a special expert in the technical department who has sat on the relevant government fact-finding commission or a market research survey giving the latest market trends, any of which would help the journalists far more than the standard handouts.

Work Elements

Most journalists agree that the telephone manners of some PR departments leave much to be desired. Some of them leave the impression that they are really too busy to deal with media enquiries and unless the journalist can use the name of a well-known programme or a national daily the service is grudging to say the least.

However, there are other PROs who are extremely friendly and helpful on the phone. This immediately puts their organization in a good light and the journalist is disposed to feel that this outfit may be a useful source of information in the future. If this friendly attitude is followed up with prompt service the good impression is stamped even deeper. Too often the executive forgets to phone back until the next day. Or even worse, the material promised does not arrive until the end of the following week. It has even been known for a company to respond to a request for information six weeks after the initial query and then to complain that their product had been left out! There also sometimes seems to be a feeling that the media could have got themselves better organized and asked for the material earlier. There is occasionally some truth in this, but very often the journalist's deadline is looming close, and the PRO is supposed to be providing a service not a favour.

Checklist for an Efficient Enquiries Procedure

1. Be friendly and helpful throughout; do not give the impression that it is all too much trouble.
2. Record the details of the request and ask for further details about the proposed story so that you can dig out the most useful in-depth material. Indicate that this is the reason for your questions.
3. Drop everything and treat the request as extremely urgent Even if you know that the answer can wait until the next day it is far better to deal with it at once. It may be forgotten later on.
4. If you need to phone back, do so as soon as possible. Phone back within hours to report progress even if you do not yet have the answer.
5. If you leave a message for someone else to phone the journalist back, check to see that they have not missed the message or forgotten to fulfil it.

6. If the request is for an expensive sample use tact in discovering whether it has a genuine background. You may not have heard of the journalist or author concerned but that does not mean that they are not engaged on a bona fide testing programme or working on a first-class magazine feature.
7. Where necessary send material by cab or messenger.
8 Check to see that both postal or hand-delivered material has arrived and whether the journalist needs any more material.

Features of Works

Getting the enquiries procedure right is only the first stage in setting up a good media relations programme. The second stage is the much more active one of going out and securing a steady stream of coverage for the company and its products or services. Start by making a list of the areas in which you think you might be able to generate coverage over a three-month period. Such a list of objectives for the PR department of a food manufacturer might look something like this:

1. Feature material on cooking with a variety of the products in women's magazines and in regional media.
2. A series of radio interviews on local radio.
3. A feature on the use of some of the products in pubs for a catering trade magazine.
4. An in-depth feature on the new soup production line in a leading food production magazine.
5. An in-depth feature on the work of the new product development team in a food technology publication.
6. A visit to the Peterborough factory-where new jobs are coming on-line-by the industrial editor of one of the national newspapers.

7. A feature on the activities of the Skelmersdale factory social club in the local media and a possible visit by the local radio station disc jockey to a social evening.

A Similar List for a Heavy Goods Vehicle Manufacturer might Look Something Like This

1. A release on the year's export success for both the heavy goods vehicle publications and all the publications covering the industries to which the goods were sold.
2. Local radio sponsorship of a motoring and good driving show.
3. An in-depth feature on the conversion of a standard line for use in a mountainous area for a leading magazine in the field of civil engineering and for publication in the country concerned.
4. An on-site demonstration of the current range of earth-diggers for publications covering public works and civil engineering generally.
5. A feature on the new managing director for the heavy freight publications.
6. A feature on safety aspects of carrying chemicals and other dangerous substances for a lorry drivers' magazine.

To achieve the list of objectives set you will need to be in constant contact with the leading media in your field and in occasional contact with all the other publications which might be useful. This contact may be by post, by telephone or by personal meetings. Some enterprising PRs have also used humorous tapes and promotional videos to put their ideas over. The choice will depend on how important you are to a magazine or radio and the magazine or radio to you and thus how often you are likely to be working with this particular publication, how physically near you are to each other and indeed how well you get on at a social level.

However, if you have creative ideas and good material, face-to-face contact is by no means necessary. Unfortunately many editors feel that this kind of creativity is absent from the activities of a number of PROs. The only material they receive is the syndicated material which is sent out to everyone on the mailing list, and there is little attempt at placing original and exclusive material.

Syndication of material can work quite well at a regional level, though even here blanket coverage can be a real waste. If for example, you are running a recipe or a beauty information service you will be able, over time, to build up a list of regional dailies and weeklies who use the material regularly. Some sophisticated services send out portfolios of material to selected users and these are updated from time to time. If the subject is one which is likely to be covered fairly regularly the expense of such an operation will be recouped. But for most products and services this sort of exercise would be too expensive. Others run food and cookery programmes on their local radio stations or even sponsor national radio slots. The success rate for syndicated material can also be increased by sending out material with themes which are relevant to the local area or which are topical.

For national media the approach must be rather different. Monthly mailings are no use at all, and ideas are needed in the first instance rather than completed material. Once you have sold an idea to an editor you can then discuss how much material you will supply and how much the newspaper or magazine will want to write or photograph for itself. Some magazines are pleased if you can produce an illustrated feature to an agreed plan. Others have a large enough budget to be able to retain their independence, and these publications will probably ask for background material only or will send a journalist to cover the story on the spot.

However, if you are to write the feature remember to check on the editor's requirements as to length, the number of illustrations, the date of issue of the article and the copy deadline. Sometimes it is worth thinking about getting a well-known person in the field to write features for you or at least to suggest his or her name to the publication. This will be a more expensive way of producing feature material but it may also make it more acceptable.

If your work is mainly in the trade and industrial area it is even more important to keep in constant touch with the leading publications in the field. An editor will appreciate it if you supply him or her regularly with information about the company, giving advance warning of changes and additions to the product range, the factory or indeed any aspect of the company's activities. A good relationship in this area can mean extra coverage since the editor will be more inclined to ring your company for quotes or for filler items. Editors have also been known to remind PROs that their exhibition details have not yet been received. Nor should you forget the media local to your offices and factories. Community relations can be extremely important but they are often relegated to the bottom of the list of PR activities.

List areas which are likely to generate coverage during a set period. Look at this list in terms of the relevant media and make a list of objectives to achieve within the period.

Send out syndicated material to specially selected regionals and place specific features ideas with nationals and specialist magazines. Be as original and creative as possible by letter or phone.

Once features have been placed take care to fulfil the editor's requirements.

Press Releases : Some PROs like to put together a newsletter to send to the media, outlining all the things that have happened to their company over the previous three or four months. These are often quite stylishly produced with a scanner and desk-top publishing packages. The idea is that journalists will pick up just those stories which are of particular interest to their publications.

The problem is that these newsletters are often so well produced that they look far too much like sales promotion material and they may indeed be of use in selling-in to the trade. Journalists are likely to bin this type of material before they even read it, assuming that it will be full of puffs and exaggerated claims.

Far better to forget the clever design and pretty colours and stick to the news. Write up the facts following the Who? What? Why? Where? When? If possible include some information on forthcoming events as well as past history and make sure that the latter is not too out of date.

It is quite permissible to include ideas for features, but it is a waste of time to write the whole piece. It is better to negotiate the placing of the complete material into those sections of the media that are likely to use it.

Various Angles : Though entertaining is not an essential part of the media relations programme it can help to smooth the way. Discriminate in your entertaining. If you are taking a journalist to lunch you should know exactly why you are doing it and what you expect to achieve from it. Even more important, you should know what you have to offer. Journalists will not appreciate your wasting their time, however good the lunch. Indeed 'launching' in the old-fashioned sense is on the decline. So do not be surprised if a journalist simply cannot find the time to join you.

Reasons for individual entertaining might include any of the following:

- Briefing editors or journalists on changes and

developments within your organization which could affect the industry as a whole.

- Briefing a newly-appointed editor or specialist writer on your company and its activities and the service you have to offer.
- A 'thank you' for successful cooperation throughout the year, usually coupled with a briefing on the coming year.
- An introduction for yourself to editors or specialist writers in an area of the media which is new to you.
- A general briefing for editors or journalists with whom you are not often in contact, usually coupled with ideas for specific features.
- To introduce new senior members of your organization to key journalists.

The question of where to entertain is a function both of your budget and the inclination of your guest. It might be a pleasant gesture to ask your guest where he or she would like to go. On the other hand, if you have reasonable in-house facilities this might be a better venue as it will be free from distraction.

It is sometimes even more valuable to entertain a group of journalists together. This can serve both as a briefing meeting and as a discussion group. It is a good idea, for example, to gather together representatives of your immediate trade or industrial publications, together with specialist writers from the national media, at a briefing lunch on the forthcoming year. Such an event enables the senior personnel within your company to meet the leading journalists in the field and to tell them first hand of the company's plans for the coming year. The journalists can ask their questions direct and can also air any grievances or problems in an informal atmosphere.

It is important that the senior management is briefed to be

as open as possible at such meetings, otherwise the value of them tends to be diminished. The representatives of the media should see the meeting as a constructive activity and not just a propaganda exercise.

Another example of extremely useful group entertaining is illustrated by a luncheon arranged by an organization which was moving into sports sponsorship for the first time. Leading journalists covering the particular sport were invited to attend the lunch and to give their views on how the sponsorship could best benefit the sport and on how they would like to be kept in the picture. The lunch also served the purpose of introducing the company's executives to this particular section of the media, and much was learnt about how to get the most out of the sponsorship.

Some companies operating in the consumer field have also seen the value of group luncheons in generating special features around products which are not very exciting and which do not really merit a series of individual lunches. Journalists must be told that this is a speculative lunch with only a small information content and that the genera! intent is to discuss the subject in broad terms with the injection of a few ideas from the PROs. The discussion around the table often generates even better feature ideas which can be taken up by one of the journalists present.

The trick is to ensure that there are no magazines represented which compete directly with each other. A luncheon to talk about nail care and nail care products might take in one representative of each of the following types of publication: general women's interest magazines, teenage publications magazines, holiday magazines, regional newspaper, London office women's editors, retirement publications and secretarial magazines. There is very little clash of interests here and it will be quite obvious which magazine will be interested in which idea.

Checklist for Informal Entertainment

1. Entertain only if you have a good reason for doing so and only if you have something of value to impart to the guest.
2. Decide whether it will serve your purpose better to entertain individually or in a group..
3. Make sure that colleagues who are to be present from sections other than the PR department are fully briefed on their role and on what can and cannot be said.
4. Have a variety of ideas ready to throw into the conversation and listen carefully to the resulting discussion. Make a note of all requests made for further information and of any interest expressed in ideas for features.

Whatever the means of communication has been, it is important to follow up properly. If a specific idea has been discussed over the phone confirm the details in writing. If an outline idea has been discussed over the lunch table ring up to carry it further, and if you have floated an idea by post and heard nothing phone up to see if it has fallen on stony ground. And when an idea has been fully agreed make sure that you deliver on time. But whatever you do, do not send out a general mailing and then ring up and ask whether the recipient is going to use it or not. If they are, your phone call will merely be a slight irritant, but if there is no appropriate slot at that particular time your call could cause enough irritation to prevent the material ever seeing the light of day.

It is worth mentioning here that the PRO's job should be a two-way one. So far we have been talking about the flow of information from the company, but it can be equally important for management to receive information on how the world is thinking about the company and its activities, about rival companies and about the industry in which it operates. Thus a press monitoring service becomes even more important. If your organization is involved in foreign markets then reaction in these countries would also be important.

The Media Relations department may also be called upon to act as a general information service, in addition to media directories you may need to keep company and financial directories-*Who's Who* and the like. These may be physical or electronic.

The choice of electronic reference works includes CD-ROMs such as *Microsoft Encarta*. This is a kind of electronic encyclopaedia which you can use to find all kinds of facts and figures. Your electronic database might also include the *Oxford English Dictionary*, *Grolier's Academic Encyclopaedia* (US) or *Microsoft Bookshelf* (half a dozen standard US reference books).

Alternatively you can subscribe to a variety of services such as CompuServe which provides access to large commercial databases such as Reuters News, Associated Press On-Line and Dun and Bradstreet. Others include the Financial Times 'Profile', British Telecom's 'Gold', 'Prestel' (which will also get you into the French 'Mintel') or 'Gateway' the international airways guide, all of which offer a variety of services. 'Profile', for example, holds every word published since the early 1980s in every national newspaper save a couple of tabloids and a few of the more important regional newspapers. BBC Enterprises have also made their database available.

The Internet is another vast source of information and it is growing all the time. Whole newspapers and magazines, complete books, hotel and restaurant guides, tourist information, weather forecasts-the list is endless-can all be downloaded from the Internet. A useful book which will give you some idea of what is available on the Internet is *The New Rider's Official Internet Yellow Pages* published by New Riders Publishing.

The choice of which kind of electronic reference base to use will depend upon the time taken to access it and the cost. The Internet is often the cheaper option but it can take a long time to find the information you need.

The Principalities : In essence, the mass media are the tools or technologies that facilitate dissemination of information and entertainment to a vast number of consumers. They are the tools of large-scale manufacture and distribution of information and related messages. These tools 'mediate' the messages; they are not the messages themselves. However, Marshall McLuhan, the media prophet, liked to proclaim that 'the medium is the message', though the title of one of his books suggests rather that 'the medium is the massage.' The media are technologies; they are also messages and massages. They can also be looked at as industries, as cultural or entertainment industries. While cinema, radio, television, cable, and the press can easily be recognised as 'mass media', it requires some stretching of the established meaning of the term to include recent technologies (sometimes termed the 'new media') such as pagers, cellular phones, satellites, computers, electronic mail and the internet as 'mass media'. More correctly, these new media may be termed 'interactive media' for they are not as much transmission technologies from one source to many receivers, as interactive technologies, which involve feedback, exchange and participation.

'A mass medium' says Wilbur Schramm, 'is essentially a working group organised round some device for circulating the same message, at about the same time, to large numbers of people.' Such a definition excludes the folk media, group media, and interpersonal communication such as rumour, education and preaching, where communication is not 'mediated' by a 'device'. Further, the pejorative term 'mass' (a way of looking down at people as 'masses') suggests that the modern media are 'experienced' not by individuals and groups in terms of their own cultures but as part of the 'mass' and as 'mass culture.' The term 'mass' also suggests that people's interaction with media is homogeneous, inactive and unquestioning. In communication studies today, however, the term 'mass media' has come to be a useful collective phrase, though it slurs over the distinctions among the various media.

As generally interpreted the 'mass' media are the press, cinema, radio and television. But books, magazines, pamphlets and direct mail literature and posters also need to be included in the label. They are so termed because their reach extends to vast heterogeneous masses of the population living in a wide and extensive area of a country. The means they employ to communicate messages to the masses are technological—printing machines, records, cameras, cable, modems, computers and satellites. Their communications are thus interposed and mediated; they are not as direct or face-to-face as in interpersonal exchanges.

The organs of the mass media are technological means of transmitting messages to large numbers of people. Indeed, they are much more than that. As they are very expensive media, (particularly the cinema, radio, television, video, cable, computers, and satellites) they have to be run by institutions like the Government or well financed private commercial bodies. They require a group of people to organise and administer, to produce, distribute and constantly maintain in working order the whole set up of, say, a studio, a transmitting centre, or a publishing house.

Yet another feature of the mass media is that they are founded on the idea of mass production and mass distribution-the marks of an industrial society. Copies of newspapers and magazines, for instance, are printed in thousands (some national and regional dailies in India have a circulation of over half a million) and are circulated over a vast area. But to enjoy a mass audience, the media have to cater to a taste that is not very 'cultured' or sophisticated. What the mass media therefore reflect and propagate is a popular culture. The culture made popular by Hindi films in our cities is a case in point. With the rapid expansion of television and video in cities and towns, popular culture is likely to take on new forms; the 'myths' of our culture will find expression in ever-new ways.

But the mass media in India are in fact a minority media as access to them is still restricted because of poverty, low literacy levels, and familiarity with Hindi and English, the major languages used in the various media; moreover, reach is limited to populations living in metros and large cities. The folk media, in contrast, have a wide audience; they are media close to the hearts and minds of the people, suited to a poor country, and help facilitate identification and participation.

Modern mass media serve functions very similar to those fulfilled by traditional media in some ancient societies, and in some developing countries today. Western media theorists generally identify three major functions; surveillance of the environment, interpretation of the information and prescription for conduct, and the transmission of heritage. The developmental and liberation or empowerment functions, or even the ritualistic or celebratory functions of the media rarely find mention in Euro-American media theory. South American media theorists have contributed to our understanding of media for 'liberation' while African and Asian scholars have explored the relevance of media to 'national development.'

Moral Principles : Surveillance of the environment relates to information or 'news' about happenings in society. The mass media carry out this function by keeping us posted about the latest news in our own region and around the world. In rural societies, however, the word-of-mouth method is still the most credible means of spreading news.

But the mass media cannot or should not stop at watching the horizon for us, through news bulletins or through advertisements of documentaries. They need, and often do help us to correlate our response to the challenges and opportunities which appear on the horizon and to reach consensus on social actions.

In rural India, the panchayat meetings help the village elders to decide on the challenges and the opportunities.

The mass media help us to keep the culture and heritage of our society alive, and to transmit it to others. This is what the media should ideally do, but often don't. Folk media serve a similar purpose in developing countries.

A fourth function is the vital function of entertainment. Entertainment has been a legitimate function of the traditional folk media, but the mass media provide it with a vengeance. They help to pass the time, and to relax with family and friends.

Anthropologists of culture and communication discern a symbolic function of the media: the media provide a 'shared symbolic environment.' George Gerbner, for instance, sees television as the central symbol of American culture today. Horace Newcomb and other 'culturalists' (such as James Carey and Robert White) perceive the media as providing a ritualistic and 'liminal' experience.

An equally vital function is that of the mass media helping to sell goods and services through sponsorships and commercials. The commercial function has indeed been served well, perhaps too well, especially in the United States, where the networks would have to close down if the support from commercials were to dry up. At the same time, it would be suicidal to let this function dominate the mass media at the expense of the other four functions. India too promotes the commercial function, and though it has not allowed its representatives to take over the programming of radio and television, the influence is still strong. This is equally true of the press and its dependence on advertising.

In the developing countries of Asia, Africa and Latin America, the mass media, which include traditional media have a different function to perform. In a word, development communication i.e., communication that focuses on the information needs of the poor and the oppressed, and their socio-economic and cultural interests.

While these may be the five functions of the mass media, it does not necessarily follow that audiences go to them for the same reasons. In his book The Play Theory of Mass Communication, William Stephenson argues that fun is both the greatest impact and the greatest public service of the mass media. Audiences use them as a form of play, or lila. Victor Turner, the anthropologist, believes that the media provide a 'liminal' ritualistic experience. James Carey, Horace Newcomb and others of the 'culturalist' school have developed this approach further by analysing the television experience in terms of 'ritual.'

So, for a good number of the audience, the mass media may be marvellous time-fillers, like listening to the radio while cooking or while driving, or reading during a long train journey. Further, some people use the media to fulfil psychological and social needs. They perhaps get vicarious enjoyment out of sex and violence in the media, and use the media to get topics for conversation at work, or to solve their own problems.

Still others might seek information, merely to be well informed, or perhaps to learn how higher-status people dress and live. Or, they might watch advertisements on TV not so much to know more about a product as to assure themselves that they have bought the best product. These are the 'uses and gratifications' of the media.

So whatever functions the media pundits say the mass media have, the people will continue to use them in the way they (the people, not the pundits) like. It is in this sense that audiences are 'active' rather than 'passive' receivers.

Ethics of Journalism : Western theories of the mass media (particularly of the news media) were first propounded by Fred Siebert, Theodore Peterson and Wilbur Schramm in their book Four Theories of the Press.

These theories have now come to be termed 'normative' in the sense that they 'mainly express ideas of how the media ought to, or can be expected to, operate under a prevailing set of conditions and values.' So, strictly speaking they are hypotheses rather than theories. These 'theories' were first enunciated in the United States during the height of the 'cold-war' against communism and the Soviet Union. They were thus part of American propaganda and only loosely based on actual practices in the media. They idealise the American practices, which are touted as being democratic and socially responsible, and deride 'Soviet' and 'Communist', practices as being 'dictatorial' and 'authoritarian.' They do not take into account the 'public service' models of print and electronic media widely accepted in Western Europe, and in many countries of Asia and Africa.

The 'original' four theories of the press/media are authoritarian theory, libertarian theory, social responsibility theory, and Soviet media theory. Each of them suits particular political and economic circumstances, and focuses not so much on the relationship between the press and readers as on the relationships between the press and Government. The major concern is with ownership and control rather than with different perspectives of Journalism or the people's right to information. Siebert, Peterson and Schramm limit their analysis to 'four' theories; three more need to be added to the original four to take account of circumstances in the developing countries of Asia, Africa and Latin America. The last three could be termed 'Developmental or Alternative Theories' of the media.

According to this theory, the mass media, though not under the direct control of the State and the ruling classes, must do their bidding. The press and other media are expected to respect authority, to be always subordinate to established power and authority, and therefore should avoid offending the majority or dominant moral, political and economic values. Journalists lack independence and freedom; their reports have to be submitted for advance censorship. This censorship is justified on the ground that the State must always take precedence over an individual's right to freedom of expression. Such censorship is more rigidly enforced in times of war and during 'internal' and 'external' emergencies. It needs to be noted that both dictatorial and democratic regimes resort to such authoritarian control of the media. The strictness with which the Official Secrets Act is enforced in Britain and in India is a case in point.

The basis of this 'free press' theory goes back to 17th century England when the printing press made it possible to print several copies of a book or pamphlet at a comparatively low price. In contrast with the authoritarian theory, libertarianism is founded on the fundamental right of an individual to freedom of expression. Western liberal democracies swear by this belief. The First Amendment in the American constitution is an embodiment of this theory; it flows from the individual's right to life, liberty and the pursuit of happiness.

The individual, not the State or society, is supreme, and popular will (vox populi) is granted precedence over the power of the State. The argument is that 'truth' can be arrived at only through the free expression of diverse points of view, no matter how erroneous. The great apologists of this theory were John Milton, the epic poet (in his Aeropagitica) and John Stuart Mill (in his essay, On Liberty). A free press is seen as essential to a free society and the dignity of the individual. Moreover, the freedom to publish is often linked to the right to property, and the free market system.

In practice, however, the theory provides the prerogative of free speech only to the rich and the powerful elites of a society. The marginalized groups do not have access to, and indeed, cannot afford the means or the tools of free expression. What happens on the ground is that media merchants and media monopolies (e.g. the big newspaper chains, the television companies) exploit that freedom to expand their empires. Market forces rather than public good mould the kind of information to be purveyed. The theory thus protects media owners rather than the rights of editors and journalists, or of the public. What the theory offers, in sum, is 'power without social responsibility'.

This theory can be said to have been derived from the Hutchins Report (entitled 'A Free and Responsible Press: A General Report on Mass Communication: Newspapers, Radio, Motion Magazines and Books'). The Hutchins Commission on Freedom of the Press (1947) was established and financed by Henry Luce of Time Magazine at a time in the history of American Journalism when press barons like Luce sensed that government regulations on 'yellow journalism' were round the corner. Moreover, the years following the Second World War witnessed the rise of the Democratic Party in the United States, the restraints on business under the New Deal, and the strengthening of the trade union movement. The American press (which was known to be largely pro-Republican) feared that the federal Government would issue legislation to regulate the 'freedom of the press', despite the First Amendment.

Robert Hutchins, the Chairman of the Commission, was the Chancellor of the Chicago University at the time, and he was assisted by twelve others who were experts in different fields. The Report appeared in two volumes: the first on newspapers, the second on the other media.

The Commission found that the free market approach to press freedom had not met the informational and social needs of the less well off classes; in fact, it had increased the power of a single class. There was little expression of diverse views; the emergence of radio, film and television also suggested that some public control and some means of accountability had become necessary.

Thus, the theory had its roots in the view that the media had certain obligations to society-to serve its needs, rather than that of the free market. Hence the need for high professional standards; of truth, accuracy, objectivity and balance. Self-regulation and also state regulations were imperative. Public interest was a greater value than unregulated freedom of expression. So news offensive to religious and ethnic minorities, or news likely to lead to social violence needed to be underplayed. The Hutchins Report led to the establishment of Press Councils, the drawing up of codes of ethics, anti-monopoly legislation, and to press subsidies to small newspapers. State and public intervention in the exercise of free expression was therefore considered legitimate under certain circumstances.

This theory is derived from Lenin's application of Marx and Engel's dictum in The German Ideology that, 'the ideas of the ruling class are in every epoch the ruling ideas.' The media are thus a means of 'mental production' of the ideology. Hence the need for their control by the working class, that is, through the Communist Party, so that the interests of the working class rather than those of the ruling or elite class are projected.

In a Socialist society, therefore, the media should be used as tools to 'socialize' the people; the primary functions of the media are to educate, inform, motivate and mobilize citizens, and to support 'progressive' movements everywhere. What is expected is 'objective' (or 'scientific') presentation of society. Censorship and restriction on the media are legitimate for the media are accountable to the State, to the public and to the

Party. The public is encouraged to provide feedback, as it is only in this way that the media will be able to serve the public interest.

The 'four theories of the press' are not fully applicable to the experience of the non-aligned countries of Asia, Africa, and South America. While in most Asian and African countries, the media (especially the broadcast media) are owned and run by the State, in Latin American countries, commercial ownership of all the mass media is the norm. A common factor in the experience of the majority of the non-aligned countries is the dependence on industrialized countries for both hardware and software. Another common factor is the commitment of these nations to social and economic development on their own terms; they would like to employ the mass media as tools for 'development', for 'nation-building.'

The larger national interest and the public good are of paramount importance to them. So certain freedoms need to be curbed in the interest of say national integration, and economic and social development. Hence the stress on 'development communication' and 'development journalism'. According to development theorists, journalists have the responsibility to support national governments in their efforts at eradicating illiteracy, promoting family planning, promoting national integration, and increasing production and employment. The weakness in the theory is that 'development' is often equated with government propaganda.

Latin American critics (notably Paulo Freire, Reyes Matta, Luis Beltran, Diaz Bordenave and Valerio Fuenzalida) of commercialized ('commodotized') media have come out strongly against the top-down, one way and non-participative character of contemporary mass media. Like the development theorists, they lay stress on the positive uses of the media, on the need for 'access' and the 'right to communicate.' They insist on the need for local and community participation in media and news production. The people must speak for themselves, they argue, not through professional journalists and producers.

What is vehemently opposed also is commercial, political or bureaucratic control of the media, which exist to serve audiences, not the interests of government or commercial enterprises. The 'demassification' of the media, according to this theory, is as vital as 'democratization.' The ultimate purpose is to put the media in the hands of communities (as in people's radio) for their own 'liberation' through a process of 'conscientization.' Thus is created, in Reyes Malta's words, a 'critical national audience.'

Mutual Relationship : Successful media relations involves understanding the media,. how they work and what their requirements are. It also involves relating this knowledge to the needs of your own organization and the objectives of its media relations programme. It is important to work out the best strategy and to plan accordingly.

This book is essentially practical. It is concerned with the tools, the organization and the planning of the media relations programme. But it also seeks to show how a thorough knowledge and understanding of the media can make your efforts more effective.

There is, after all, no point in spending a fortune on trying to communicate an important story if you are telling the wrong people, in the wrong way, at the wrong time. Putting yourself in the recipient's place and deciding exactly what will be of interest and what will not will be much more useful from everyone's point of view.

This kind of practical knowledge of the media will put you in a better position to build up a harmonious and helpful relationship with those sections of the media which cover your organization's particular activities. And this relationship will in turn help you to establish a smooth communications channel between media and management.

Unfortunately, the senior managements of some organizations tend to view the press or media relations department as a buffer between the media and themselves. This can only lead to trouble. Very often the Public Relations Officer (PRO) is not qualified to answer detailed and possibly highly technical questions. Nor does he or she have the authority to answer for the company on important issues. Such an attitude inevitably leads to an unnecessarily bad press and a lack of cooperation by the media on future occasions.

Rather, the PRO should be the means by which the two sides can talk to each other more easily and with more understanding. You must stick to your professional guns in telling senior management what the consequences of their actions in the media relations field are likely to be. You must, however, also follow up such a stand with sensible advice on dealing with the media and be on hand to see fair play.

Of course, there are occasions when certain sections of the media behave with some dishonesty and as PRO you must watch out for signs of such a situation arising and warn your management in time. But the vast majority of dealings with the media will not be like this, and management must be encouraged to be as open as possible.

Building up a favourable relationship with the media often involves building up a good personal relationship with key journalists in your field. You cannot hope to achieve this if you are not convinced yourself. If you do not think you can be committed to an organization's activities, do not work for it. Honesty is as important at this level as it is on individual issues.

This applies equally whether you are planning to work directly for the organization or for its PR consultants. Indeed everything in the book applies to both situations, for they differ only in their organization and lines of control. To all intents and purposes a PR consultant must act as though he or she works directly for the client organization. 'Public Relations Officer' has also been taken to be synonymous with Press or Media Relations Officer' for the purposes of this book.

Of course a harmonious relationship with the media does not mean that everything will always go smoothly. Sometimes your objectives and those of your media friends will be in conflict and this is where your powers of diplomacy will be tested to the full. Competent journalists will be probing critically. That is their job. Yours is to present the facts in the most favourable light for your organization and, if the problems are severe, to ensure that ultimately your organization's worst story receives the best hearing.

A good example of successful media relations concerns a multinational oil company, one of whose oil tankers was wrecked, causing extensive spillage along the Californian holiday beaches. Sales at petrol stations immediately started to fall. The company instituted an expensive and wide-ranging mopping up programme including very quick cleaning of the popular beaches and a bird sanctuary, a marine life survey and a restocking operation. Full details of the disaster and the company's prompt action were relayed to the media at once and this, coupled with the previously good relationship between the oil company and the media, ensured that most of the coverage was concentrated on the mopping up operation. This resulted in the company being seen as a responsible, socially conscious organization rectifying an inevitable disaster, rather than as an irresponsible multinational with no concern for the environment. Sales not only recovered but exceeded the previous norm.

There are times when the disaster is less obvious to the public view and this is when there is a strong temptation to deny everything. The short answer is, don't allow your management to do so either. If you or any of the representatives of your organization do lie, your reputation in the media will be shattered and its loss will precede you into whatever industry you go. It is very rare for the truth not to emerge, given time, and once a journalist has been castigated by his or her editor for believing your lies the journalist will, understandably, never trust you again. In future, the journalist will be suspicious of everything you and your organization have to say and will tell associates to be wary too.

Successful media relations, then, means understanding the people with whom you want to communicate-producers, editors and journalists-appreciating their problems, needs and audiences and treating them with honesty, efficiency and common sense. It is this principle that underlies all the detailed information and advice.

The term 'media relations' refers to the communication Pattern between an organization and those sections of the media which are interested in its activities. Such communication may be concerned with anything and everything which happens within and around that organization. It may also be concerned with local and national issues, with finance and legislation and with public opinion.

Communication between organization and media may be initiated by either side, but from the organization's point of view media relations is concerned with achieving the most favourable coverage possible. This can sometimes be achieved by reacting to individual happenings or to media enquiries, but at best this approach is haphazard and at worst it is inefficient and potentially dangerous.

It is far better to plan a media relations programme within the framework of your organization's objectives as a whole. This not only helps to channel your efforts into the most effective areas, but also ensures that everyone who comes into contact with the media knows what their organization is trying to achieve.

Real Situations : The first step is to define and analyse the problems in order of priority and then to set objectives to be achieved. The problems will, of course, vary according to the field in which your company or organization is operating and what it is trying to achieve. However, for a manufacturing company the problems might include any of the following:

- The product range is seen as too expensive.
- The proper use of a new product is not really understood.
- The company has a reputation for bad service.
- The company is moving into a new high technology field and needs to upgrade its scientific image.
- The company is not thought of as a good employer.
- The more expensive end of the product range is not being retailed through the right kind of outlets.
- There is an important technical development behind the introduction of a new product which is not fully appreciated.
- The company is thought of as being old-fashioned.

All these and other problems will come in as feedback from the marketing and other departments. Obviously they need to be countered and an objective must be set. Ideally objectives should be measurable and achievable. If you set unobtainable objectives you will be seen to have failed even if you do a wonderful job. To some extent this is also true if the objectives are not measurable.

Whatever you do not try to link your objectives to sales. There may be a great temptation to do this as part of a justification for the very existence of the media relations programme. But you are unlikely to be able to show a link which is directly attributable to your activities and you will be encouraging the view that media relations is simply a cheap form of advertising.

If an objective is to be measured effectively it needs to be defined clearly. There is no point in stating that the objective is 'to increase awareness' or 'to change an attitude'. This is not enough. You must include the answers to the questions 'of what?' and 'by whom?' which will lead you into defining your target audiences. The answer to 'who are you trying to influence?' will in turn lead you on to 'how are you going to reach them?', and once you have reached this stage the programme starts to become viable.

Here is a very simple example of the start of a media relations programme for a small company producing torches.

Market research has shown that the company's torches are seen as dependable but rather old-fashioned and there is little awareness of the newer products which have been introduced to fit the contemporary life-style.

Objectives

1. To increase awareness of the more recent products.
2. To show that these products are up to date and invaluable to the modern man or woman.
3. To give the company a more go-ahead image, while retaining the dependable aspect.

The torch-buying public includes the following markets:

- Women buying torches for domestic and car use.
- Men buying torches for similar uses.
- Industrial buyers, for security services.
- The police and the armed services.

The media reaching the ultimate target audience include the following groups:

- Women's interest programmes and publications.
- Men's and general interest programmes and publications.
- Motoring programmes and press, and the caravan and holiday press.
- Security and safety publications (both consumer and trade).
- Police and armed services press.

This sort of analysis makes the rest of the programme much easier to plan. Working against the background of known developments and plans for the torch company for the coming year a single idea for each area will start the programme off. There may, for example, be plans to launch a new pocket or handbag version of one of the company's torches; if it is sufficiently different from anything else on the market this could form the basis for an onslaught on the women's interest press.

The frustration of life without a torch, illustrated by either a feature or a demonstration, could interest the men's press, and special car fitments for fixing a torch inside the car would be of great interest to the motoring media. Similar ideas for features, visits and events could be thought up for the remaining areas.

A plan like this not only shows up the priority areas and assists a sensible organization to plan its work-load; it also shows where effort should be concentrated and helps in the measurement of success.

Massive coverage may look good but it is less valuable if it appears in media which are not seen by your ultimate target audience. There could even be occasions when extended coverage in a large number of regional and provincial newspapers is much more useful than a short piece in *The*

Times. The temptation is, of course, to impress management with national press coverage, but this may not always be the most effective approach. It may be good for your ego, but is it good for the company?

Once you have an outline of your media relations programme worked out, and preferably written down, you will be ready to start thinking about the detailed use of tools such as media lists, press releases, competitions, press receptions, workshops, visits and special events.

However, the media relations programme does not end here. It must be assessed. Is the right message reaching the right people in the right volume or are you wasting your efforts talking to the wrong audience or giving the wrong signals? There are various ways of evaluating a media relations programme.

9

Structural Setup

Newspaper Format

Editor : (a) relations with owner, individual proprietor; partners; private or public limited company or charitable trusts; relations with publishers, printers and public; (b) need for clear line of authority and division of responsibility for policy and production process, relations with staff of Editorial Department and with the Business Section (advertisement, circulation and accounts); Promotion (public relation); Circulation (readers' preferences) and Printing Department (for flow of copy, etc.);

Structure Depends on Nature of Organization : (a) single edition; (b) multiple edition (printing only), multiple edition (chains); multiple-language editions—Joint Editor, Managing Editor, Associate Editor, Executive Editor, Guest Editor — (for book page, arts, fashion, etc.);

Editorial Conference : Editor and Assistant Editors (News, Views, News-Views, Magazine, Art, etc.); News Editor;

News Editor : Deputy, Chief Sub, Senior Sub, Sub-Editor, Sports, Conference Editor — managerial function (flow of copy to press, make-up etc.); editorial function; liaison with reporting section; selection and distribution of copy to sub-editor with instructions on length, headline, etc.

Sub-Editor : main tasks—qualifications (general, technical), need for alert mind, quick decisions, cool temper — relations with other colleagues, with superiors and the printing department; rights —Working Journalists Act; professional training; efficient discharge of his tasks, whatever his position in the hierarchy, decides his progress—individual and professional.

Editing General Principles

News Editing : Process by which information is presented to readers in entertaining way for their enlightenment on current affairs—rush of modern life newsflow varied and of complex implications —extraction of relevant material from this vast newsflow.

Reader's Requirements : News is what man is interested in as an individual and as member of a society — food, shelter, clothing, transport, religious and social differences, national and international problems, differences of publication owing to differences in locale, complexion of population, etc., variety of publications — for laymen and experts, etc., — Form Follows Function.

Fourth Estate : Fourth Estate is the press of England. What are the other three estates? Lords, Temporal and Spiritual and Commons — modern newspapers not mere chroniclers of news but interpreters as democracy requires well informed and enlightened public opinion —catering to popular interest not enough, public interest must be considered.

Basic Responsibilities : Salesmanship aspect — reader as customer — financial viability — advertisement and circulation — warning on threat to freedom of press and hazards of journalistic profession for advertiser's pressures and public lobbying—responsibility to reader —reliable information, entertaining presentation, and enlightenment.

Code of Ethics

Reporter vs. Editor : Why editing ? Reporter gathers news and is primarily responsible for selection and bright and brisk presentation — but editor makes sure the account is well stressed, organized, uses aids like headlines, pictures, charts, sketches etc. to draw the reader's attention — reporter not infallible, rush in getting news makes report defective — editor acts as second mind.

Five W's and one H : Main Factors—what, who, when, where, why and how—editor rearranges details to dramatise value —meticulous examination of details—eliminates editorial expression from news—news is sacred but comment is free — check-up on details —simplicity of language and style deletes trivia, absurdities, irrelevancies, emotionalism, propaganda — care to avoid identification of the speaker and reporter. Coordination with other news of the day.

Warning : In rearranging and rewriting reporter's copy.

Editor should preserve the spirit and personality of the reporter and as far as possible, the words of the reporter—no change for mere changes sake — change only to make the news element a unity, cohesive and emphatic, for greater impact on the reader.

Copy Matter

Copy Received by : 1. post; 2. telephone; 3. telegram; 4. cable and wireless; 5. teleprinter circuit — news agencies; 6. monitoring of radio and television programmes; 7. lift journals.

Types of Copy : 1. City — local news from own reporter or news agencies; 2. District and mofussil correspondents; 3. State and Union capitals; 4. Foreign news from abroad; 5. News, Views, News plus Views:— special articles from own correspondents — Letters to Editors, official information, crime, education, etc.

Copy Content : 1. political, economic and social developments; 2. statements and speeches — press conferences and interviews; legislature proceedings; 3. arts, film, drama, etc.; 4. sports; 5. commerce; 6. gossip — personal column; 7. births and deaths-accidents-sickness-morgue; 8. weddings — birth anniversaries, etc.; 9. human stories from occasional correspondents.

Sources of Copy : 1. Government, the biggest source in India — Secretariat and other offices, Collectorates; 2. Public sector and private sector firms — industries; trade unions; 3. Political parties and politicians; 4. Economic and social organisations; 5. Universities, College managements and students, teacher bodies; 6. Syndicated copy articles, comic strips, etc.; 7. Public utility services; 8. Embassies of foreign countries.

"Tasting" copy for "Slant", Colour and Advertisement passing off as "News"

Distinction between News and Propaganda : Difficult to draw a line, while suppression as well as overmuch publicity will hamper the journalist's service to his readers, total withdrawal is bad; essence of propaganda is selection and spread of ideas or news to induce a desired belief or action — transmission or opinion to influence people — the selectiveness pertains not only to content but also to the decision in what page, in what proportion and in which position and with what typographical emphasis the news should appear.

Propaganda Devices : They are *Amoral* like any other tool of knowledge — either for or against particular cause, person or event —1. Name Call, 2. Glitter, 3. Transfer or usurpation of ideas, functions like fast, Crusades; 4. Testimonial from VIPs—Tyranny of minority opinion, 5. Band Wagon — use of religious symbols, colours, music and slogans — tyranny of majority; 6. Card-stacking giving selective stimuli; and 7. Conspiracy of silence.

If these devices do not accord with the responsibilities of the journalists, they should not be adopted. If the propaganda is harmless, or helpful and does not affect professional standards and is subversive of the above responsibilities, then they may be considered innocuous and used.

Distinguish between colourful and coloured reports.

What was mentioned above is what the journalist should avoid. What follows is what he should guard against, that is, in the above, he should avoid making the readers victims of his propaganda; and in what follows, he should avoid becoming a victim of propaganda by others.

1. Handouts — picked news; 2. Made News — circumstances are created to give publicity to an idea, to a prominent person or organisation etc.; 3. Hoax; 4. Camouflaged public service; 5. Polluted news; 6. Free publicity, professional publicity-mongers— problem of inclusion of who gave the news and why — the inclusion will remove the poisonous effect of such propaganda.

Buying space for advertisement should not be confused with the pressure to invade news columns — difficulties in drawing a strict line — should hotel names be used in accidents or receptions, so also hospitals, lawyers, doctors, etc. — police reports require mention of police personnel if they are news sources.

Change from region to region, state to state readership differences even within the family, influence of edition time, place of occurrence, developing news, essential and non-essential aspects, advt. and dummy.

Gate-keeper's Function : (a) What item should go into the publication; (b) in what detail and length; (c) where it should go on page; (d) with what typographical emphasis; (e) role of aids like pictures, cartoons, sketches, tables etc. How to make the reader concentrate on what the editor thinks is important and should be read immediately.

For selection of news relates to the specific aims of the publication, maintenance of standards of the profession and catering to the tastes and interests of the readership — popular versus public interest.

Criteria for Selection of News : Immediacy or timeliness, immediate import of interest, writing about strikes etc., preparing the reader to meet an eventuality, background information about what has happened or is about to happen — Cauvery waters and famines etc.

Proximity : (a) geographical news from one's own birthplace of where one studies or works: familiarity; (b) ideological: one's interests, ideological affiliation ; specialists etc.

Prominence : Activities of prominent people, ministers, actors, etc., events in prominent localities: overshadowing nature in Indian Press.

Physical conflicts like communal and caste clashes, wars among nations, war against diseases, inventions and discoveries produce changes, beneficial or harmful — fibre replaces cotton, automation renders people jobless, reservation, dissatisfaction.

Removal of slums, new slums for old, pangs of progress, new problems.

Events for which the reader is least prepared— if Smt. Indira Gandhi announces retirement from public life etc. —

suspense over actor's condition — snags in spacecraft will be concern to people till the snags are removed.

Sex : Issues like sex education, sexual jealousy, murder, etc.—discoveries about sex motivation — use of sex hormones.

Oddity : Odd behaviour of prominent persons — millionaire willing away his fortune for gods; ear-boring ceremony for cat etc.

Role of emotions, issues of universal interest —suffering elicits sympathy, but false sympathy is dangerous — a man sacrificing his life for another, animals in distress, prevention of cruelty to animals in drug industry, should it be done or not. News of value may not always be apparent. It has to be sought after.

Creation of News Interest : Editorial campaign for the benefit of the community.

How much and what kind of crime news should be printed ?

Newspapers probably are reproached more for reporting crime news than for any other reason. The critics say that newspapers make crime by reporting crime.

The factors which make crime news may be summarised as follows :

Prominence of Persons : Wealth and position count in any kind of story, but especially when there is proof of wrong doing.

Prominence of Place : The same test applied to familiar things and places whenever they serve as background.

Property Loss : If all other factors balance, the property loss gauges the news value.

Mystery and Suspense : As long as the police are baffled, news interest thrives and expands. The moment the case is solved, interest dies.

Unique Circumstances : Anything startling, novel, or peculiar especially if it relates to the motive that promoted the act, strengthens the news bond.

Emotional Pull : Police reporters probably unearth more human interest stories than any members of the staff, with the possible exception of reporters.

Gruesomeness and Melodrama : The first lesson a crime reporter learns is that he must eliminate repellent details from his copy. If he fails to do so, the sub-editors will do it for him. This means little colour.

News Desk : There are two kinds of news editors. There is the passive news editor who reacts like a chief clerk in a government office through whom everything must pass, but who does not initiate or inspire any action. Then there is the active news editor who initiates and directs the operation of news gathering. The active news editor's work produces the news on which the paper exists; the page for topical features; the inspiration for dramatic pictures, cartoons and illustrations; and the occasion and theme for the commentaries, columns and leaders.

An active news editor's job is to sell his readers what his fellow beings have been doing since the last issue of his newspaper appeared. How can a news desk be made active ? Mainly in checking the stock sources of news :

1. Government and official news; News about the head of the State, Cabinet, the Legislature and the Administration.
2. Meeting of the legislature, local bodies and subsidiary agencies of Government such as State, Corporation, etc.
3. Functions attended by Ministers, Officials, V.I.Ps.
4. Activities, movements and statements of people already

known to the public or interesting to the public such as businessmen, entrepreneurs, scientists, educators, sportsmen, filmstars, cultural and religious leaders, etc.

5. Accidents, crimes, litigation, police.
6. Health and hospitals.
7. Births, marriages and deaths.
8. Money and business.
9. Cultural and religious events.
10. Science and economic news.

These ten themes span a wide range of human activity and interest and should be rigorously exploited to develop news possibilities.

A fundamental general rule for active news editors to remember. It is not enough for a newspaper to report what the Government and the public does. It must report what the public feels, thinks, hopes and fears.

Our newspapers make nothing like enough use of illustrations. This makes them weak in two fundamental ways. They are not telling the news as effectively as they could. And they are failing to use one of the fundamental means of bringing colour and variety: the forbidding greyness of their newspapers.

The old Chinese proverb is still true today : One picture is equal to a thousand words. Not all photographers are genius but an ordinary run-of-the-mill photographer will respond and can produce good news pictures if he is told what to look for. But to begin with, he must, of course, have sufficient technical knowledge to take good pictures.

The newspaperman has to bear two things in mind when he considers photographs for publication. He has to consider the photograph's technical value and also its editorial value.

Since you will almost inevitably lose some of the detail in your photographs in reproduction, what you want, technically, is a picture with sharp detail and large pattern. Look for a picture that shows crisply the various gradations of grey —the halftone — that bring out the contents on a face or a building. This sharp detail is called "contrast".

With a mediocre picture, "crop" for the most interesting part and enlarge that for reproduction. The best motto here is one used by the staff of the *Vancouver Sun* :

> "If a picture is great it deserves to be played big."
> If it's an ordinary picture it needs to be played big.

It is far easier to get a photograph technically suitable for reproduction than to find one worth printing on strict editorial values. Judgement comes into this of course but there are a number of useful tests you can bear in mind.

Does the Picture Live ? Every news picture must tell a story at a glance. The best pictures show life happening. They show suspended animation, you might say. They capture something that is there one minute, gone the next.

Is it posed ? In the very best news pictures the subject is not conscious at all of the camera. Then the people in your pictures must be active. Not the "line up" or "firing squad" pictures. You know the sort of thing a group of people lined up like condemned men facing a firing squad. They look straight into the camera. They do nothing else. What kind of story does the picture tell ?

Can you see anything ? Another reason why you should avoid the ordinarily squad group pictures is that most times you cannot even see who the people are in them. If you must use a group picture (say, of a football team) you must make it big or otherwise the individual faces will not reproduce in the newspaper.

Edit pictures for size, shape and detail. A strong vertical stress is an effective shape of picture for a newspaper.

A strong horizontal stress is also striking. Almost invariably you should make the picture bigger than you first thought.

Most newspaper photographs are improved by "cropping" — cutting out unnecessary background detail.

Crop pictures for two reasons: First, you will be getting rid of a good deal of fussy clutter.

Secondly, crop because it will give you more space to display the main points of interest.

Captions : All the rules of news writing apply to writing captions. Captions should be written in short, pithy sentences. They must tell who is in the picture, what they are doing, where they are doing it, when were they doing it, why were they doing it. Give full names to identify everyone in the picture; and be accurate.

Captions should supplement what we can see with our eyes. A caption of a picture showing Mrs. Gandhi speaking should not just say "Mrs. Gandhi speaking." We can see that. The caption should say, even in a sentence, what she addressed the people about.

Overlines or Titles : The caption supplements what we can see with our eyes. The overline never does that. It merely sums up what we can see in an arresting fashion.

News in our Time : Mass communication has given us a window on the world, and we often might not like what we see through it. But without the news, we would be without the means to correct the ills and injustices of modern-day life.

In his recent book *Eyewitness to History*, the distinguished English professor John Carey tells of how a correspondent from *The Times* of London was sent to France to cover the

Franco-Prussian War of 1870. After the decisive battle of Sedan, he rushed back to England by train and ferry boat, staying up all right to write his account of the German victory. He arrived only to find that competing newspapers had published reports of the event sent by electric telegraph two days earlier. *The Times* had literally blundered into a new era in western society — an era in which the news from almost everywhere is available to almost everyone every hour of every day.

The improvement in the transmission of the news coincided with improvements in printing and paper making technology which made possible the speedy production of huge quantities of daily newspapers that could be sold at minimal prices. Meanwhile the spread of literacy owing to compulsory education was opening up a mass market for the "peny press". Soon the ordinary people of the United States, Britain and Western Europe had a ready means of learning what was going on in the world, a privilege once reserved for a relatively small literate minority. Public access to the news had been established : from there on it was merely a series of technological steps to today's 24-hour television news by satellite.

"Arguably the advent of mass communications represents the greatest change in human consciousness that has taken place in recorded history," Carey wrote. "The development, within a few short decades, from a situation where most of the inhabitants of the globe would have no day-to-day knowledge of or curiosity about how most of the others were faring, to a situation where the ordinary person's mental space is filled (and must be refilled daily or hourly unless a feeling of disorientation is to ensue) with accurate reports about the doings of complete strangers represents a revolution in mental activity which is incalculable in its effects."

Public access to national and international news has deeply influenced popular culture, politics, and even philosophy. It has given ordinary men and women a more humanistic and tolerant outlook on life by making them empathize with all of humanity. New reports force us to look human suffering in the face, and make us want to do something about it, whether to donate money to aid disaster victims or call on our governments to put pressure on other governments to stop committing injustices. In the age of the news, no man is an island. We cannot help but be, as John Donne put it, "involved in mankind".

So pervasive is the news in western countries that it has become one of life's necessities. There are, of course, times when it is absolutely necessary to know what is happening for our own well-being, as when a hurricane is heading in the direction of where we live. But beyond immediate practical information, we need the news to help us cope with the pace and complexity of modern living. As the Canadian journalism professor Wilfred Eggleston wrote: "Survival of all living creatures requires an awareness of the changing environment .... Speedy and accurate information is required for people to react."

Out of our need for news has evolved a principle which would never have been thought of in the days before the telegraph: that the public has a right to news that can be trusted. The Canadian Royal Commission on Newspapers broached this concept in 1981 by declaring that people have a "to inform themselves" which is inseparable from their right to express themselves. Canada is one country where the right to the news is enshrined in legislation. To hold a broadcast licence, every Canadian radio station must carry news reports.

The ability to keep track of what is happening and of what is being said is central of our system of government. "A people without reliable news is, sooner or later, a people without the basis of freedom," political scientist Harold Laski wrote.

Wherever there is no political freedom, the news is always controlled — not only internal news, but news from abroad which invites comparisons with conditions elsewhere and exposes the repressed populace to "alien" ideas. No less a tyrant than Adolf Hitler objected fiercely to free reporting. "Our law concerning the press is such that divergences of opinion between members of the government are no longer an occasion for public exhibitions," he said at the height of his power.

A man of an opposite cast of mind, the American statesman Thomas Jefferson, once declared that if he had to decide between government without newspapers and newspapers without government, he would choose the latter. At the same time Jefferson was the first to admit that the freedom of the press which he so eloquently upheld could be abused. This freedom (which today covers the electronic media as well) is by no means unbridled. News organizations are not free, for instance, to ruin a person's reputation, to invade a person's privacy, or to subject a person to 'trial by publicity'. They are prohibited from doing such things by various laws.

Despite these legal constraints, news organizations remain very much responsible to themselves, and there is plenty of room for breaches of that responsibility. Newspapers, radio and television stations carry not only accounts of events, but commentary on those events. Writers and broadcasters of opinion do not need an array of indisputable facts to blacken a reputation or throw suspicion on the motives of an organization; sufficient to mix a few suggestive facts in with a lot of innuendo. A clever writer or editor with an axe to grind can paint a biased picture even in an apparently impartial report.

At one time it was left almost entirely up to newspaper proprietors and their sycophants to decide how much restraint would be applied on their ability to play with the facts, or to publish absolute falsehoods. Their papers frequently distorted the "news" to suit their own political objectives. Sensationalism ran rampant among hotly-competitive big city dailies. The truth was often slaughtered in the crossfire of their circulation wars.

For better or for worse (some say worse) the new generation of newspaper proprietors in North America are for the most part detached from day-to-day operations of papers they own, running large chains from corporate head offices. News organizations have become big businesses, whether their outlet is in print or by electronic means.

The decline of the old-time imperious press barons coincided with the rise of professional journalists who insist that their first duty is not to the boss but to the reader. Sensational dailies still exist, but beneath their splashy layout, they will usually be found to be quite scrupulous about getting their facts straight, at least in their news columns.

Today, any news organization worthy of the name pledges itself to ensure as far as possible that the news it presents is accurate, fair and balanced. While this has always been an informal understanding among ethical journalists, many organizations have adopted formal codes of ethics, and some employ ombudsmen to protect the public interest.

By adopting such self-restraint, the media have acknowledged that the dissemination of the news is not just another business. It is a form of public trust, not only because people need information to live out their everyday lives, but because the media have so much latent power. Power must be counterbalanced by responsibility, and news organizations have chosen to exercise that responsibility themselves, rather than risk the threat to democratic practice posed by having governments do it for them.

The greatest power of the media to influence public opinion lies not so much in their commentary on the news but in their selection and presentation of it. "Of course the people won't always vote the way the editorial-writers tell them on next week's sewer by law," observed the 1970 Canadian Senate Report on Mass Media; "but who decides when they'll start thinking and talking about sewers — or whether they'll worry about pollution at all ?"

Back in the comparatively simple world of 1920, the great American columnist Walter Lippmann wrote : "The news of the day as it reaches the newspaper office is an incredible medley of fact, propaganda, rumour, suspicion, clues, hopes, and fears, and the task of selecting and ordering the news is one of the truly sacred and priestly offices in a democracy."

All sorts of judgements come into play when a newspaper or new program is being produced: How long should a story be ? Should it come first, last, or in between ? Within the story itself, which points should be emphasized over others ? In a controversy, which spokesmen for which side should be quoted more prominently ? The answers to all these questions have a strong influence on what people think about issues and events.

How do editors and news directors choose what you will or will not hear about ? According to George Kennedy in his textbook *News Reporting and Writing*, there are five usual criteria: impact (what everybody will be talking about); proximity (all things being equal, something that happens a few streets away is bigger news than something that happens 1,000 miles away); timeliness (news has a short shelf life); prominence ("names make news"); conflict (as in strikes, politics, crime, sports competition); and novelty ("if a dog bites a man, that's not news; if a man bites a dog, that's news").

The yardsticks used by professionals to judge what makes news frequently come in for criticism from the public and its spokesmen. "Trouble : that's (what's) wrong with journalism's current definition of the news," complained the Senate Report on Mass Media. "There is more to life than hassle and strife, but the media's entertainment in drama, conflict and disruption prevents them from reporting it."

The trouble is that people like to hear about trouble as long as it is not happening to them, and the news is to a large extent "market driven". A perhaps apocryphal story is told in the business about a man who started a wire service which carried only good news, and promptly went broke.It is an open question whether it is the consumers or processors of news who demand that it be delivered at great speed, but certainly any news organisation that is consistently beaten to the punch on stories would fear losing the market share to more alert competitors. Many of the failings of the media can be traced to the haste with which reports are prepared.The scope for error is enormous when reporting is done in a rush, which is why newspapers and agencies obligate themselves to publish corrections when the inevitable mistakes occur. Speed breeds superficiality; when something is reported in a hurry, important details may be overlooked or misunderstood.

How to Present Real Picture? : Even when the time to prepare a report is not unduly short, there is a constant danger of getting events or issues out of perspective. At a time when life is growing even more complicated, salient facts may be lost in the shuffle of all the considerations that come into play. Also, news people see things through their own pre-conditioned perceptions, and "the observers," as communications scholar P. W. Bridgman put it. They must deal with words, and words can be slippery. They sometimes pass on their biases to readers or listeners through their choice of language.

Reporters, as opposed to opinion journalists, traditionally have tried to keep their personal feelings and opinions out of their reports, but objectivity is not without its pitfalls. There is a decided difference between the facts and the truth. It might be a fact that a person involved in a newsworthy situation says something, but what he says might not be true. Still, his words must be reported objectively in the absence of evidence that they are lies.

The school of "new journalism" that grew up in the 1960s contended that true objectivity was a psychological impossibility and should, therefore, be dispensed with. In any case, the new journalists insisted, objectivity was merely an excuse for the established media to support the status quo on questions of justice that cried out for reform.

Though it was practised in the name of democracy, subjective reporting proved to be distinctly undemocratic, which perhaps explains why it is now discredited among most mainstream journalists. Its practitioners felt free to ignore the precept that there are two sides to every story when one side did not agree with their point of view.

Worse, the freedom from the discipline of objectivity blurred the distinction between personal interpretation of the facts and pure fiction: It became just too tempting for some writers not to invent convenient "facts" when a story was (so they thought) written from such a personal point of view that no one could check up on it. In several cases, someone did check up, and found that stories had been falsified.

Although members of every profession will occasionally bring it into disgrace, the cases of fabrication seemed to confirm the views of those who regard the entire media with unwavering suspicion Such derelictions are, in fact, very uncommon. The great majority of writers and editors strive intently to ensure the integrity of the news.

People who excoriate the sins of the media frequently fail to differentiate between reportage and commentary. The media themselves sometimes contribute to the confusion by mixing the two in the form of "interpretative reporting" and not clearly identifying the line between the verifiable facts and what the writer speculates those facts might mean.

Mostly, though, people who rail against the media are indulging in the time-honoured sport of shooting the messenger. They are upset by the endless chronicle of folly and evil which journalists deliver—"the usual depravities and businesses and hypocrisies and cruelties" which Mark Twain said could be found in any morning's news. It is natural enough to want to ascribe blame for all the tumult and grief that seems to surround us. And so journalists are blamed for going out of their way to make the world look worse than it is.

This is particularly so in the case of "investigative reporting," which digs out news rather than waiting for it to happen. The public sometimes seems to have more sympathy with the subjects of revelations of misbehaviour than with the journalists who have uncovered them. "There they go again," people will say. "Why do they have to tell us these things ? Why not let sleeping dogs lie?"

The answer is that our society would be a lot worse off if media did not play such a role; the fear of being exposed is a strong deterrent to corruption. Granted, the media sometimes go too far in their pursuit of real or supposed villains. That is one reason why there are now press councils in many parts of North America. The councils are there to see that, in their lust for justice, the media do not commit injustices themselves.

The most commonly-heard complaint against the purveyors of news is that they "blow things out of proportion". In the most general terms, they certainly do. The bad news which comprises the bulk of national and international reports is out of proportion to the great mass of "good news" that is never reported. At any given hour, nine-tenths of human affairs around the world are proceeding peacefully, smoothly and safely. The stuff of headlines is the other aberrant one-tenth, or less.

Walter Lippmann said that the task of news people is to provide a picture of reality upon which men can act, but the news does not and cannot reflect the whole of reality. Still, it does give us grounds for action to build a better world. There are times when we would prefer not to know just how stupid and bad human beings can be, but if we did not know about it, we would never be able to correct the stupidity and badness. The news is a necessary evil in the advancement of civilization. It might even be said that there can be no civilization without the news.

Open to all parties, but influenced by none.

Only a courageous publisher supported by an inspired, intelligent, and dynamic editorial staff ably augmented by knowledgeable, efficient and dedicated "reporters" can find his greatest fulfilment as a newspaper man.

A newspaper cannot please everyone every day. The newspaperman must know his public : it will help if the reader knows something of the problems of the reporter and the editors, and how they go about solving them.

The newspaper is produced for commercial gain, sold under highly competitive conditions, and must have careful business management. If it is not issued for sale so as to make a profit, it is not a distinct individual, but a part or adjunct of something else. If published to advance any cause, it is an organ, not a newspaper. It cannot be independent unless it earns its living.

The perfect newspaper will be the voice of the lowly and oppressed and forgotten people, champions of the underdog. If in discharge of its responsibility especially in the present "restless world" — it occasionally troubles the public conscience, that is not to its credit. If it is a defender of civil liberty and a friend of righteous causes it is performing a worthy service. Its chief function is to hold up a mirror to the happenings of the day. If it is careful to keep the mirror clean and as flawless as possible, the reflections will be honest, clear and interesting.

Newspaper writing and newspaper reading are not jobs for people who cannot, when necessary, look at a subject objectively. The reader needs to distinguish between knowledge and guessing, between trained and casual observation, between verification and credulousness.

The urge to play up conflict in print and in conversation is widespread, and newspapers might improve their image by curbing it.

News is accurate information about any event of public or human interest, of the record of significant acts or opinions. It tells about something that is different from daily routine.

Two attributes of the good newspaper reporter today are selection and sincerity. He knows what incident to include to give his canvas the image of life, and he cannot be induced to omit an iota of what he believes to be essential.

He is neither too dainty to face facts as they are, nor too blind to discern their full significance, but he will not revel in the unhealthy or set down anything in malice. He is true to the facts whether he is writing an account of a college concert or a report of the clash of events in world politics.

The press is not free if those who operate it behave as though their position conferred upon them the privilege of being deaf to ideas which the processes of free speech have brought to public attention.

Just as the citizen tries to order his life so as to live decently, effectively and fruitfully, so a newspaper can contribute to its generation by telling the news in accord with the principles of honesty, impartiality, integrity, accuracy and fairness. The editorial writer with a sense of responsibility will try to give his readers a balanced presentation of basic facts, tell the purpose of proposed action suggest alternatives, and illuminate the whole matter by his soulful thought.

The word press signifies newspapers, magazines, journals or dailies or periodicals in general. Subject matters to publicise or as reported in the press. Press release signifies to make news known publicly or to allow news to be made known publicly. An advertisement, for instance, is released of a product recently introduced in the market.

Press release is a statement given to newspapers, reporters etc. Government corporations, institutions issue press releases to inform the public. Press and news media are powerful, and generally influential to project an image to the public. Indian Press is free press and the people have much faith in the press. The press can effectively communicate to the public.

The press transmits facts, figures, symbols to the readers. It is an objective announcement about a particular matter or event issued to the press for publication to inform the public in time. The press has every right to publish any news item intact or in condensed form. It all depends on its news-worthiness and importance. A press release is not confined only to news items of Government, politics, national and international events.

Press releases include advertisements, appointments, legal notices, growth of industry, government notifications, guidelines, achievements, activities, marriages, entertainment, rentals, seminars etc. A press release is effective only when it satisfies qualities like information, which is concise, clear, and devoid of hackneyed publicity materials.

Selection of a newspaper or newspapers for the subject matter and the circle of readers for whom it is meant are the deciding factors for the effectiveness of any press release. They are closely related with each other. Evidently the wrong selection of newspaper(s) for the publication of any fact is a matter of great significance to achieve the objectives of release. Therefore, in any press release the right selection of newspapers and its significance cannot be over-emphasised.

A few illustrations of recent press releases are as under :

Illustration 1

Office of the Andhra Pradesh

Housing Board

'Gruhakalpa' Mukarramjahi Road,

Hyderabad

Press Note : In the Notification No. 13/92 issued calling for applications for allotment of houses at Ongole, the cost of application is mentioned as Rs. 35/- and by post Rs. 25/- by oversight instead of Rs. 25/- and Rs. 35/- respectively. Therefore, it is informed that the applications can be had in person by paying Rs. 25/- and Rs. 35/- by post from the office of the Regional Housing Engineer, A.P. Housing Board, Vijaywada.

For Vice Chairman & Housing Commissioner.

Illustration 2

Wanted Distributors

A company manufacturing PCs and State-of-art new generation Fax machines wishes to appoint area-wise distributors who are : Financially sound. Professionally managed. Having good track record in the field.

Apply within 10 days with full details along with bank references.

To

The Chief Executive,

XYZ Company Limited 15,

Anandha Road Alwarpet,

Madras 600018.

Illustration 3

X.Y. GROUP Requires

Two

Company

Secretaries

For Their New Delhi Offices

The candidates must be members of the Institute of Company Secretaries of India. Past experience is not necessary. Please apply with salary expected within 10 days to :

The Managing Director

X. Y. Group Limited

12, New Colony,

Model Basti

New Delhi-110005.

Illustration 4

Steel Authority of India Limited

(A Government of India Enterprise)

Rourkela Steel Plant

Rourkela-769 011 Orissa Office of the Additional General Manager (MM)

Purchase Department Sub : Second Corrigendum

To Tender Notice No : P/Proj/Modn/4011899124 for signalling and Truck Inter Connection Package under Phase-II Modernisation of Rourkela Steel Plant.

Sl.No.2.0 First line for existing entry please read as the Tender documents will be available for sale from 30-6-1990 to 21-7-1992.

Sl.No.2.1 First line in place of 10-7-1992 please read as "31-8-1992." All other conditions of the tender notice shall remain unaltered.

Registered Office :

Ispat Bhavan,

Lodhi Road,

New Delhi-110 003.

Illustration 5

Notice inviting Tender

Sealed tenders are invited for design, manufacture, supply, erection, testing, commissioning of FEED systems for the Banbury Mixer at our Kankinara Works, West Bengal.

Tender documents can be obtained from Materials Manager (Project), at the address given below on all working days between 10.00 a.m. and 2.00 p.m. up to 21-6-90. Last date of submission of bid completed in all respects is 21-7-90.

Type Corporation of India Ltd.

(A Government of India Enterprise). 19, Jawaharlal Nehru Road, Calcutta - 700 087.

Mass Media Guidelines

1. The sacredness of human personality has to be the vital content of any mass media reporting.
2. Must ever be alive to responsible reporting in this restless world.
3. Newspapers must be open to all parties but influenced by none.
4. Only a courageous publisher supported by an inspired, intelligent and dynamic editorial staff ably supported by knowledgeable. Efficient and dedicated "reporters" can find his greatest fulfilment as a newspaper man.
5. In this imperfect world of "Man, the unknowns," people practising different professions tend to forget the Code of Ethics. Though "Journalism" is a profession, it has

to be considered as a mission. Only a sincere "opposition" and an aggressive press could be the guardians of democracy.

6. From being a "reporter" he should endeavour to combine velocity and facility and become a "social scientist".
7. The perfect newspaper will be the voice of the lowly and oppressed and forgotten people, champion of the underdog. Its chief function is to hold up a mirror to the happenings of the day. If it is careful to keep the mirror clean and as flawless as possible, the reflections will be honest, clear and interesting.
8. The urge to play up conflict in print and in conversation is widespread, newspapers might improve their image by curbing it.
9. News is accurate information about any event of public or human interest, or the record of significant acts of opinions. It tells about something that is different from daily routine.
10. The press is not free if those who operate it behave as though their position conferred upon them the privilege of being deaf to ideas which the processes of free speech have brought to public attention.
11. Just as the citizen tries to order his life so as to live decently, 'effectively and fruitfully, so a newspaper can contribute to its generation by reporting the news in accord with the principles of honesty, impartiality, integrity, accuracy and fairness.

Favouring Factors

Not only does the newspaper have greater merit than the radio because it is the older of the two media, but also because of the special advantages and conveniences offered by it. The radio listener has to adjust himself to the timings and place of the station, while the reader can take his paper wherever he likes, go through it at leisure and re-read a part which he likes. Even the appearance of the "Radio-Newspaper" and its possible development does not alter the position because the newspaper can give much, much greater variety.

In this era when prompt supply of news is of paramount importance, the radio sometimes beats the newspaper in the game. But even this occasional beating only whets public appetite to read more and at greater leisure about important developments in the reader's favourite newspaper. The ghost that the radio and the press are rivals has been laid to rest long ago.

Illiteracy which is a large chink in our armour, is no obstacle in the case of the radio as it is in the case of the newspaper. The vast areas of the countryside can be opened up and brought under the educative influence of the radio by installing more community sets. The regional radio stations lay more and more emphasis to rural programmes.

Radio-mindedness is limited mainly by one's paying capacity. If the radio sets could be made and sold at cheaper rates and the Central, State and other local taxes on them are brought down, it will be a boon to the lower and middle classes and to people living in the villages.

Despite competition from the radio and the TV the newspaper is undergoing a tremendous revolution not only in respect of new ideas and new methods in editing but also in the introduction of new printing procedures and machines. The major consideration of the print media today is how to catch the interest and attention of the reader so that he continues as ever to wait anxiously for the morning newspaper. There is an attempt to put greater variety in coverage, more human value stories and the lighter type of matter which may inform, instruct and provide entertainment at the same time. Newspapers are becoming more and more humanized.

With the printing revolution already going fast, newspapers, especially weeklies, fortnightlies and monthlies, are using modern methods of offset printing in which many colours are combined to give a better visual effect.

A country's political system (stemming from the political ideology) is obviously related to the direction and speed of a country's total national development. If this assumption be true, then media and national development join in a kind of symbiotic relationship of a complex nature. It is this symbiotic relationship that has been consuming more and more time and effort of researchers and theorists in the related fields of journalism, sociology and political science since about the middle of this century.

Editors and writers are a highly individualistic group who maintain fairly high standards of competence and integrity in evaluating information they pass on to their readers. Newspapers are as much a public utility as water, electricity, gas or transportation. Because they are essential to the smooth functioning of a political democracy and a free enterprise economic system, newspapers keep the public interest foremost in their day-to-day judgement of news.

Outside Newspapers

The legislature, the judiciary, the executive and the press are the four pivotal pillars on which modern democracy is built. The press, as the Fourth Estate, it should safeguard the principles of democracy by effective dissemination of information. The press plays a paramount role in a democracy, it is not known as the Fourth Estate for nothing. Secularism, socialism, democracy, self-reliance and constitutional values are the important factors to move towards liberalisation of Indian newspaper industry. There should not be any discrimination on the grounds of religion, race, caste or creed.

> "The approach to foreign media has been governed by considerations of larger national interest and has ever been and ought not to be treated merely as an issue of economic policy".
>
> (N.Ravi, The Hindu).

Controversial Elements

There is a great deal of controversy and views on the concept of foreign print media. It is nothing but liberalisation of newspaper industry like other economic sectors liberalised and globalised. In other words it is the presence of foreign press on Indian soil. Allowing foreign print media is giving permission to the big foreign newspaper business concerns to commence publishing in India it is a step towards globalisation with liberalisation. The free entry of newspaper and periodicals permits foreign print media to print and publish news and views from India. As a result foreigners directly print and distribute their news. Free foreign print media is possible only with the Government policy of liberalisation to the newspaper industry. The trend in media ownership in recent global village is towards large and free foreign newspapers.

The concept of going global has become most popular in recent years in media industries as print, film, broadcast, cable, satellite, marketing and advertising organisations have been expanding their activities across frontiers. Globalisation of newspaper industry with liberalisation policy represents nothing more than trans nationalisation which affects substantially domestic activities.

Communication is the heart of all social interactions. Our worlds in its communication dimension consists of nations affiliated to United Nations. The basis for globalisation is that people cannot live in isolation and human solidarity.

In the year 1955 the Government withheld permission to foreign nationals to own newspapers in India. In the year 1956 the Government laid down that foreign news agencies have to operate in the country by collaborating with Indian news agencies and not directly. The entry of foreign print media also had been thoroughly examined by the first press commission. The ban on foreign nationals running newspapers in the country was imposed during the period of Jawaharlal Nehru. According to Mr. Justice Sarkaria,' 'the ban was imposed in the national interest when the nation's integrity and security was endangered by fissiparous forces operating from within and outside the country".

The major problems of newspaper industry in this country are:

1. Declining sales.
2. Increasing competition.
3. High price.
4. Uneconomic rates.
5. Time and language.
6. Lack of direct servicing wires to all newspapers.
7. Liberalisation policy helping electronic media to huge sums by way of advertisement revenues.
8. Multiple channel.
9. Foreign satellite.
10. Video and cable TV.
11. The advertisement rates of the Government advertisements are uneconomic and lowest commercial rates.
12. Introduction of colour pages by some newspapers, which small newspapers cannot afford.

The recent trend is that the advertisement revenue which other wise would have gone to the print media is now being diverted to the electronic media. The advertisements rates fixed for Government advertisements through Directorate of Advertising x and Visual Publicity (DAVP) are not reasonable. Print media have been facing the problem and challenges from radio, television and is now computing with the electronic media in the form of internet, cyberspace.

There has been a wide debate over the open door proposal for foreign media and its possible threat to the Indian free press. There are different opinions and wide spectrum of views. Editors, and media barons, politicians and intellectuals, and even readers form a part of the wide spectrum of views, divided down the line.

There are supportive of the entry of foreign print media and some objected the same. While some people say the entry of foreign media is not a harmful, while others perceive a threat to Indian free press. On the other hand some people adopts middle path, in view of globalisation, opening the doors to foreign publishing houses may not pose much of a problem provided adequate steps are taken to ensure that their operations are regulated and controlled to safeguard national interest.

No unanimity may emerge on controversial and sensitive issue like this, because it is a question of defending sovereignty, upholding national tradition in a multi-cultural and multilingual country like India. Allowing free entry of foreign print media may, however, require an amount of national consensus.

The ideas and opinions are so sharply divided over whether or not to allow the entry of foreign print media in India. There is no consensus of unanimity on the matter. Opinions widely differ between journalists, politicians, lawyers, academicians and social activities. Interestingly enough the trend is against the entry of foreign media.

It is all above theoretical proposition and it is difficult to see how the Netty of foreign media would work and help Indian press with highest level of professional conduct, standards, latest technology.

However, under the following paragraphs, the merits and demerits of foreign print media are presented.

The Merits

1. Foreign print media would help to get huge investment, new technology and varied expertise and experience. For improving the printing technology and publishing technique and for giving boost to Indian journalism, foreign media are partly recommended, it brings in capital, technology and professional advise.
2. Foreign and Indian press working together would help expand the perception of Indians on multifarious issues of global nature. The open door policy permits a wholesome view of cultural cross currents taking place, in a global village.
3. Allowing foreign print media promotes a healthy competitive spirit and entrepreneur ship in Indian newspaper industry.
4. In a free global village foreign entry into newspaper industry, anybody can own a paper.
5. Allowing the foreign print media in the country in the name of liberalisation would help expanding knowledge.
6. The advent of foreigners into a newspaper industry would bring about an improvement in professional standards of journalism and communication by way of stiff competition. The entry of foreign media would help in widening the perception of the Indians in the matters of both national and international.

7. Foreign newspapers offer higher salaries, perks, and better working conditions, better prospects, career opportunities, greater mobility, better working environment. Thus foreign media will snatch the cream of the Indian journalist by offering better monetary benefits.
8. Foreign print media promote fast declining cultural values. The presence of foreign media reflects credible global cultural revolution brought about by sophisticated printing, photo-type and electronic technology.
9. Be global and by global is the order in these days of information revolution and communication age.
10. The target readership of the foreign news papers would mainly be the english reading urbanites.
11. There is no fear of professional competition. Indian journalists are professionally competent with anyone in the world. In respect of standards and professional code the Indian journalists are not lagging behind.
12. Some of the newspapers in India are tied up with some business houses which filter the news and fair views. While some newspapers are bias of political parties and religious sects. The foreign media eliminates this environment in view of competition, standards and other commercial considerations. The problem of politically biased and editorials tailored to sub-serve the politico-business interest may exit from Indian newspaper industry.

The inflow of well known foreign newspapers will not only destabilise the english language Indian newspaper, but also the regional and small language propers through advertisement revenue diversion and readership. It is not advantageous to the vernacular press which may vehemently oppose the idea of entry of foreign media which would be a total disaster as it would irreversibly damage the pluralistic and relatively independent national press.

The Demerits

Be Indian and by Indian is the Indian slogan. The father of the Nation Mahatma Gandhi advocated Swadeshi in all fields.

1. The foreign press would definitely pose a direct danger to the Indian language newspapers. In fact Indian language newspapers are the real moulders of the public opinion.
2. The concept of liberalisation and globalisation by no means have any relevance to the newspaper industry liberalisation, globalisation of newspaper cannot be equated in the same category of other economic sectors, it is a sensitive media of information and sensitive political matter. This sector is not an economic commodity.
3. The entry of foreign media would affect integrity, and security endangers by fissiparous forces operating from within and outside the country.
4. Giving foothold in the country to the outside newspaper, would endanger the free flow of information by Indian media holding different views.
5. As a powerful outside foreign may not show concern for Indias interest.
6. Editorial policy of foreign newspapers a cannot be controlled, as a result poses a greater danger of national security.
7. Presently small newspapers have been grapple a host of operating problems. The entry of foreign print media may very much affect adversely the small newspaper

industry. So the entry of foreign news agencies is a real threat to the small papers. These papers already have been facing problems like competition, low circulation, paltry advertisement revenue and TV and radio drained the newspaper industry's advertisement revenues.

8. Allowing the entry of foreign media implies foreigners claiming right of freedom of expression which is fundamental right guaranteed by the constitution of India to the Indian citizens only but not to the foreigners. Every country has its own laws and constitutions to protect their respective print media and right of freedom of expression, thus provisions of Article 19 would be thrown open to non-citizens. Thus entry of foreign media into India may have some legal implications. Article 19 of the Constitution stipulates that all citizens shall have the right to freedom of speech and expression. The provision of restriction of ownership of the press to citizens alone is correct one. Foreign corporations are not Indian citizens and hence have no fundamental right to force into our territory.

9. There is also an evident danger of foreign element taking advantage of a free entry to propagate terrorism, separatism, casteism and create social bitterness through publications. The anti-national element would exploit the advantages of press liberalisation to endanger the country.

10. Foreign print media are threat and would pose to nation's security and culture, national integrity, interest, tradition and native way of life. It amounts to cultural invasion.

11. Open door proposal allowing print media would adversely affect country's political and social through resulting foreign rule over Indian minds.

12. Foreign agencies publishing newspaper involves distribution of their news, only through the Indian means.
13. Foreign print media would definitely influence electorate and may endanger democracy.
14. Views are also there that foreign newspapers may lead to serious dent in the circulation and readership.
15. Indian newspaper and magazines are getting government advertisements, hence foreign media is a threat of the advertisement word.
16. It is quote possible to impose a restriction by foreign print media that the employees of the foreign-owned media should be foreigners.
17. The All India Newspaper Employees Federation, PTI Employees Union, National Union of Journalists, UNI Employees Federation and Media Watch Group, in the year 1994 express their opposition to the entry of foreign media on several grounds. There was a "Campaign against Entry of Foreign Media" (CARFORM) in 1994.

To Sum Up :

To summarise is foreign print media globalisation inevitable?

Is it necessary to globalise print media ?

Is global village homogenised ?

Are hybridised, synthesised and urbanised culture promote national interest ?

Globalisation of press or foreign media is not the same category as other economic sectors. Newspapers, through a part of national economic aspect, should not be considered like economic commodity, capital, technology etc. Because it is not an extension of economic policy, the press has social, cultural, national traditional values and commitments.

The conscious of social responsibility of the newspapers of a particular country should not be ignored. The media of the country ideally reflect the social and cultural values of the country, but foreign media do not. There is no doubt about the fact that the so called global society permits to know other cultures and civilization. Foreign print media may be permitted to a very limited extent and in a restricted way to ventilate fair views under close monitoring. Parameters should be prescribed not causing harm to national integrity and friendly foreign relations.

The overwhelming majority of minus points submitted above indicate creation of an unfavourable environment that may likely be created with the foreign print media. But still it is not a conclusive opinion. The entry on scientific, technical, educational and informative newspapers and journals can restrictively be permitted. Foreign publications should not be given blanket permission. Strict guidelines, code and standards can be prescribed. The screening procedure promotes quality publication and undesirable publications should be removed. Lower price and greater control over publications, ensuring majority Indian ownership by holding shares holding positions in the Board of Management and editors are some of the safeguarding measures.

Thus the issue is a sensitive. But invasion of foreign media poses a serious danger to the country's independence, sovereignty friendly relations, communal harmony.

Structure Similar to Industry

Electronic communications were killing print. That judgement has proved wrong or at least premature. True, the antenna of the media picked up tremors in the mid-1970s indicating that Americans' reading and writing skills were declining, and by concentrating public attention on alarming statistics and assertions of decline, the media moved the tremors up the Richter scale. Popular and expert opinion quickly blamed television as a major villain. Particularly as the apparent decline coincided with a drop in newspaper circulation. The analysts so explained the statistics as to raise doubts that the decline was real; experts disagreed about whether or not a problem in fact existed, and if it did, just how serious it was; and historians pointed out that concern about declining literacy had surfaced before and seemed cyclical in nature. Nevertheless, the message through the media was that indeed Johnny could not read or write, and schools and universities were put on notice to do something.

Then the media picked up other tremors in society and moved on. Because it lacked dramatic visual appeal, the "story" of declining literacy lent itself more to examination by the print than the electronic media, so illustrating an important point. Although the media all perform the same functions, they cannot in every instance perform them equally well. To some extent their competition for audiences and advertisers is at one another's expense, but each possesses sufficiently unique attributes for supplementary and complementary roles to survive. This chapter, discusses a dynamic not a dying communications technology.

Area of Large Market : The creation of mass markets, which only large and costly units could service efficiently, has led inevitably to a contraction of ownership in many cities and towns and thus to the development of newspaper chains. The high point in the number of newspapers published in the United States came in 1909, when there were 2600 daily publications. On this situation, magazine publisher Frank Munsey commented, "There is no business that cries out so loud for organization and combination as that of newspaper publishing. For one thing, the number of newspapers is at least 60 percent greater than we need."

Munsey dreamed of a national chain of 500 newspapers and tried to start it by buying newspapers in New York, Washington, Boston, Baltimore, and Philadelphia. Although his chain failed, he pioneered an accelerating trend in twentieth-century publishing.

In the first half of the twentieth century, more than 2000 new daily newspapers (including those changing from weekly to daily) were started. But, during the same period, 1947 daily newspapers suspended publication to become weeklies, 547 disappeared through merger or consolidation, and at least 302 local combinations took place. At the same time the number of newspaper chains increased from three, publishing 62 newspapers, to 70 publishing 386, with more than two-fifths of the daily and one-half of the Sunday circulation. In the 1950s there were scarcely more than 100 cities with competing daily newspapers. Of the 1500 cities with daily newspapers in 1977, only 2.5 percent-fewer than 40-had competing newspapers. By then the nation's 168 chains owned three-fifths of the nation's 1756 daily newspapers and controlled 71 percent of the circulation.

According to journalist historian Frank Mott, consolidation of newspapers is not a strictly recent tendency, it can be found in all periods. But since World War I, the skyrocketing cost of newspaper publication has been a strong influence in accelerating the tendency to consolidate.

Melville E. Stone established the Chicago Daily News in 1876 with a few thousand dollars capital; in 1925 it sold for $13 million. In 1963 two Omaha dailies were sold for $43 million, and in 1967 Newhouse Newspapers bought the Cleveland Plain Dealer for $53.4 million, Knight Newspapers paid $55 million for two Philadelphia papers in 1969. In 1976 Rupert Murdoch, the Australian press baron, paid, according to Folio magazine's estimate, $30 million for the New York Post at a time when all three New York dailies were losing circulation (between March 1974 and September 1976, the Times dropped from approximately 910,000 daily to 802,000, the Daily News from 2.12 million to 1.93 million, and the Post from 650,000 to 489,000).

In the typical American town in earlier days, more newspaper publishing ventures were attempted than the economy could support. Some newspapers-for example, those founded solely as voices of political parties or other interest groups-went out of business simply because they could not win general community support. Others were founded by people who went into the business apparently on the assumption that to make money it was only necessary to "buy newsprint white and sell it black." They soon discovered that, aside from the problems of editing a mass medium, such factors as rigid advertising and circulation rates made newspaper publishing a dubious enterprise at best. For the new entrant today the problems are even more formidable, particularly in metropolitan areas. Not only has population shifted increasingly to the suburbs, with businesses and service industries in pursuit, but inflation in the 1970s was forcing more and more families to stop subscribing to more than one newspaper.

Both in procuring their raw material and in marketing their products. Newspaper publishers exhibit the familiar behaviour of monopoly and oligopoly. As buyers they use the customary pressures for keeping down costs; as sellers they maintain rigid advertising and circulation rates, discriminate by rate differentials, and practice block selling of space in morning and evening newspapers in combination. The typical newspaper pays out for newsprint roughly one-third of its revenues, which is just about what it receives in circulation revenue. Practically all newsprint is sold in carload lots under long-term contracts, mostly to large publishers. Those who cannot afford carload lots get their newsprint from jobbers, brokers, and paper merchants at open market prices, which are sometimes higher by 10 percent or more than the carload rates.

Procuring syndicated features and wire services is no less difficult for the new entrant. The syndicated feature business is dominated by four major companies: AP news features, King Features, NEA Service, and United Features. Most franchises provide for exclusive territories. Furthermore, package selling enables large publishers to buy up rights to more features than they print. Oligopoly is similarly a chief trait of the two wire services.

The new newspaper is confronted in many markets by chain organization. Chains, especially of large newspapers, have certain special advantages: Notably, they make wider use of editorial and feature writers: it is easier for them to obtain new funds from the capital market; they engage in block merchandising of space to national advertisers, in centralized and large-scale research, and in bulk purchases of newsprint, ink, and equipment; they are better able to make maximum use of specialized technical and managerial services, and of electronic automation-central computers can serve all papers in the chain. Despite these centralizing tendencies, American news institutions, and newspapers in particular, have been local rather than national because of "a peculiarity in American political organization and the prevailing pattern of family money spending." Ben Bagdikian has written:

> More governmental functions are left to the local level in the United States than in other developed countries. Schools, property taxes, land use, public health, large areas of business regulation, and many other political and social activities are controlled by locally elected and locally controlled bodies... These locally controlled policies have maximum immediate impact on family life, such as schooling for children, design and location of homes, routes of local highways, and rates of personal property taxes. Such decisions are made by a complicated but highly localized set of political bodies.

The United States has no national newspapers. The closest approximations are the Wall Street Journal, which in 1977 reached across the nation to 1.46 million people interested mainly in financial news, and the New York Times, one quarter of whose 854,000 daily subscribers in 1977 lived more than 100 miles from New York City. To a much lesser extent, the

Washington Post also reached beyond the capital, but it did not compete seriously in national and international circulation with the times. In the late 1970s the Times was spending $35 million a year (the Post was spending $19 million) to support the world's largest full-time news staff-641 journalists (550 in New York, 40 in Washington, 19 scattered throughout the United States, and 32 abroad). There are fatter American newspapers than the Times (the average news hole-the space devoted to editorial words-of the Times in 1977 was 160 columns a day; the Washington Star printed 185 and the Chicago Tribune 218 columns a day), but they rely typically on wire service and syndicated material for much of their content. Almost everything in the Times is staff written.

These huge newspapers with an impact beyond their cities of publication form a tiny minority of American daily newspapers; only half a percent of all dailies have more than 500,000 circulation. Seventy percent of U.S. dailies have circulations of 25,000 or less; 53 percent are published in cities with populations less than 25,000. Although the New York Times has an influence in the United States and abroad out of all proportion to its size, the statistics in the tables below present a clearer perspective on the newspaper industry as a whole and vividly make Bagdikian's point about the localism of newspapers.

As Americans' disposable income has risen, retail stores and service enterprises have kept pace at the local level in competing for this income, typically by advertising through the local newspaper. In 1976 advertisers spent $33.6 billion in all media. Newspapers got $10.2 billion or 30 percent of that, 25.6 percent local, only 4.4 percent national. Because of family spending patterns, the population shift to the suburbs, and the mushrooming suburban shopping centers, a relatively new newspaper category has emerged: the shopper's guide or shopper or throwaway. A typical daily newspaper has a ratio of about 65 percent advertising content to 35 percent news and feature content. Shoppers, by contrast, contain 75 percent or more advertising content, and many are distributed free. And their numbers are growing. The U.S. Suburban Press, Inc., had 850 of these shoppers with a total circulation of 11.3 million in early 1976.

To curb shoppers' eating into their advertising revenues, established newspapers were supporting efforts by some states to exclude shoppers from the tax privileges enjoyed by "traditional" newspapers. In New Jersey state tax officials were struggling to come up with a satisfactory definition of "newspaper." The rise of the suburban press, whether as traditional newspaper or shopper, challenged the domination of major metropolitan newspapers, many of which began developing their own suburban or zone editions in the 1970s to compete for readers and advertisers.

The localism of newspapers and their efforts to attract and hold readers in a competitive market have made the newspaper in many respects a more direct descendant of the early magazine of the nineteenth century than is the contemporary magazine. The word "magazine" is derived from the French word magazine, 'meaning "storehouse," and early magazines were miscellanies of information and amusement. In its growing consumer orientation and emphasis on "news you can use," today's local newspaper is very similar. Readers of all ages can usually find something to interest them in the paper's coverage of local events and activities, in its local and syndicated features, comics, and games, and in its local retail ads and listing of local entertainment. Even the large metropolitan newspapers that concentrate on public affairs and appeal to a readership far beyond their cities of publication-the new York times, Washington Post, the Wall Street Journal, and the Christian Science Monitor-publish a miscellany of serious and entertaining content more diverse than that of a general-interest magazine.

In fact, it seemed in the late 1970s that newspapers had to publish more of such "soft" new and feature material to stave off circulation declines. By adding a section three days a week in 1976 and 1977—Living, a section on food and wine, on Wednesdays Home, on furniture, interior decorating, and gardening, on Thursdays, and Weekend, a guide to entertainment and the arts, on Fridays- the New York Times reversed its circulation decline, increasing circulation from a daily average of 821,000 in 1976 to 854,000 in 1977. Not only did more people buy the Times on the days with added sections-35,000 more than on unsupplemented days-more advertisers bought space. The Times sold more advertising in May 1977 than in any previous month in its history.

To some their local orientation offsets the standardization of American newspapers. Yet whatever character a publisher or editor or the community itself confers on a local newspaper, economy dictates a heavy reliance by almost all on wire and news services for national and international news and on syndicates for features, columns, and comics. Studies have long shown that the comics sections, and particularly the Sunday comics, are among the best-read sections in the paper. A study reported by N.W. Ayer and Company in 1976 found that more than 50 million copies of Sunday comics are distributed to American homes every week, where they are read by over 100 million people. And two organizations, Metro Sunday Comics and the Puck Group, supply over 76 percent of those copies.

Not only do these centralised sources of news and entertainment make for an essential similarity in newspaper content from place to place, but the news-writing techniques and formulas of the wire services-typically a summary lead paragraph followed by the facts in order or decreasing importance-have influenced reportorial style in such a way that even local stories read alike. The chemistry of the city council members and the nature of the issues they discuss may differ dramatically between Lompoc, California, and Brunswick, Maine, but the way in which the Lompoc Record and the Brunswick Times Record report them is unlikely to differ much. Researchers have argued, in fact, that because of professional norms concerning definitions of news and the inverted pyramid style of reporting, reporters ignore the colour, flavour, and very human disorder and tedium of city council discussion in favour of a concise, objective account of the decisions taken. The effect of this approach, the researchers argue, is to shore up the authority of local government by creating the impression that it is consistently acting decisively and rationally.

Even though the great majority of daily newspapers-approximately 85 percent-have circulations under 50,000, and may therefore appear small enough to serve as personal vehicles for strong-minded, colourful publishers who can stamp the newspaper with their own personalities, the forces of industrialization and urbanization accelerating after the Civil War virtually killed the dominance of flamboyant publishers like Bennett, Pulitzer, and Hearst whose paper were personal, idiosyncratic extensions of themselves. Most newspapers today are corporate and impersonal enterprises.

Examples of the colourful breed of the nineteenth century survive, of course. In New Hampshire, William Loeb, the publisher of the Manchester Union Leader, uses his statewide newspaper with vigorous partisanship against political candidates of whom he disapproves. Rupert Murdoch, the Australian publisher of the New York Post, seems a reincarnation of much of the best and worst of Pulitzer and hearst.

In Las Vegas, Herman M. Greenspun, publisher of the Las Vegas Sun, has carried an adventurous life into his paper. Editor & Publisher gives this account of the extraordinary derring-do of his fight for Israel's survival in 1948. He plundered a naval depot in Hawaii, and, posing as an agent for

Generalissimo Chiang-Kai-Shek, seized a yacht at gunpoint. He then filled a ship at Tampico Bay with 6000 tons of contraband rifles, machine guns, howitzers, cannons, and tons of ammunition, and sailed to Israel. He was convicted in 1950 of violating the U.S. Neutrality Act and stripped of his civil rights. President John Kennedy pardoned him in 1961. Before becoming publisher of the Sun, Greenspun worked as publicity director for the Flamingo Casino, owned by hoodlum Bugsy Siegel, who was later gunned down.

Since then Greenspun has campaigned against gangsters in Las Vegas, and as a result of his investigative journalism and his trenchant front-page column, "Where I Stand," has been hit with more than 100 lawsuits, so becoming the most sued publisher in the nation. He was one of the first publishers to attack Joseph McCarthy, the anti-Communist senator from Wisconsin in the early 1950s; he was the only newsman to testify before the Senate Watergate committee-he said he knew of a $100,000 campaign contribution to Richard Nixon from billionaire recluse Howard Hughes.

Newspaper publishing has other characters, but the generalization holds: Most newspapers are impersonal, corporate enterprises that reflect the middle-class values of their mainly middle-class owners. Not only does the scale of their enterprise distance many publishers from the daily operation of the newspaper, but the professionalization of journalists also sets publisher and reporter apart. The rise of journalism education and of organizations such as the newspaper Guild and the Society of Professional Journalists, Sigma Delta Chi, has to some extent institutionalized journalists' ethics and reinforced conventions such as objective reporting, adherence to which has given reporters a measure of independence from publishers' whims.

The Underground Press Largely to protest middle-class values and accepted journalistic responsibilities and conventions and to express their protest in vivid, unrestrained language, an "underground" press flowered in the late 1960s and early 1970s, giving the lie fleetingly to the generalization that newspapers are impersonal, middle-class businesses. There were only four in 1965, but Robert Glessing counted approximately 3000 underground papers that had published at one time or another between 1965 and 1972. Some underground papers built circulations in the tens of thousands, among them the highly successful Berkeley Barb. In 1969 wrangling between the owner.

Max Scherr, and his staff became public, revealing just how lucrative such an operation can be. It also revealed that, like the capitalists of the commercial press; some underground journalists are money-conscious. A large group of Scherr's helpers broke away and began to publish the Berkeley Tribe, but not before their negotiations to buy the Barb had reached figures in the hundreds of thousands. It will not do to assign sweeping significance to the underground press. Ray Mungo, one of the founders of the Liberation News Service, which provided material for underground newspapers, has written:

> Lots of radicals will give you a very precise line about why their little newspaper or organization was formed and what needs it fulfills and most of that stuff is bullshit, you see the point is they've got nothing to do, and the prospect of holding a straight job is so dreary that they join the "movement" and start hitting up people for money to live, on the premise that they're involved in critical social change blah blah blah. And it's really better that way, at least for some people, than finishing college and working at dump jobs for constipated corporations: at least it's not always boring... that's why we decided to start a news service-not because the proliferating underground and radical college press really needed a central

> information-gathering agency staffed by people they could trust (that was our hype), but because we had nothing else to do.

At the same time, it is important to recognize the real strengths of this new journalism. It provided a forum for ideas that were not considered, or not considered adequately, in conventional media. The undergrounders also provided a view of a different life style and afforded different and valuable perspectives. What this new journalism proved was that a vast distance stretched between the conventional media and important segments of the public. There was a time when a newspaper or magazine served its own small public.

The circulation was relatively slender, but editors spoke directly to the central interests of their readers, and they could usually count on reader loyalty. Anyone who cherished another point of view might attack, and a publication that posed a threat might be destroyed-the abolitionist papers, for example-but most people simply subscribed to publications that squared with their own prejudices and idiosyncrasies.

When the conventional media became large and few, however, and editors we're trying to attract mass audiences, separate voices could no longer be raised so readily in a free marketplace of ideas. Many underground papers succeeded in building close relationships with their readers, at least in part because they revived the art of speaking to a relatively homogeneous audience.

One important technique was to present news in heavily subjective prose: "A growing revolt against the selfish and reactionary American Medical Association came to a head here," began an article on Open City a Los a Angeles paper. "Objectivity is a farce" said Thorne Dreyer of Liberation news Service, Jeff Shero, former editor of The Rat, said, "We make our biases clear. That frees our writers to talk about their guts."

Bibliography

Angharad, N. Valdivia : *A Companion to Media Studies*, Blackwell, New Delhi, 2004.

Aronson, James : *The Press and the Cold War*, Beacon Press, Boston, 1970.

Ashby, Eric : *Introduction to Educational Technology*, Sterling Publishers, New Delhi, 1981.

Bard, F. Eraser : *An Introduction to Journalism*, MacMillan Co., New York, 1958.

Brown, J.W. Lewis R.S. and F.F. : Harclebroad : *Instruction Materials and Methods*, McGraw Book Co., New York, 1964.

Brown, James : *Media and Educational Planning*, McGraw Hill Book Co., New York, 1964.

Chaffee, S.H. and Berger, C.R. : *Handbook of Communication Science*, Sage Publications, London, 1987.

Cohen, B.C. : *The Press and Foreign Policy*, Princeton University Press, Princeton, N.J., 1963.

Dash B.N. and G.M. Tripathy : *Essentials of General Psychology*, MacMillan, London, 1999.

Dieu, Zeide, H. : *Educational Technology and Development of Education*, UNESCO.

Due, R.C. : *Teaching Techniques ASC Newsletter*, Utkal University, Bhubaneswar, 1990.

Emery, Edwin : *The Press and America*, Prentice-Hall, New Jersey, 1997.

Emest, C. Hynds : *American Newspaper in* 1980s, Hastings House, New York, 1980.

Fiske, J. : *Introduction to Communication Studies*, Methuen, London, 1982.

Gagne, R.M. : *Conditions of Learning*, Holf & Rinehart & Winston, New York, 1965.

Gerbner, G : *Mass Media Policies in Changing Cultures*, Wiley, New York, 1977.

Giner, S. : *Mass Society*, Martin Robertson, London, 1976.

Grey, Elizabeth : *The Story of Journalism*, Longmans Young Books, London, 1968.

Husen, Torsten, : *International Encyclopaedia*, Pergamon Press, Oxford, 1989.

James, S. Kinder : *Audio-Visual Materials Television*, American Book Co., New York, 1959.

Jayapalan, N. : *Journalism*, Atlantic Publishers, New Delhi, 2001.

Knightley, Phillip : *The First Casualty : The War Correspondent as Hero, Propa-gandist and Myth Maker*, Harcourt Brace Joronovich, New York and London, 1975.

Kulkarni, S.S.: *Introduction to Educational Technology*, IAET, New Delhi, 1986.

Lowman, J.: *Mastering the Techniques of Teaching*, Prentice Hall of India, New Delhi, 1987.

Mac, Iver, R.M. & Page C.M. : *Society and Media*, MacMillan, London, 1950.

Mark, C. Jaylor & Esa : *Imagologies Media Philosophy*, Routledge, UK, 1996.

Mayer, T. : *Preparing Objectives for Programmed Instruction*, Palo Atlo, California Fearon, 1962.

McFarland H.S.N. : *Psychological Theory and Educational Practice*, Blackwell, London, 2000.

Menon, Narayan : *The Communication Revolution*, National Book Trust, New Delhi, 1976.

Moven, Kiran : *Studies in Educational Broadcasting*, Deep & Deep Publications, New Delhi, 1996.

Mujuni, J.P. : *Studies in Media Education*, Deep & Deep Publications, New Delhi, 1995.

Narayan Rao S. : *Educational Psychology*, Atlantic Pub., New Delhi, 2001.

Ogburn W.F., Nimkoff M.E. : *A Handbook of Journalism*, Kegan Paul, London 1947.

Ottaway A.K.C. : *Education and Media*, Routledge & Kegan Paul, London, 1962.

Ottaway, A.K.C. : *Press and Society*, Routldge and Kegan Paul, London, 1962.

Pachori, Sudhis : *Jan Sanchar Madhyaam : Bhasha*, Rohit Publishers, Meerut, 1990.

Panickkar, K.M. : *The Foundation of New India*, George Allen & Unwin, London,1963.

Pant, N. C., Joshi M. K. and Jitendera Kumar : *Hindi Patrakarita ki Roop Rekha*, Kanishka Publishers, New Delhi, 2000.

Parikh, R.D. : *The Press and Society*, Popular Prakashan, Bombay, 1965.

Parkar, E.B. and Mahananda, A. : *Communications Policy for National Development*, Routledge and Kegan Paul, London, 1977.

Rau, M.C. : *Social Change and the Unchanging Press*, Government of India Publication, New Delhi, 1982.

Reston, James : *The Artillery of the Press : Its Influence on American Foreign Policy*, Harper & Row, New York, 1967.

Sharma, G.D. & Ahmed, S.R : *Methodologies of Teaching in Colleges*, Sterling Publishers, New Delhi, 1988.

Sharma, G.D. : *Dynamics of Higher Education in India,* Deep & Deep Publishers, New Delhi, 1993.

Smith, Anthony : *The Newspaper—An International History,* Thames and Hudson, London, 1979.

Verma, Adarsh Kumar : *Management Mantaras of Journalism,* Kanishka Publishers, New Delhi, 2001.

Vigneshwara : *Our New Rulers,* B.G. Paul & Co., Madras, 1961.

Vilanilam, J.V. : *Reporting a Revolution,* Sage, New Delhi, 1989.

Waldrop, A. Gayle : *Editor and Editorial Writer,* Rinehart & Co., New York, 1955.

Warwick, D. : *Modular Curricula : International Encyclopaedia,* Pergamon Publications, UK, 1994.

Wolseley, Roland E. : *Journalism in Modern India,* Asia Publishing House, Bombay, 1964.

Zachariah, Aruna : *Media Power : People, Politics and Public Interest,* Kanishka Publishers, New Delhi. 2001.

Index

Q

R

S

T

❑❑❑